Praise for DEMO VOLUME TWO

"Best thing I read: I'm happy DEMO is back — it's a good Vertigo comic-book series from Brian Wood and Becky Cloonan where each issue is its own story, so you can (and should!) just jump right in. If you like the new issues, there's a compilation of all "classic" DEMO issues you should check out."
USA TODAY/Pop Candy

"One of the most interesting introspective series... about having heightened abilities or heightened powers... each issue focuses on a different person... plagued with some supernatural or superhuman ability... just awesome."
FRESH INK/G4

"A worthy successor to the original."
COMIC BOOK RESOURCES

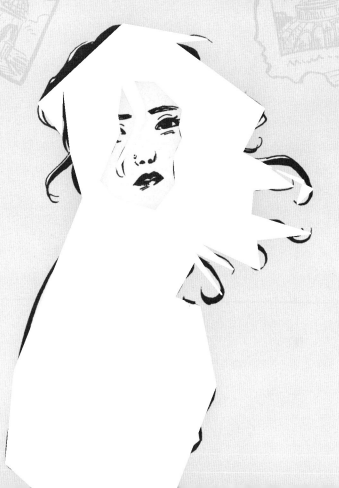

DEMO

WRITTEN BY
Brian Wood

ILLUSTRATED BY
Becky Cloonan

LETTERED BY
Jared K. Fletcher

DEMO CREATED BY
Wood & Cloonan

Karen Berger SVP-Executive Editor

Will Dennis Editor-Original Series

Mark Doyle Associate Editor-Original Series

Bob Harras Group Editor-Collected Editions

Robbin Brosterman Design Director-Books

Curtis King Jr. Senior Art Director

DC COMICS

Diane Nelson President

Dan DiDio and **Jim Lee** Co-Publishers

Geoff Johns Chief Creative Officer

Patrick Caldon EVP-Finance and Administration

John Rood EVP-Sales, Marketing and Business Development

Amy Genkins SVP-Business and Legal Affairs

Steve Rotterdam SVP-Sales and Marketing

John Cunningham VP-Marketing

Terri Cunningham VP-Managing Editor

Alison Gill VP-Manufacturing

David Hyde VP-Publicity

Sue Pohja VP-Book Trade Sales

Alysse Soll VP-Advertising and Custom Publishing

Bob Wayne VP-Sales

Mark Chiarello Art Director

Cover design by Brian Wood
All artwork by Becky Cloonan

DC Comics
1700 Broadway, New York, NY 10019
A Warner Bros. Entertainment Company.
Printed in the U.S.A. First Printing.
ISBN: 978-1-4012-2995-5

SUSTAINABLE FORESTRY INITIATIVE

Certified Chain of Custody
Promoting Sustainable
Forest Management
www.sfiprogram.org

Fiber used in this product line meets the sourcing requirements
of the SFI program. www.sfiprogram.org SGS-SFICOC-0130

Contents

1

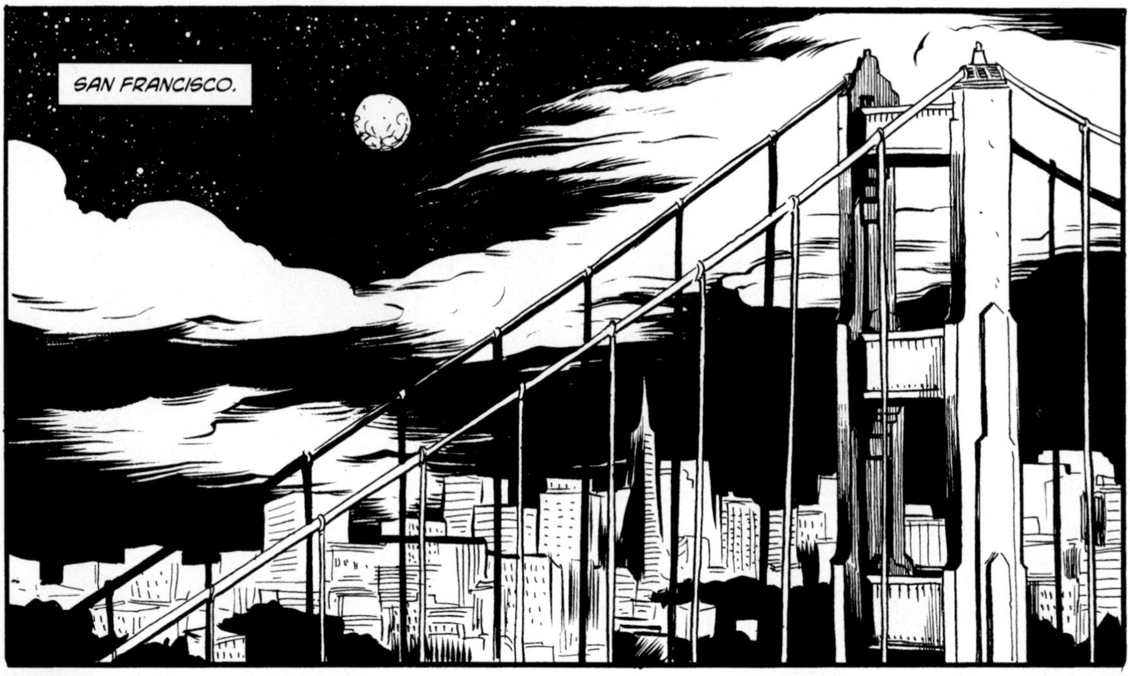
SAN FRANCISCO.

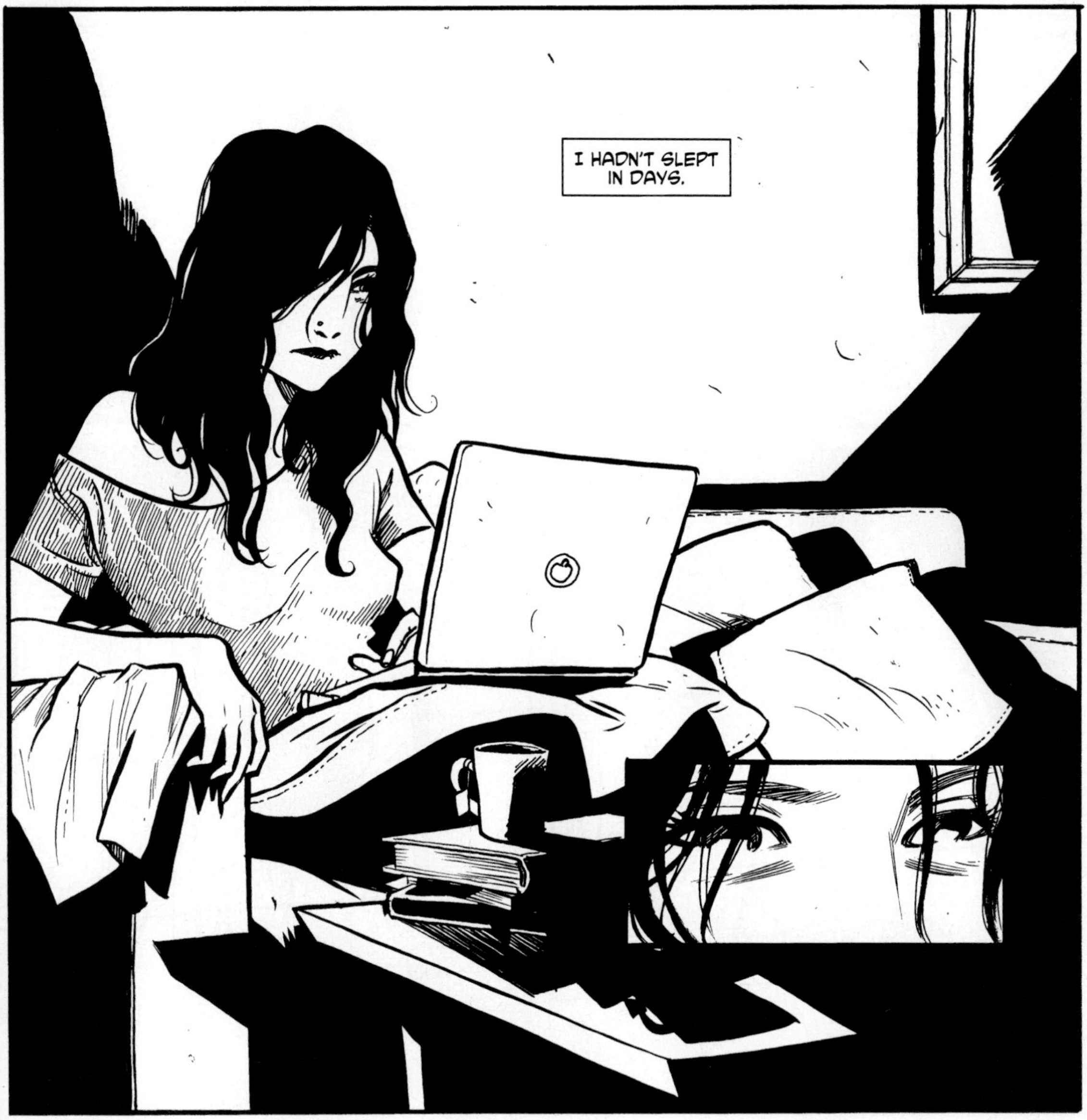
I HADN'T SLEPT IN DAYS.

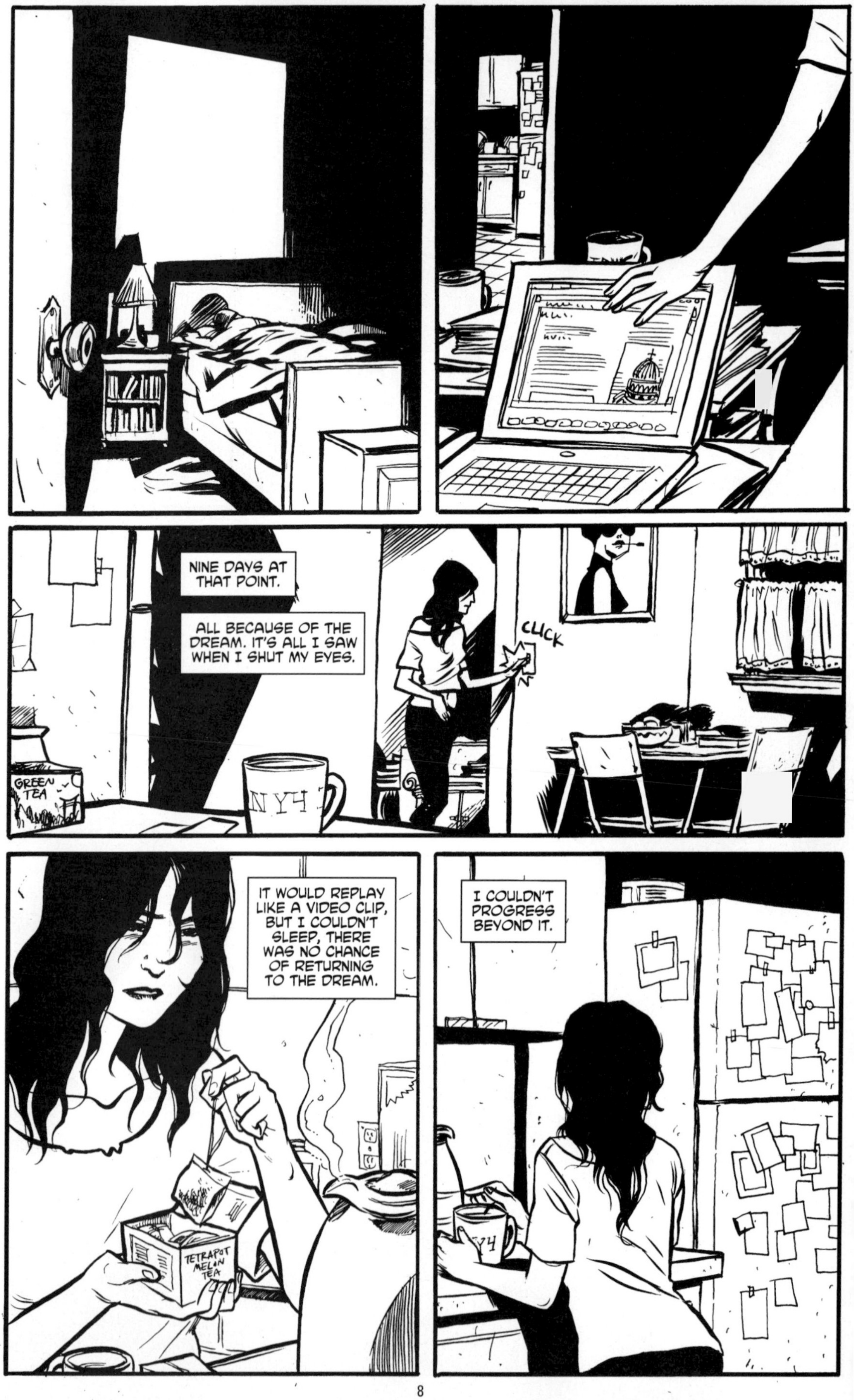
NINE DAYS AT THAT POINT.
ALL BECAUSE OF THE DREAM. IT'S ALL I SAW WHEN I SHUT MY EYES.
CLICK
GREEN TEA
NY4
IT WOULD REPLAY LIKE A VIDEO CLIP, BUT I COULDN'T SLEEP, THERE WAS NO CHANCE OF RETURNING TO THE DREAM.
TETRAPOT MELON TEA
I COULDN'T PROGRESS BEYOND IT.
NY4

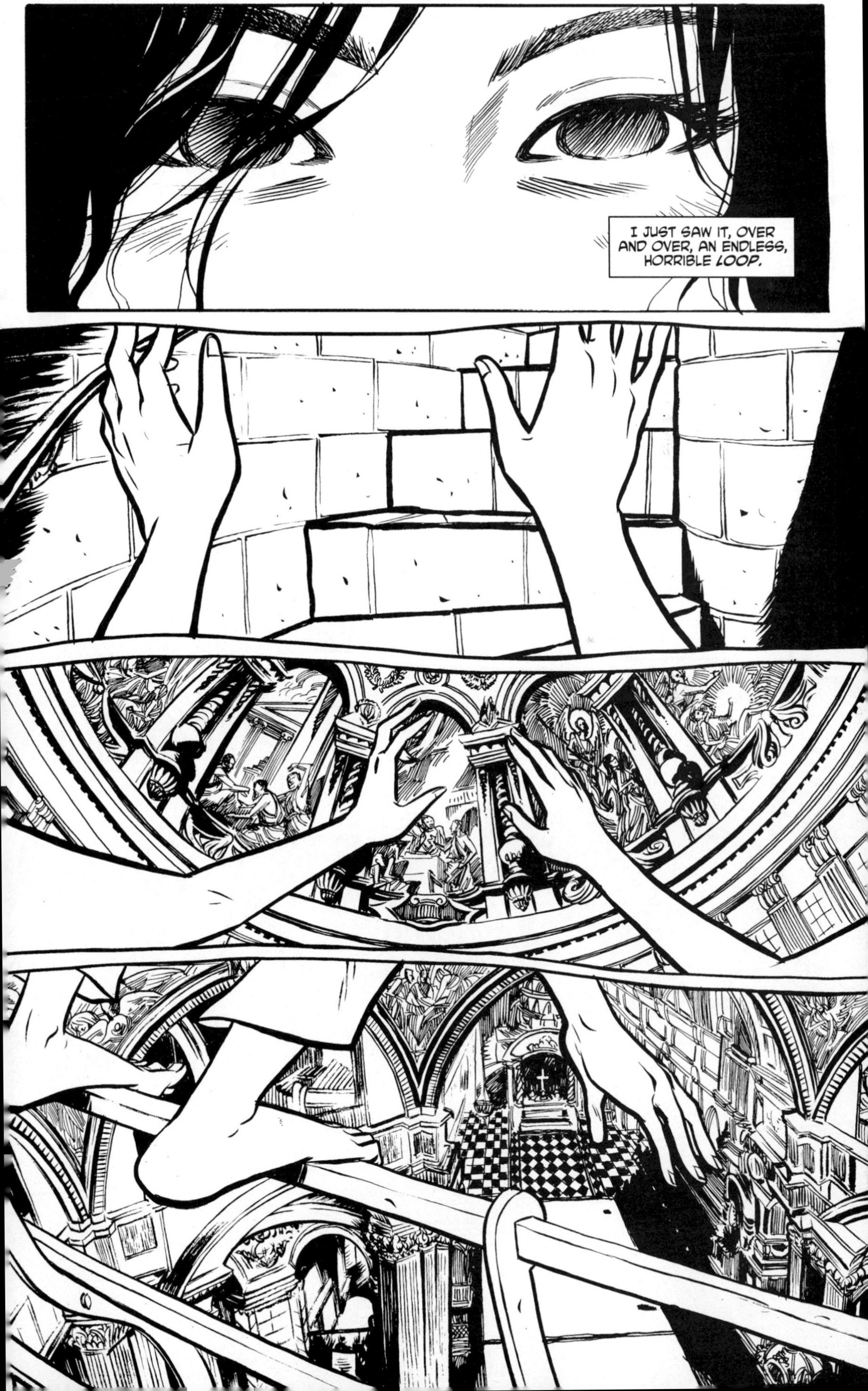
I JUST SAW IT, OVER AND OVER, AN ENDLESS, HORRIBLE LOOP.

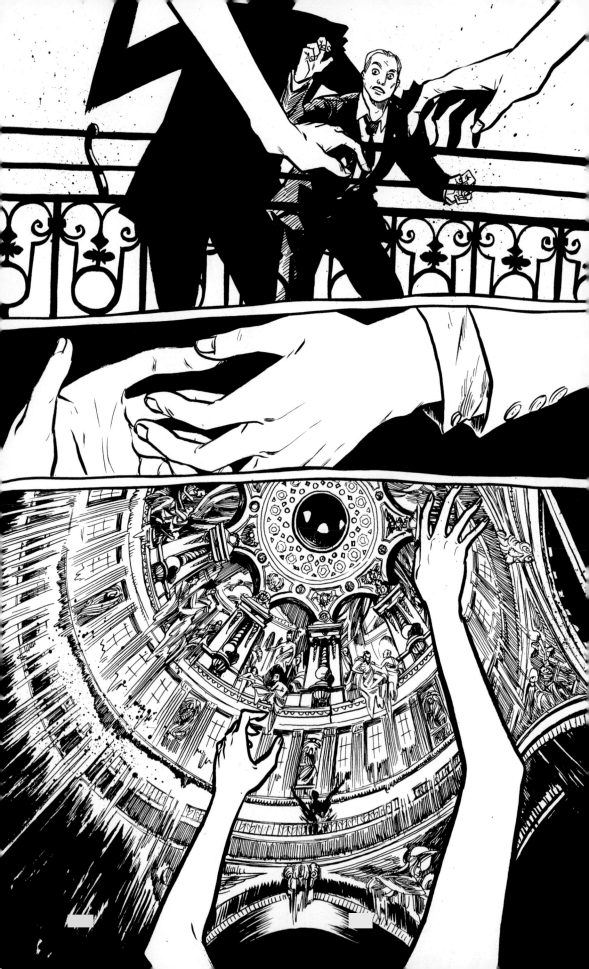

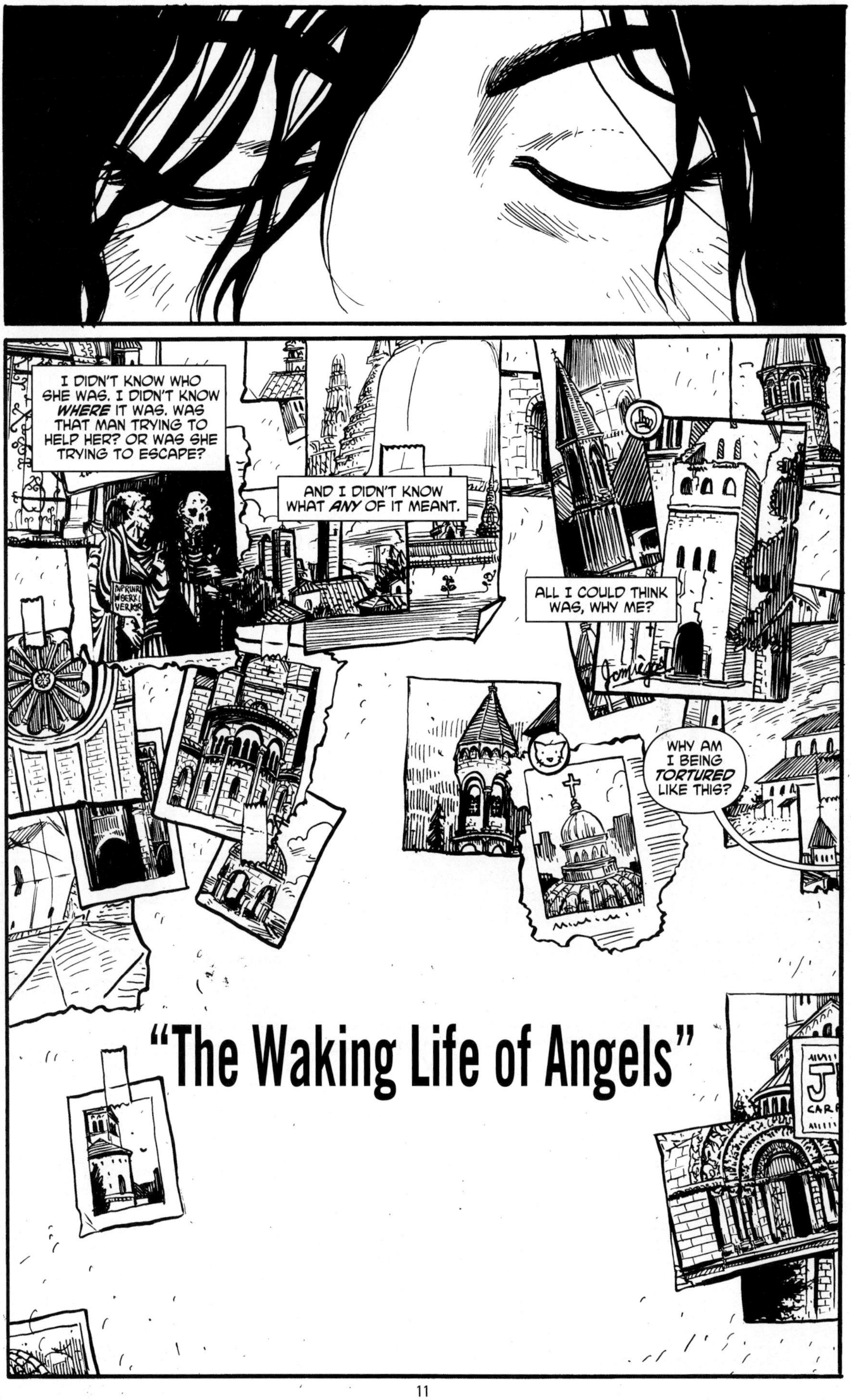
I DIDN'T KNOW WHO SHE WAS. I DIDN'T KNOW *WHERE* IT WAS. WAS THAT MAN TRYING TO HELP HER? OR WAS SHE TRYING TO ESCAPE?
AND I DIDN'T KNOW WHAT *ANY* OF IT MEANT.
ALL I COULD THINK WAS, WHY ME?
WHY AM I BEING *TORTURED* LIKE THIS?
"The Waking Life of Angels"

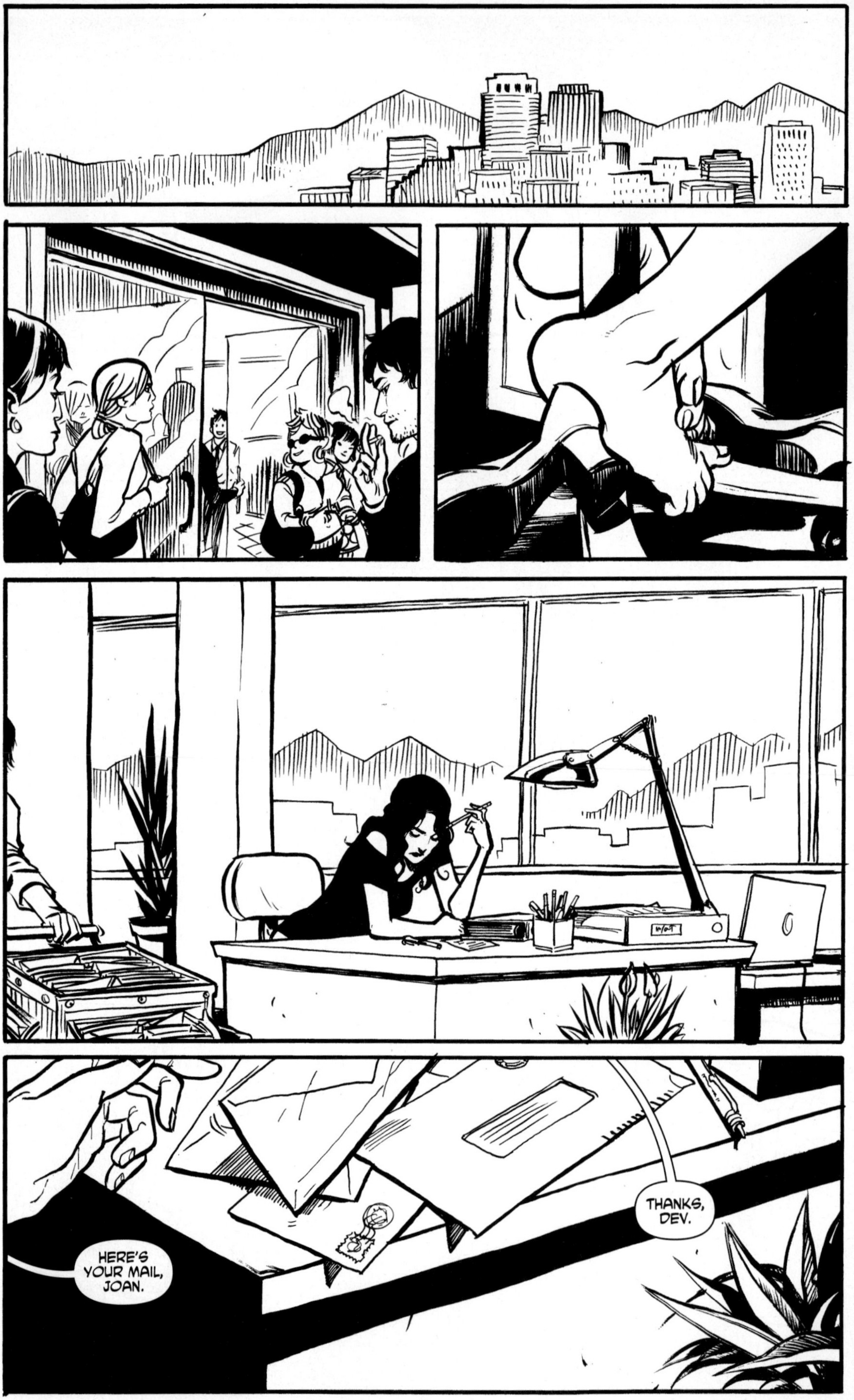
HERE'S YOUR MAIL, JOAN.
THANKS, DEV.

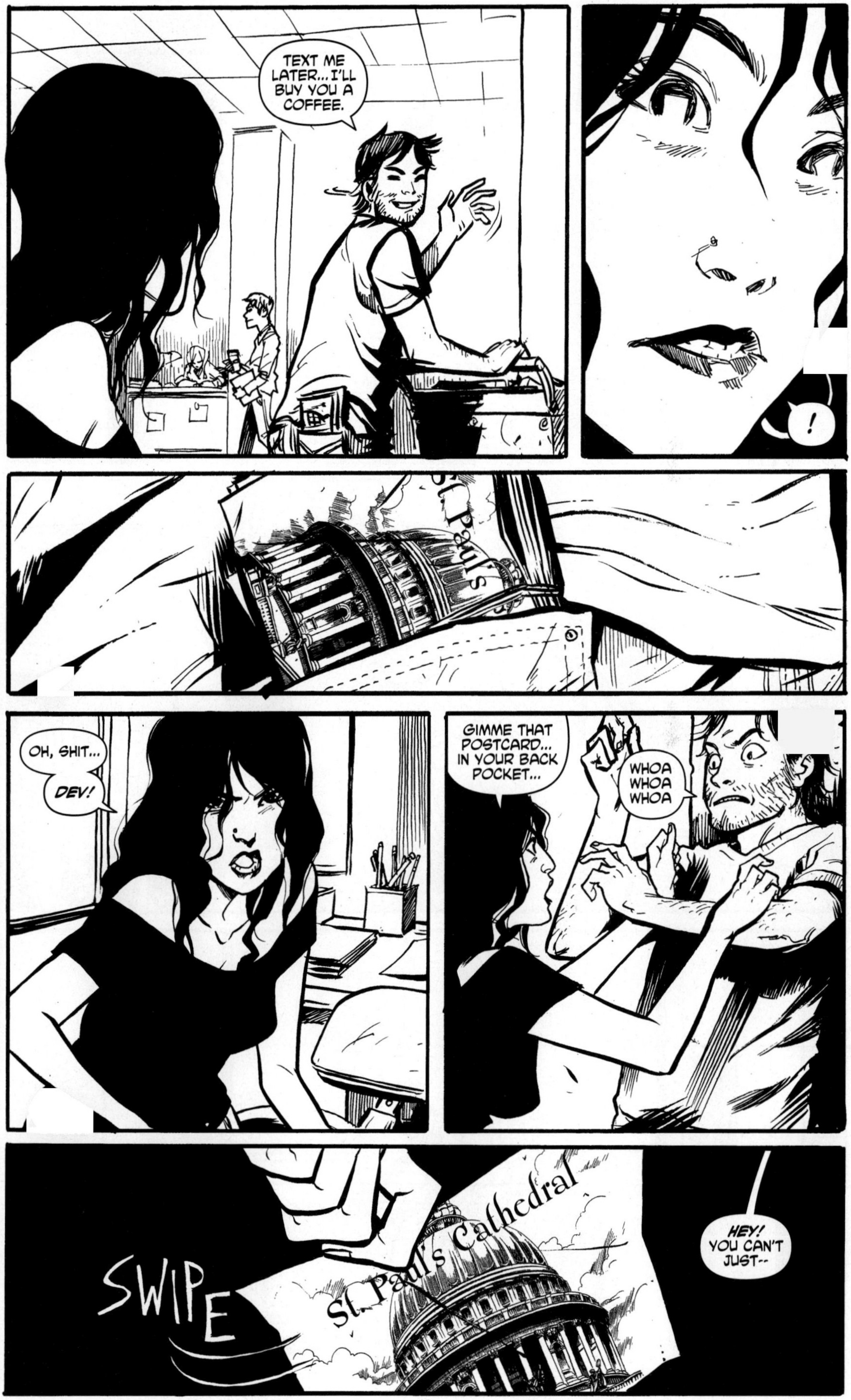
TEXT ME LATER... I'LL BUY YOU A COFFEE.
!
St. Paul's
OH, SHIT...
DEV!
GIMME THAT POSTCARD... IN YOUR BACK POCKET...
WHOA WHOA WHOA
SWIPE
St. Paul's Cathedral
HEY! YOU CAN'T JUST--

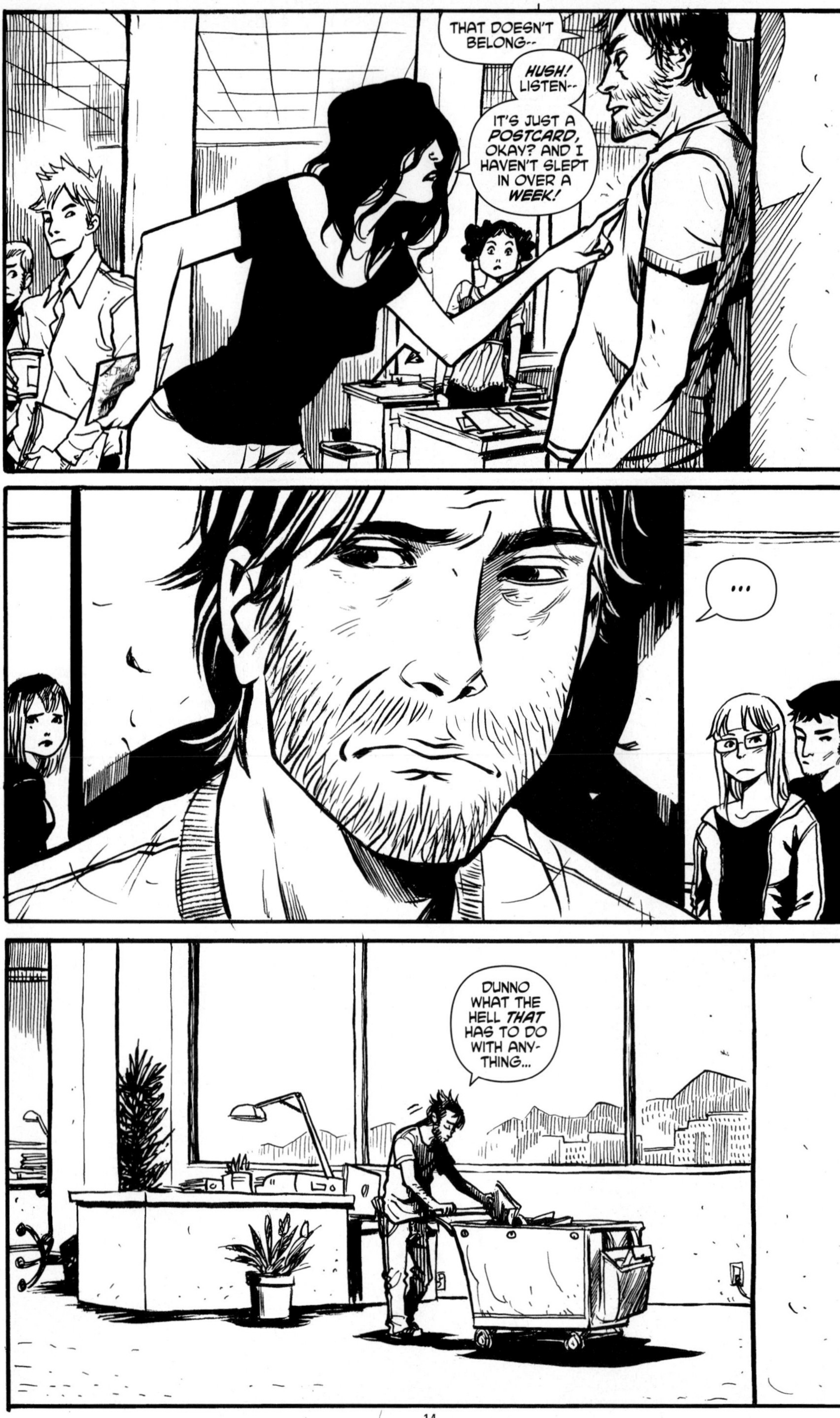
THAT DOESN'T BELONG--
HUSH! LISTEN--
IT'S JUST A POSTCARD, OKAY? AND I HAVEN'T SLEPT IN OVER A WEEK!
...
DUNNO WHAT THE HELL THAT HAS TO DO WITH ANY-THING...

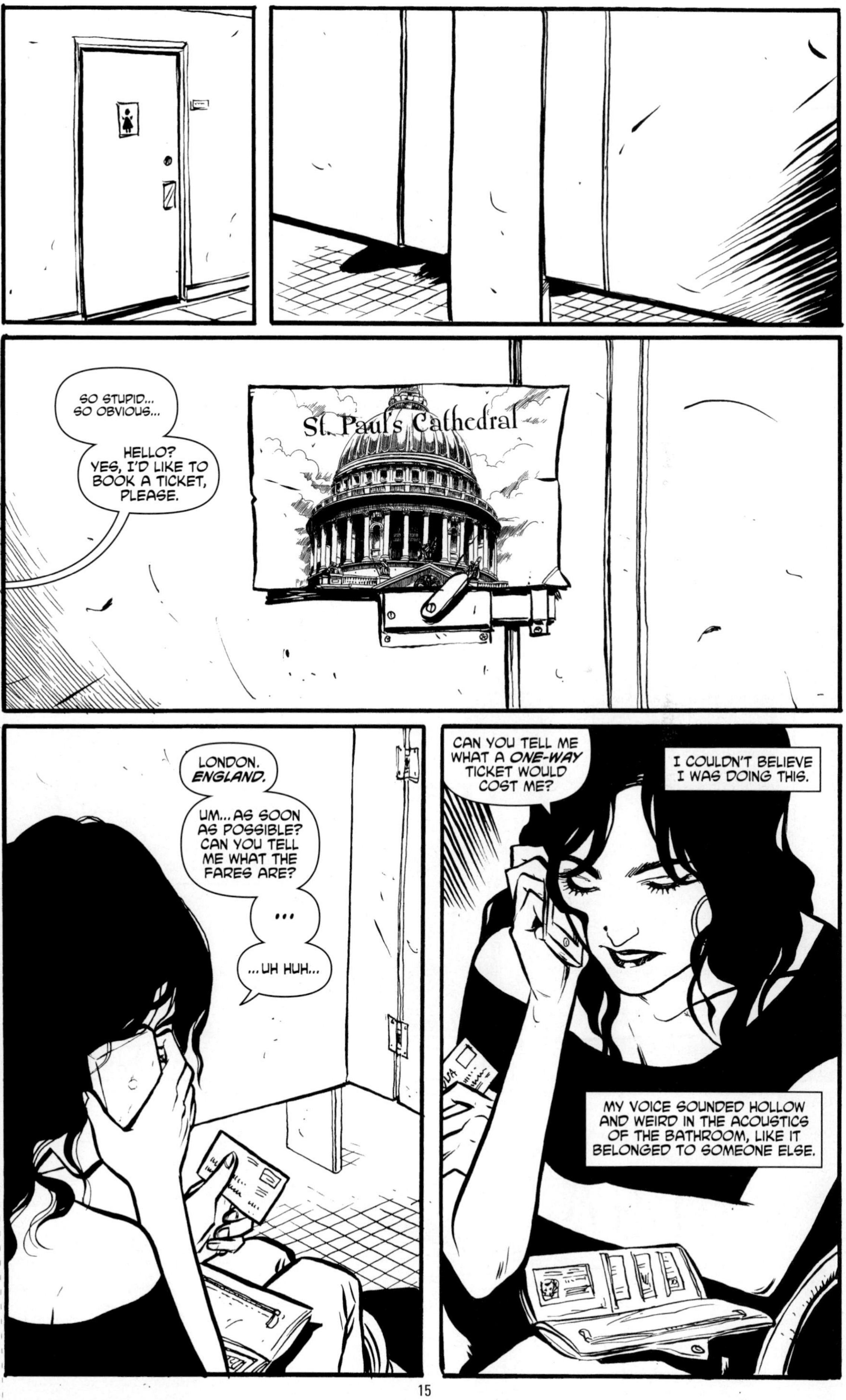
SO STUPID... SO OBVIOUS...
HELLO? YES, I'D LIKE TO BOOK A TICKET, PLEASE.
St. Paul's Cathedral
LONDON. *ENGLAND.*
UM...AS SOON AS POSSIBLE? CAN YOU TELL ME WHAT THE FARES ARE?
...
...UH HUH...
CAN YOU TELL ME WHAT A *ONE-WAY* TICKET WOULD COST ME?
I COULDN'T BELIEVE I WAS DOING THIS.
MY VOICE SOUNDED HOLLOW AND WEIRD IN THE ACOUSTICS OF THE BATHROOM, LIKE IT BELONGED TO SOMEONE ELSE.

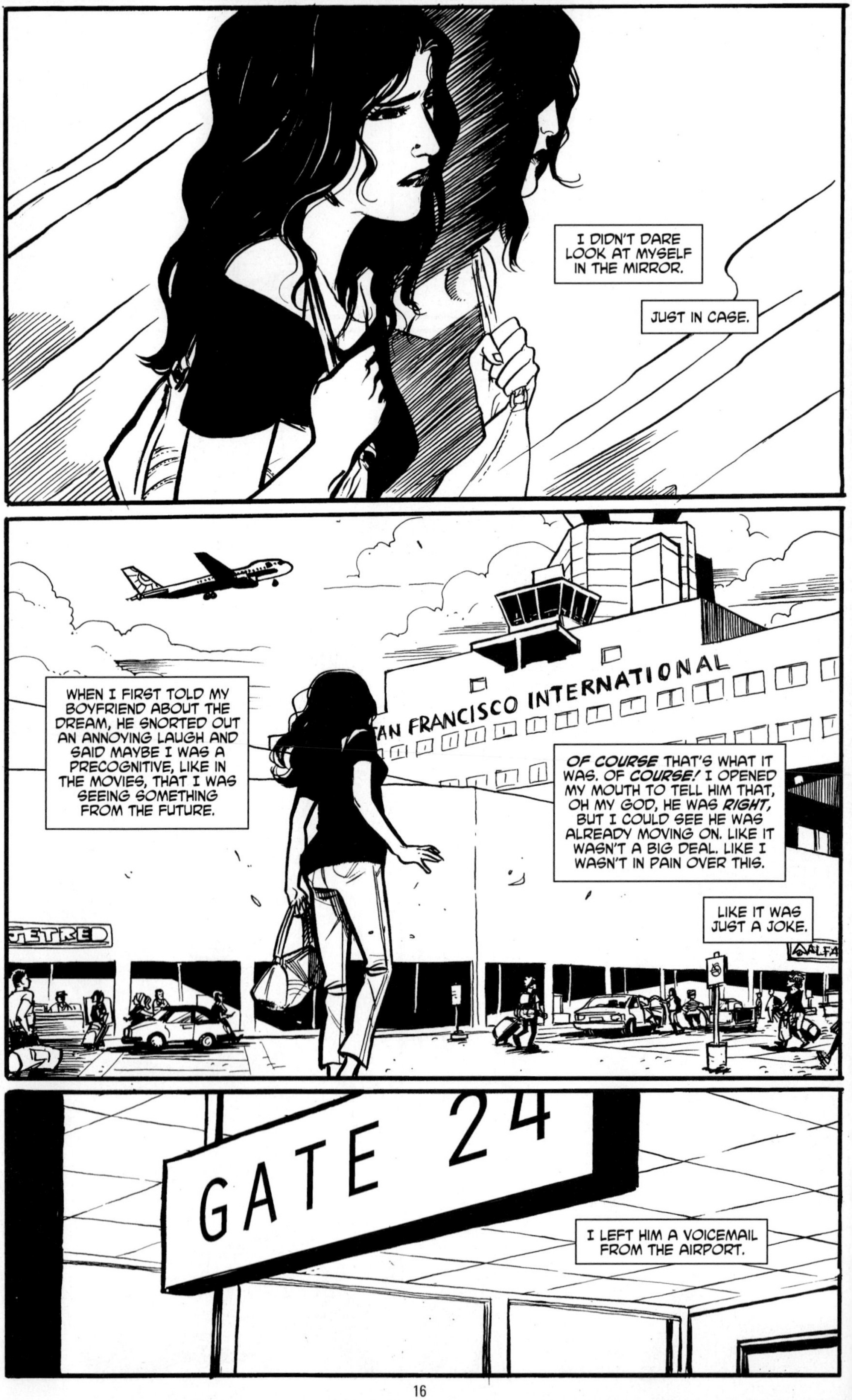
I DIDN'T DARE LOOK AT MYSELF IN THE MIRROR.
JUST IN CASE.
WHEN I FIRST TOLD MY BOYFRIEND ABOUT THE DREAM, HE SNORTED OUT AN ANNOYING LAUGH AND SAID MAYBE I WAS A PRECOGNITIVE, LIKE IN THE MOVIES, THAT I WAS SEEING SOMETHING FROM THE FUTURE.
AN FRANCISCO INTERNATIONAL
OF COURSE THAT'S WHAT IT WAS. OF *COURSE!* I OPENED MY MOUTH TO TELL HIM THAT, OH MY GOD, HE WAS *RIGHT,* BUT I COULD SEE HE WAS ALREADY MOVING ON. LIKE IT WASN'T A BIG DEAL. LIKE I WASN'T IN PAIN OVER THIS.
LIKE IT WAS JUST A JOKE.
GATE 24
I LEFT HIM A VOICEMAIL FROM THE AIRPORT.

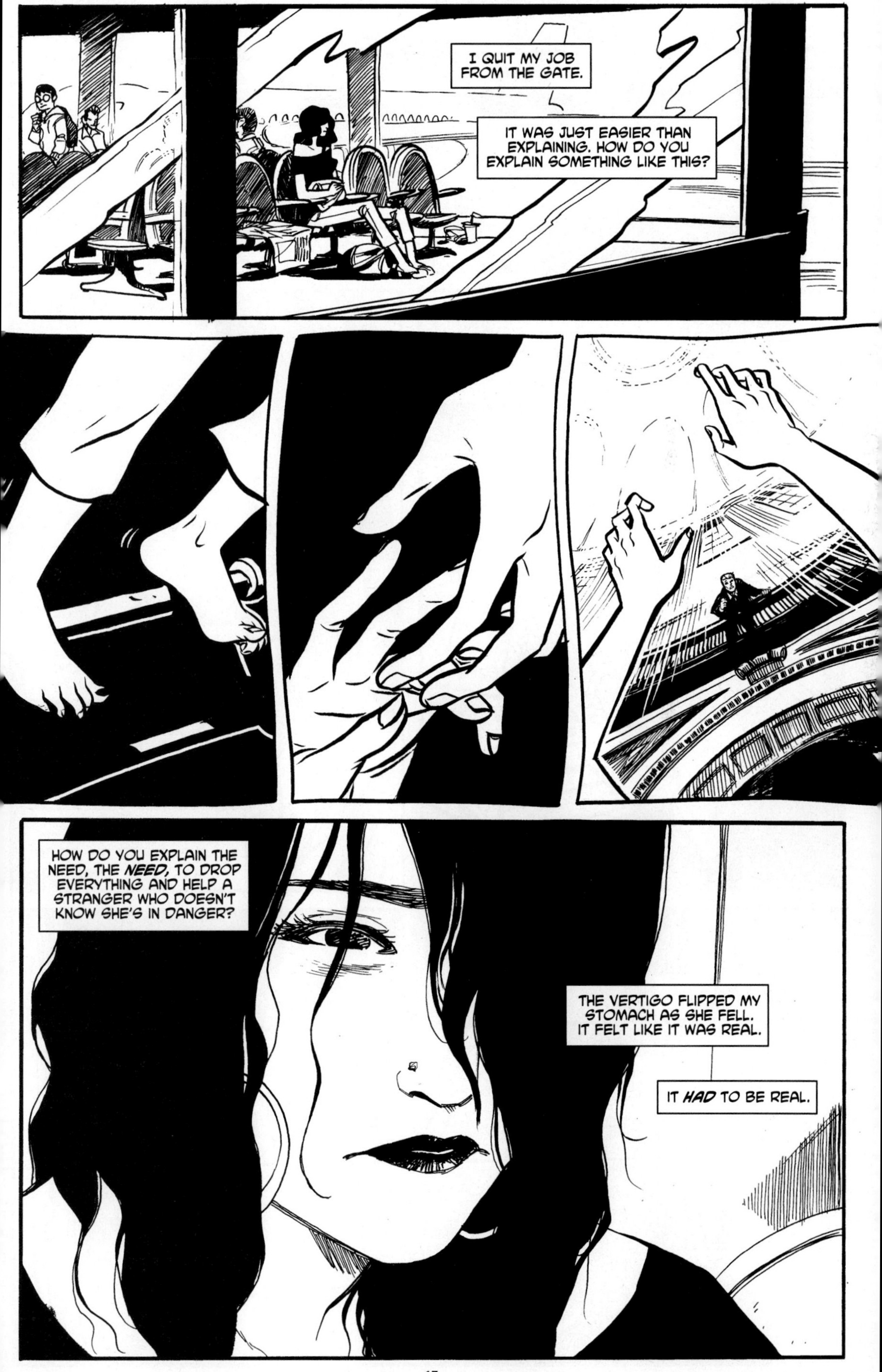
I QUIT MY JOB FROM THE GATE.
IT WAS JUST EASIER THAN EXPLAINING. HOW DO YOU EXPLAIN SOMETHING LIKE THIS?
HOW DO YOU EXPLAIN THE NEED, THE *NEED,* TO DROP EVERYTHING AND HELP A STRANGER WHO DOESN'T KNOW SHE'S IN DANGER?
THE VERTIGO FLIPPED MY STOMACH AS SHE FELL. IT FELT LIKE IT WAS REAL.
IT *HAD* TO BE REAL.

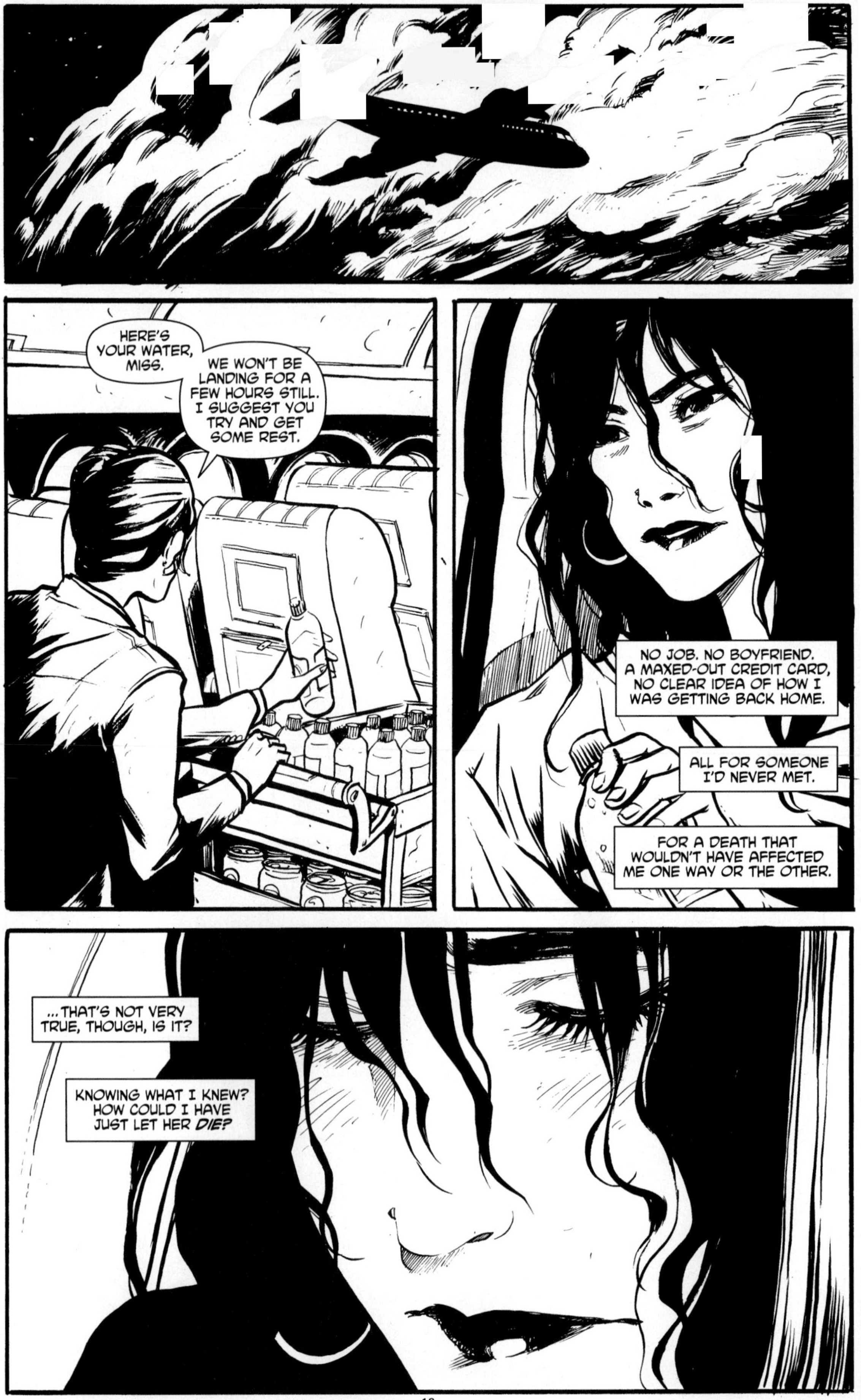
HERE'S YOUR WATER, MISS.
WE WON'T BE LANDING FOR A FEW HOURS STILL. I SUGGEST YOU TRY AND GET SOME REST.
NO JOB. NO BOYFRIEND. A MAXED-OUT CREDIT CARD, NO CLEAR IDEA OF HOW I WAS GETTING BACK HOME.
ALL FOR SOMEONE I'D NEVER MET.
FOR A DEATH THAT WOULDN'T HAVE AFFECTED ME ONE WAY OR THE OTHER.
...THAT'S NOT VERY TRUE, THOUGH, IS IT?
KNOWING WHAT I KNEW? HOW COULD I HAVE JUST LET HER *DIE?*

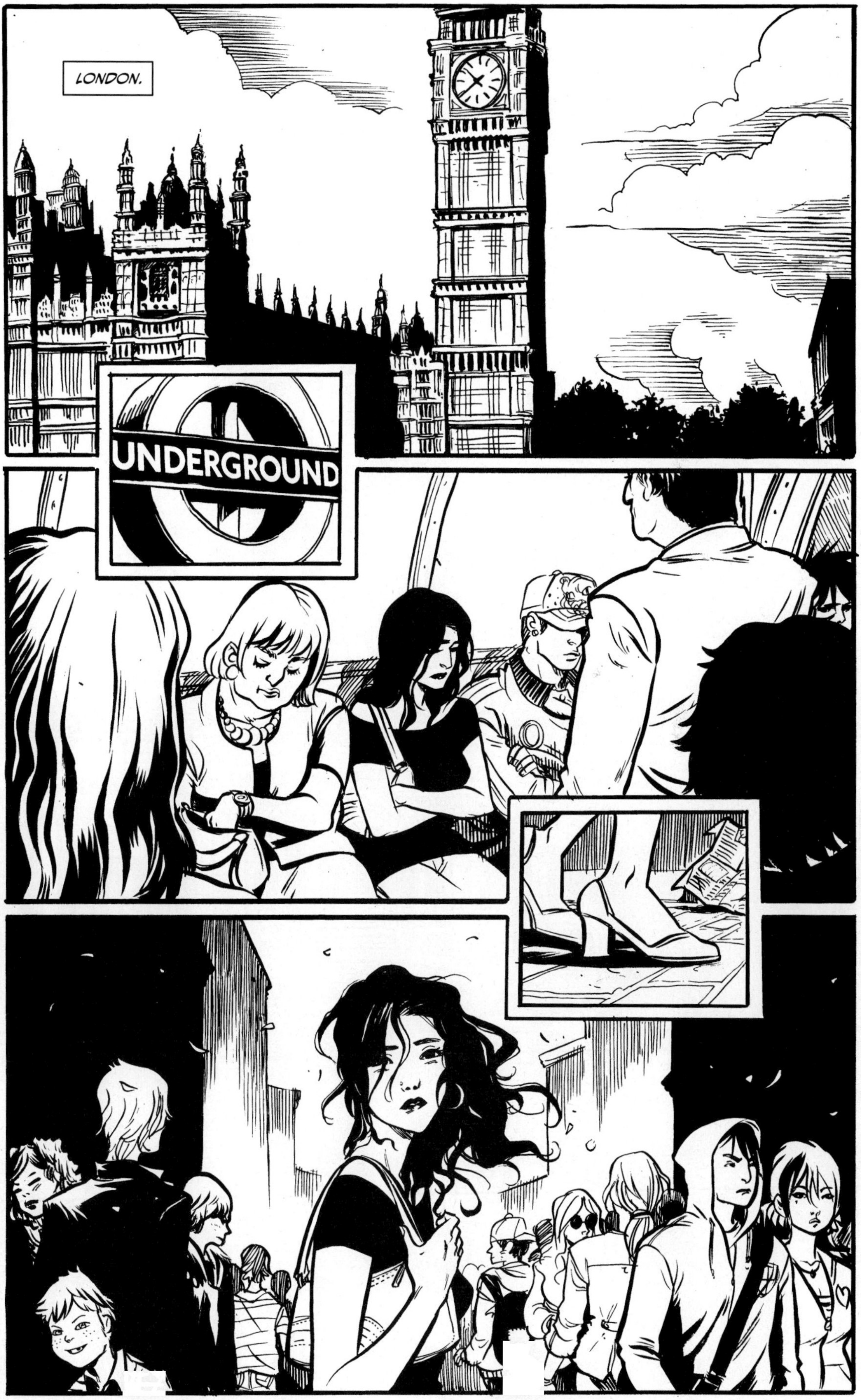
LONDON.
UNDERGROUND

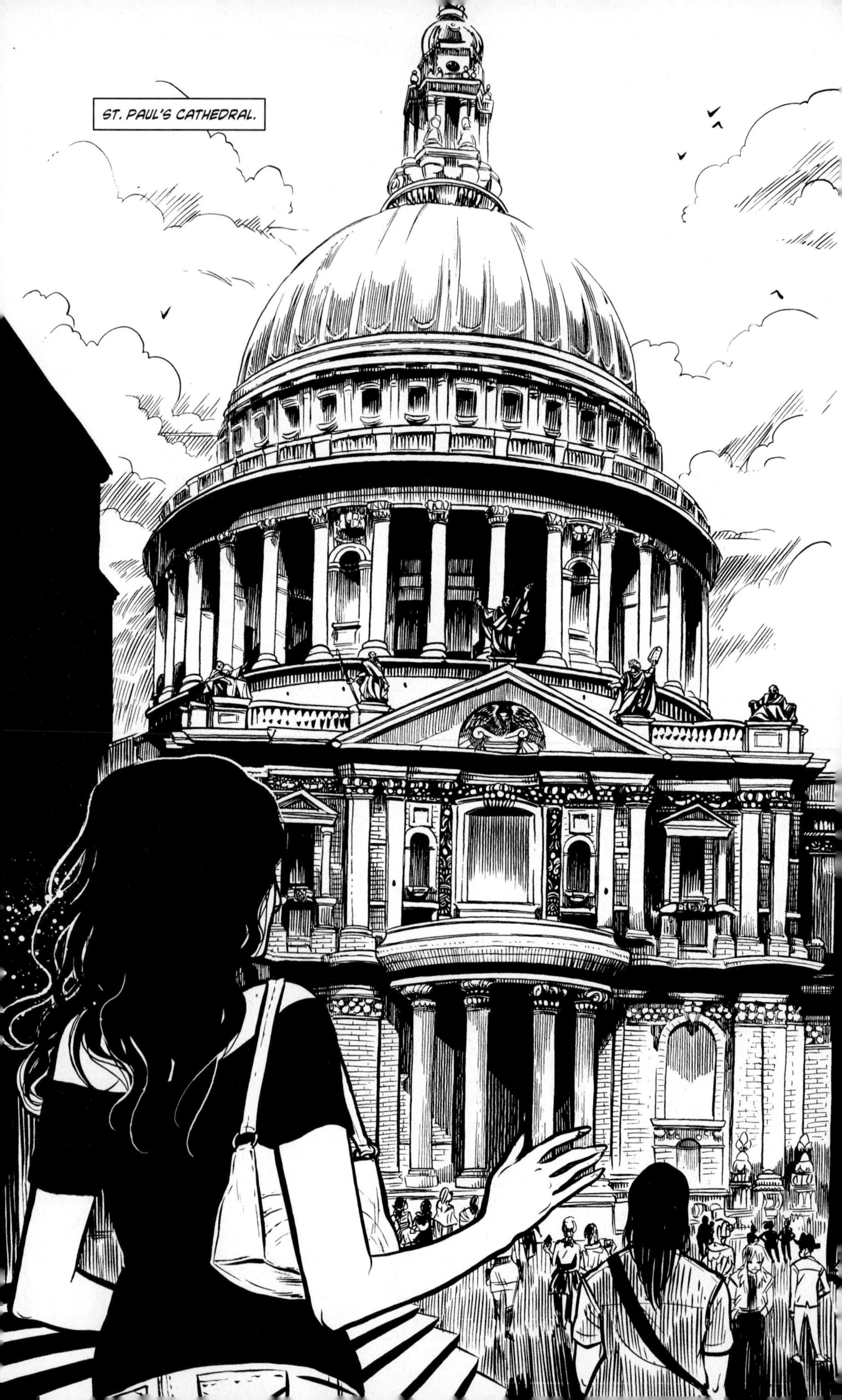
ST. PAUL'S CATHEDRAL.

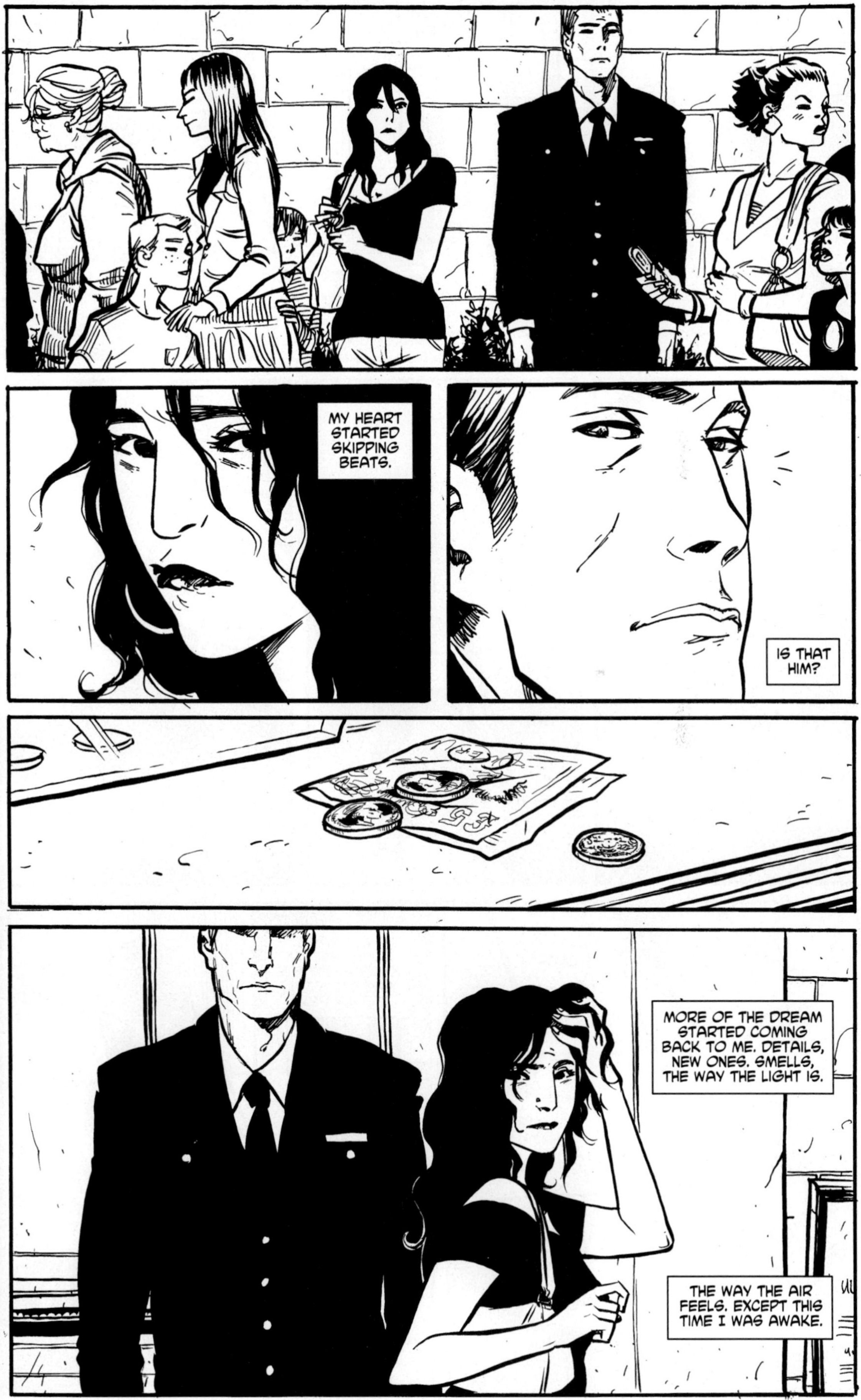
MY HEART STARTED SKIPPING BEATS.
IS THAT HIM?
£5
MORE OF THE DREAM STARTED COMING BACK TO ME. DETAILS, NEW ONES. SMELLS, THE WAY THE LIGHT IS.
THE WAY THE AIR FEELS. EXCEPT THIS TIME I WAS AWAKE.

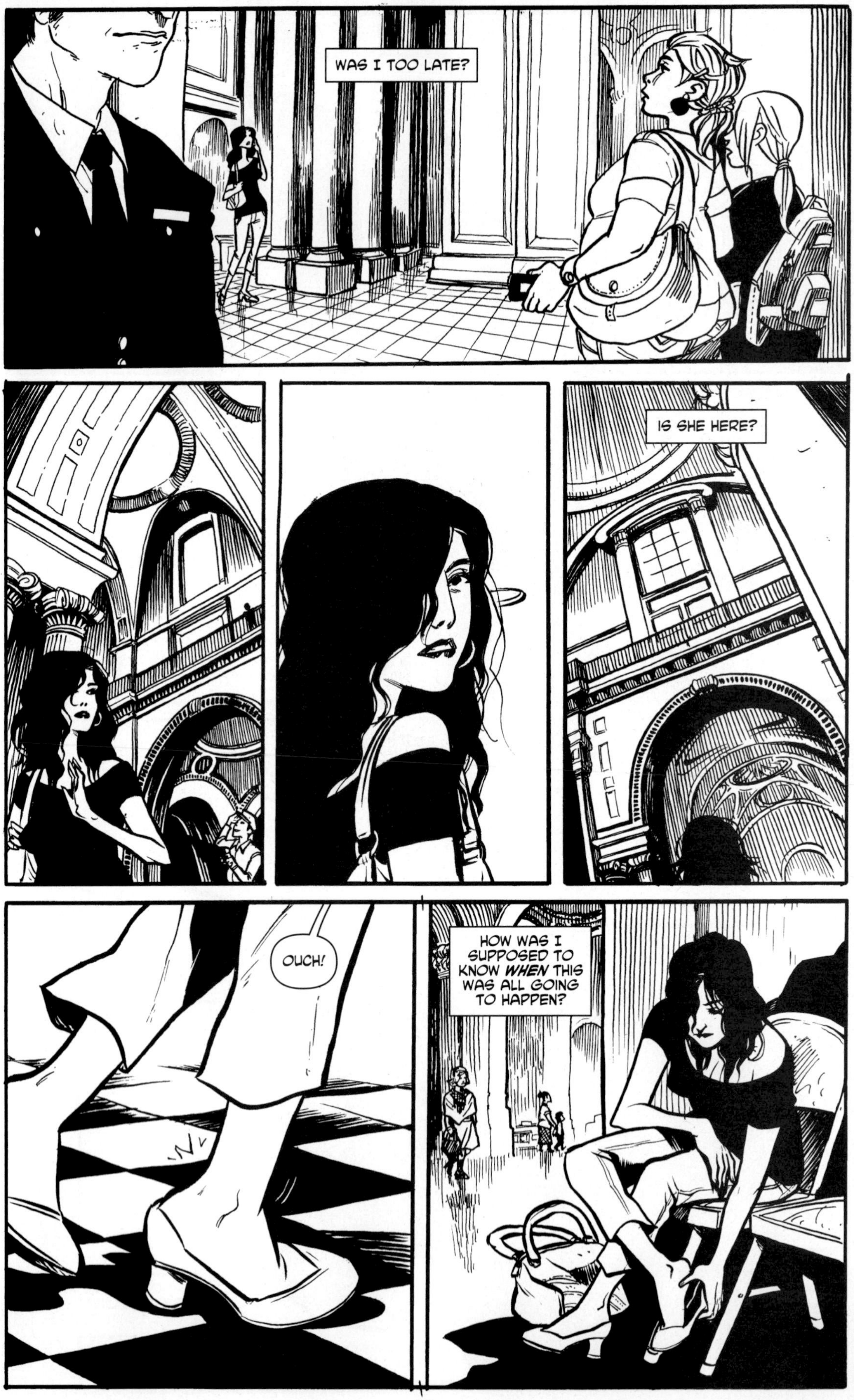
WAS I TOO LATE?
IS SHE HERE?
OUCH!
HOW WAS I SUPPOSED TO KNOW *WHEN* THIS WAS ALL GOING TO HAPPEN?

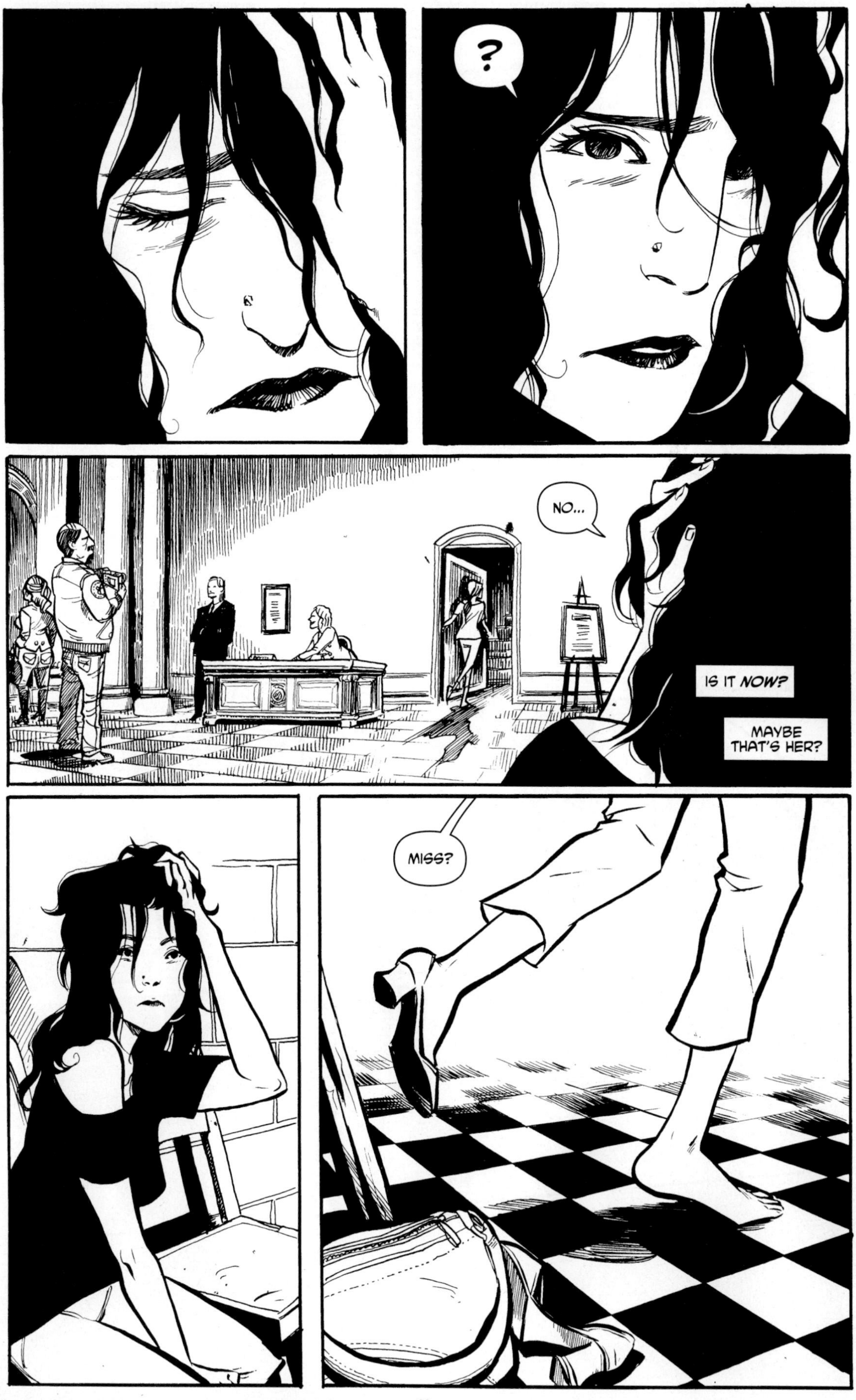
?
NO...
IS IT NOW?
MAYBE THAT'S HER?
MISS?

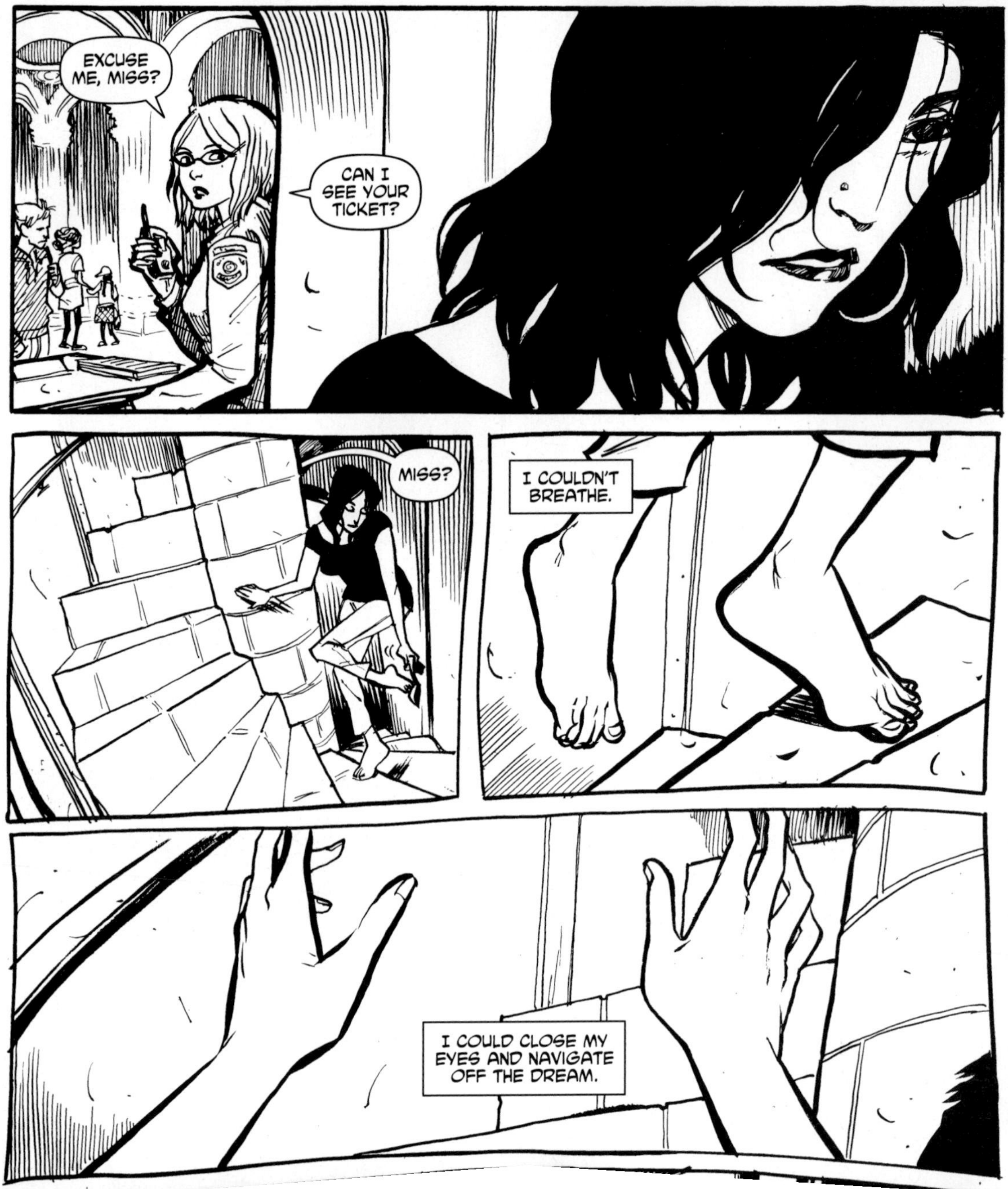
EXCUSE ME, MISS?
CAN I SEE YOUR TICKET?
MISS?
I COULDN'T BREATHE.
I COULD CLOSE MY EYES AND NAVIGATE OFF THE DREAM.

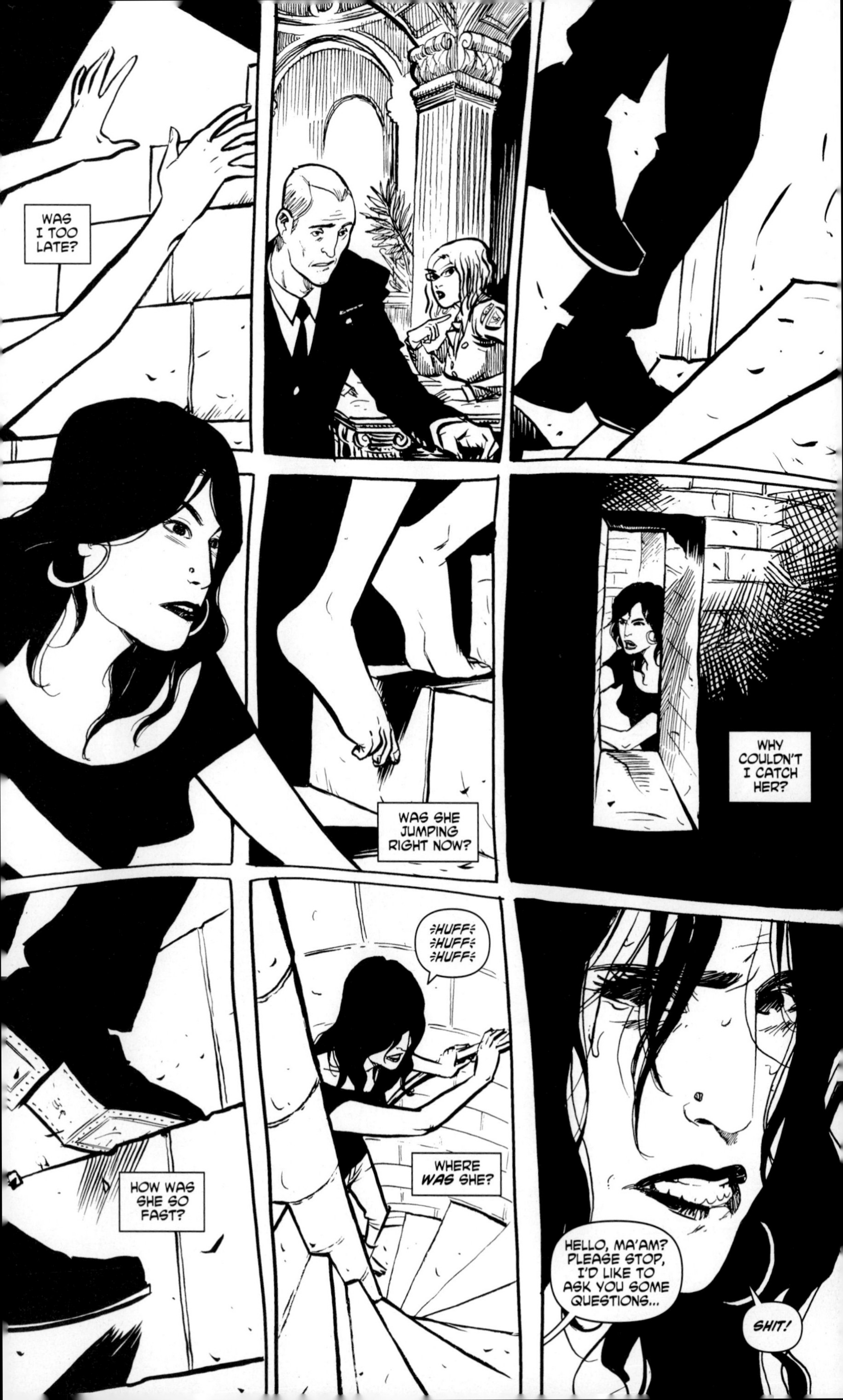
WAS I TOO LATE?
WAS SHE JUMPING RIGHT NOW?
WHY COULDN'T I CATCH HER?
HOW WAS SHE SO FAST?
HUFF HUFF HUFF
WHERE WAS SHE?
HELLO, MA'AM? PLEASE STOP, I'D LIKE TO ASK YOU SOME QUESTIONS...
SHIT!

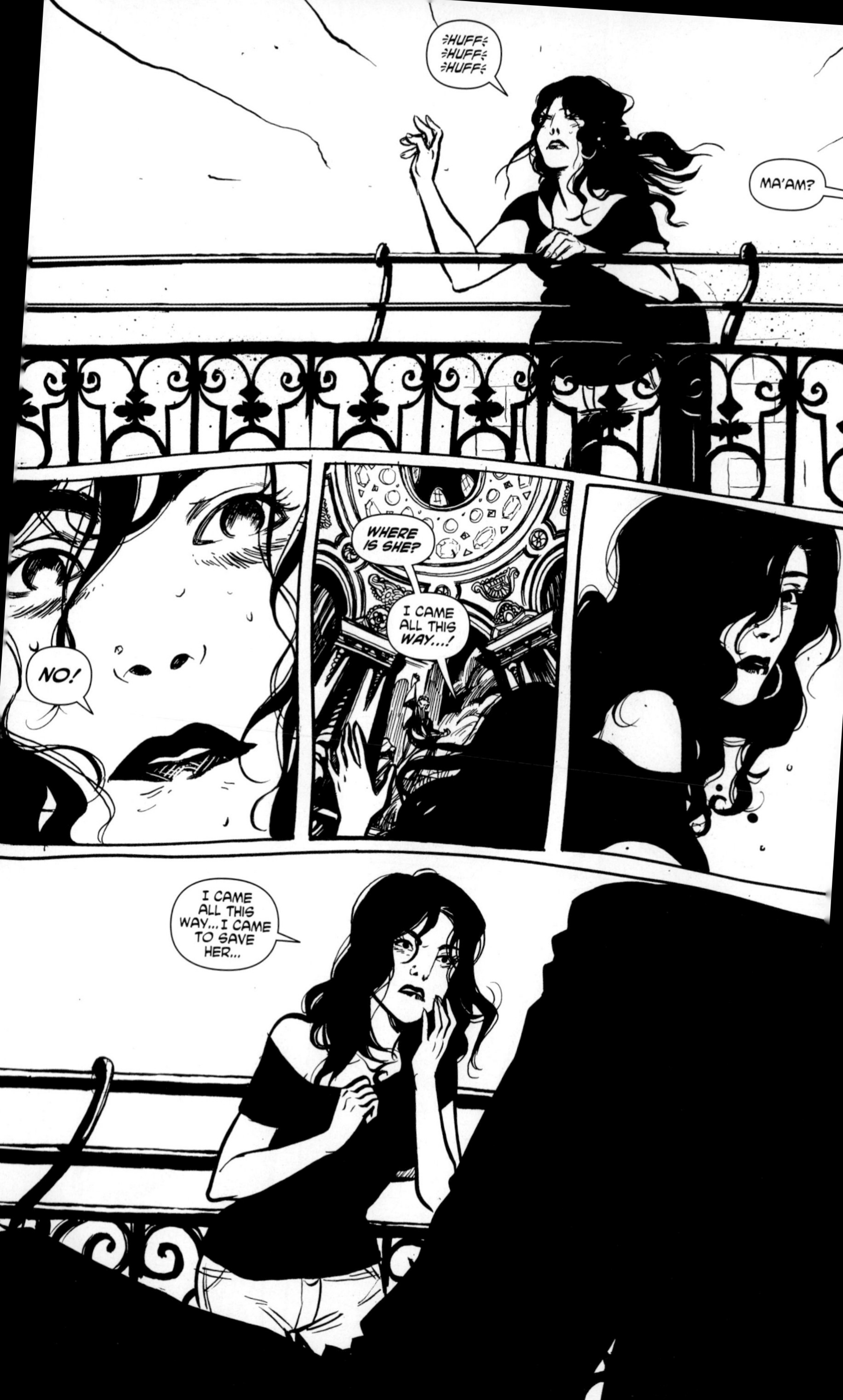

HUFF
HUFF
HUFF
MA'AM?
NO!
WHERE IS SHE?
I CAME ALL THIS WAY...!
I CAME ALL THIS WAY...I CAME TO SAVE HER...

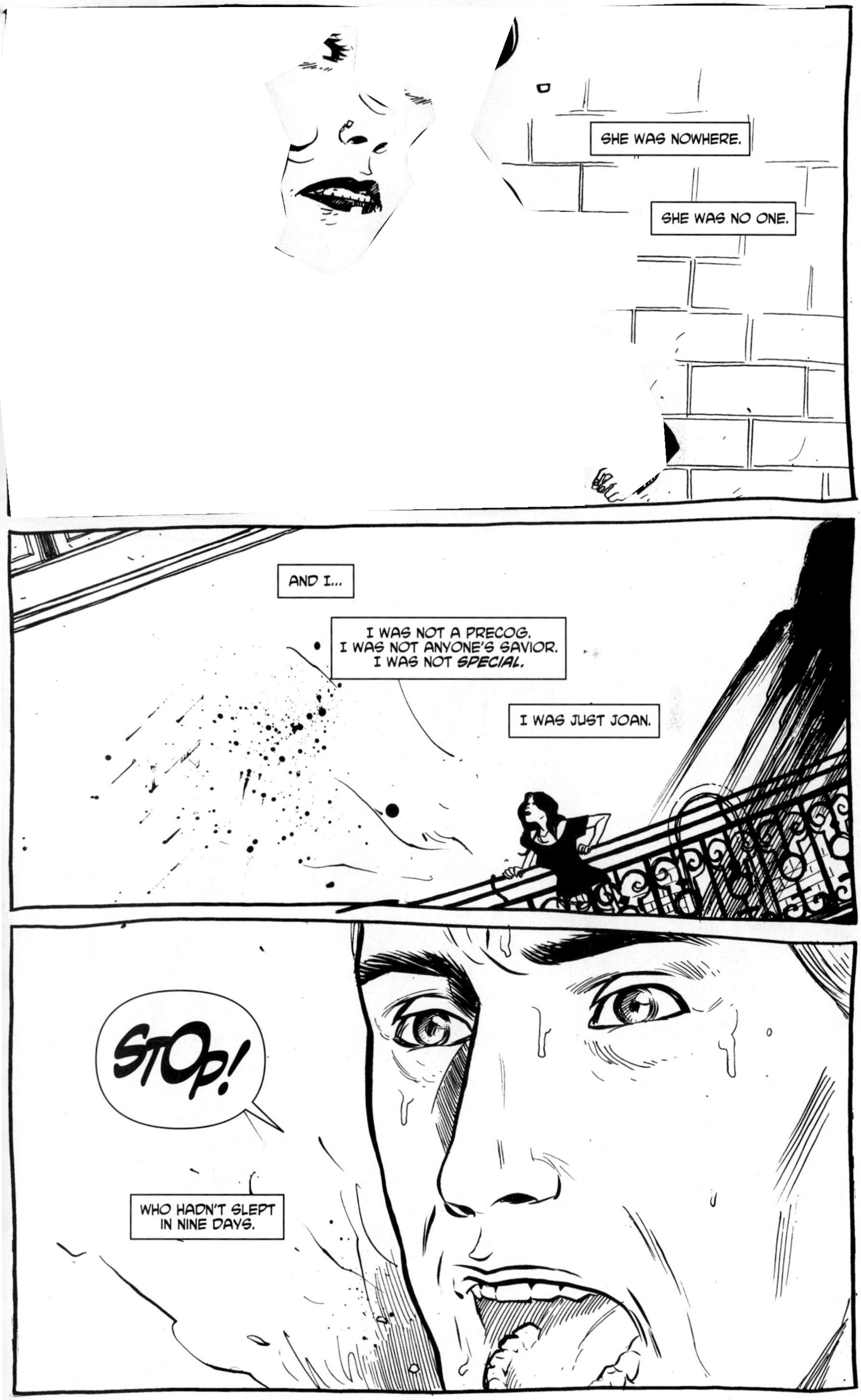
SHE WAS NOWHERE.
SHE WAS NO ONE.
AND I...
I WAS NOT A PRECOG. I WAS NOT ANYONE'S SAVIOR. I WAS NOT *SPECIAL.*
I WAS JUST JOAN.
STOP!
WHO HADN'T SLEPT IN NINE DAYS.

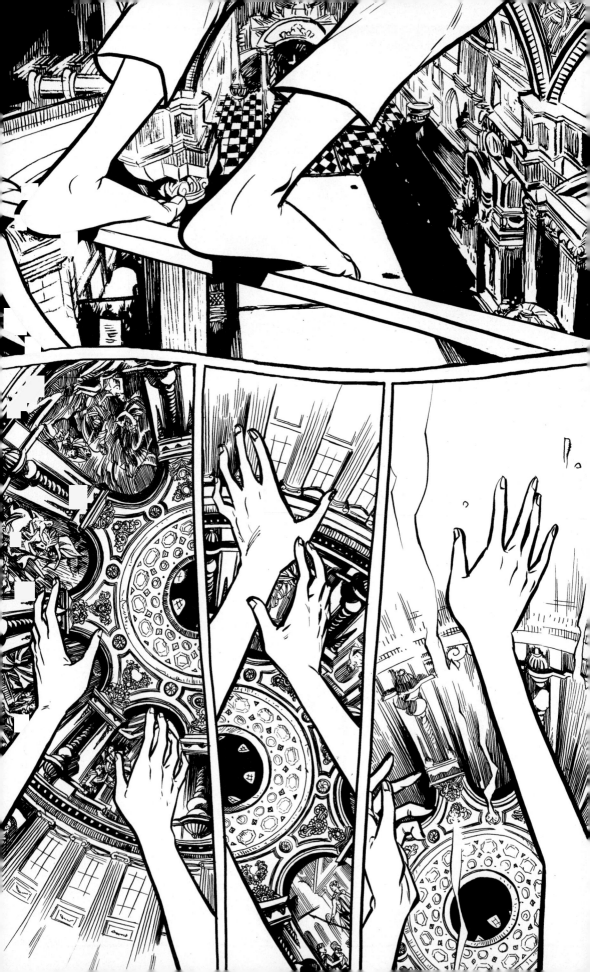

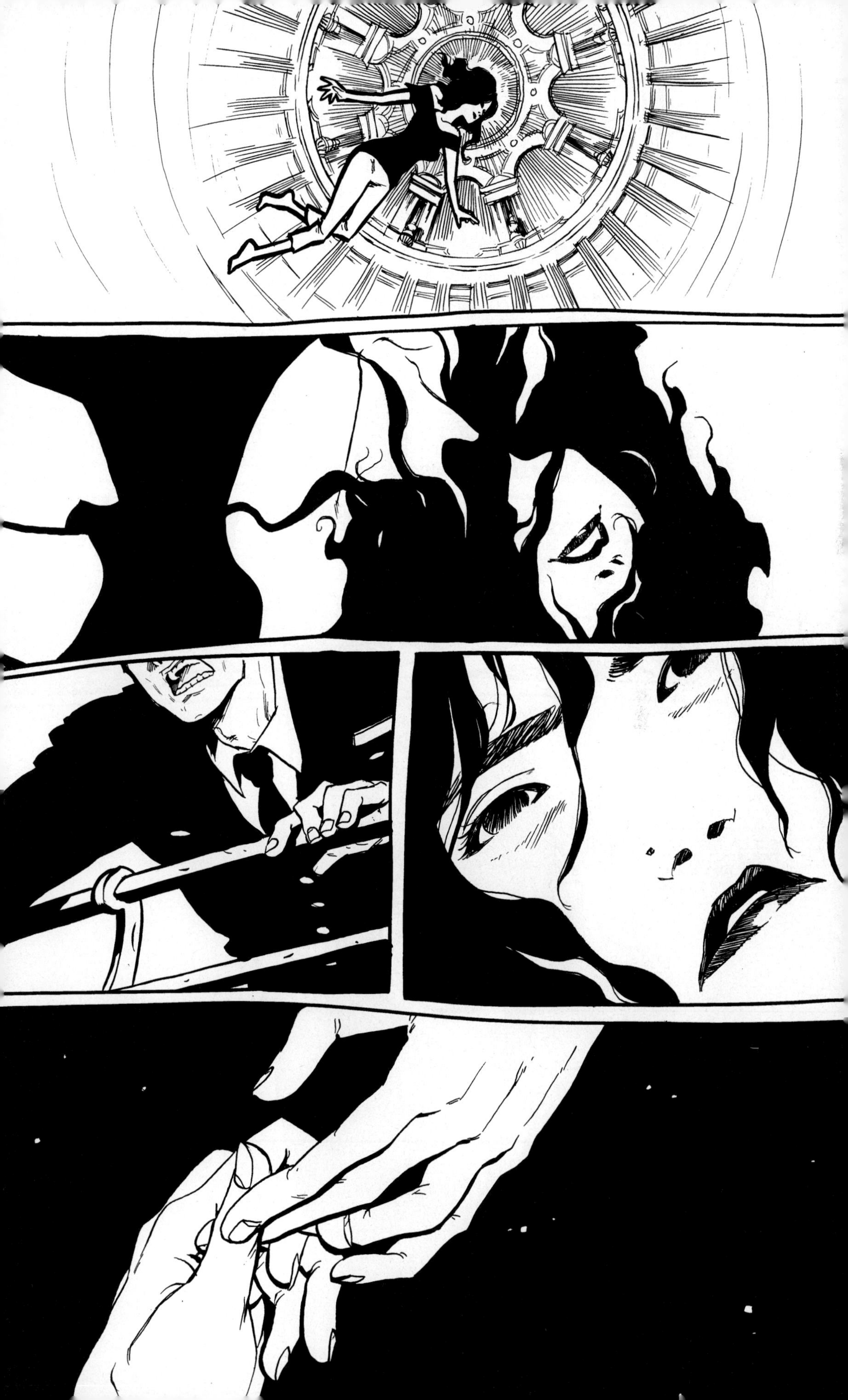

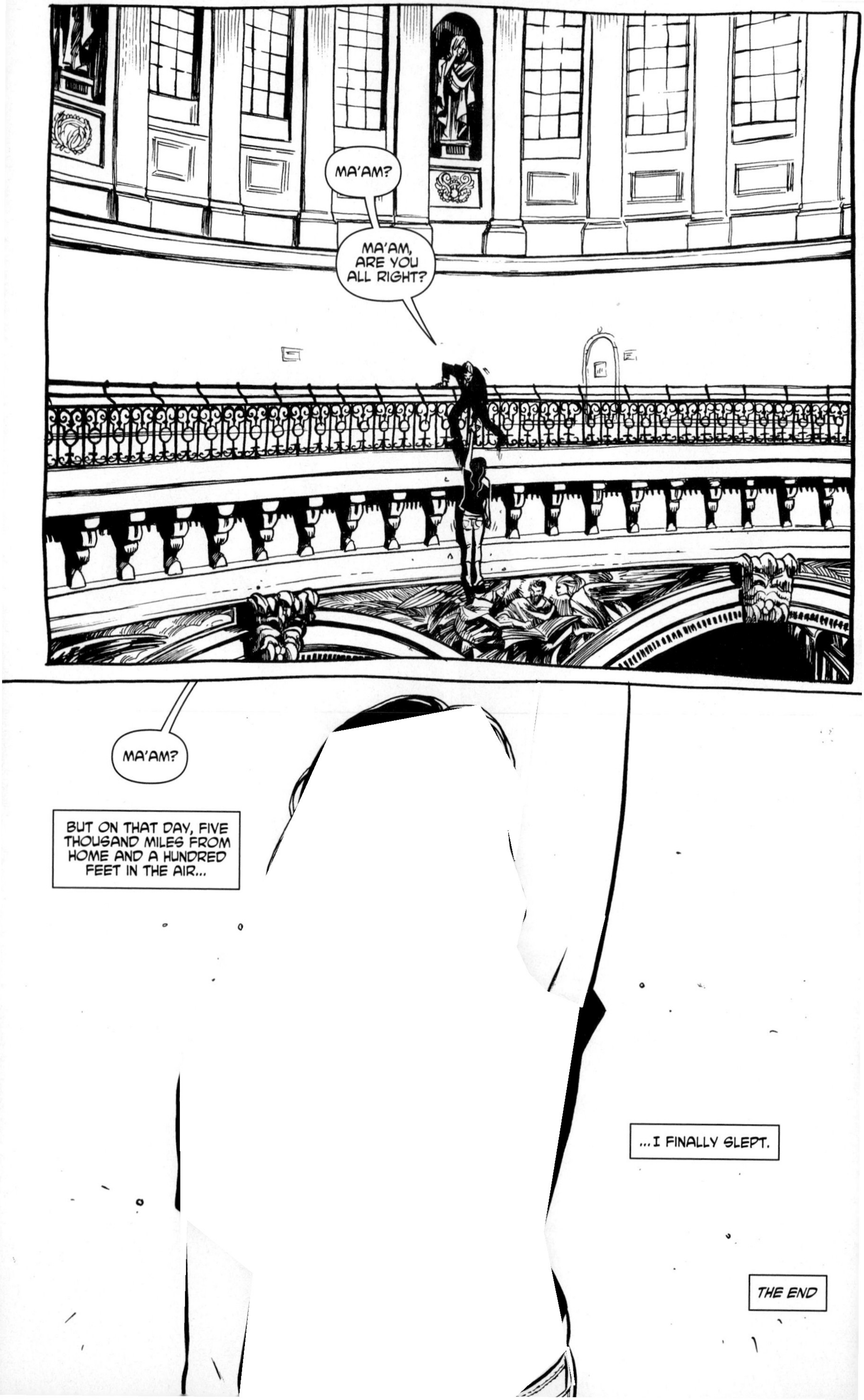
MA'AM?
MA'AM, ARE YOU ALL RIGHT?
MA'AM?
BUT ON THAT DAY, FIVE THOUSAND MILES FROM HOME AND A HUNDRED FEET IN THE AIR...
...I FINALLY SLEPT.
THE END

2

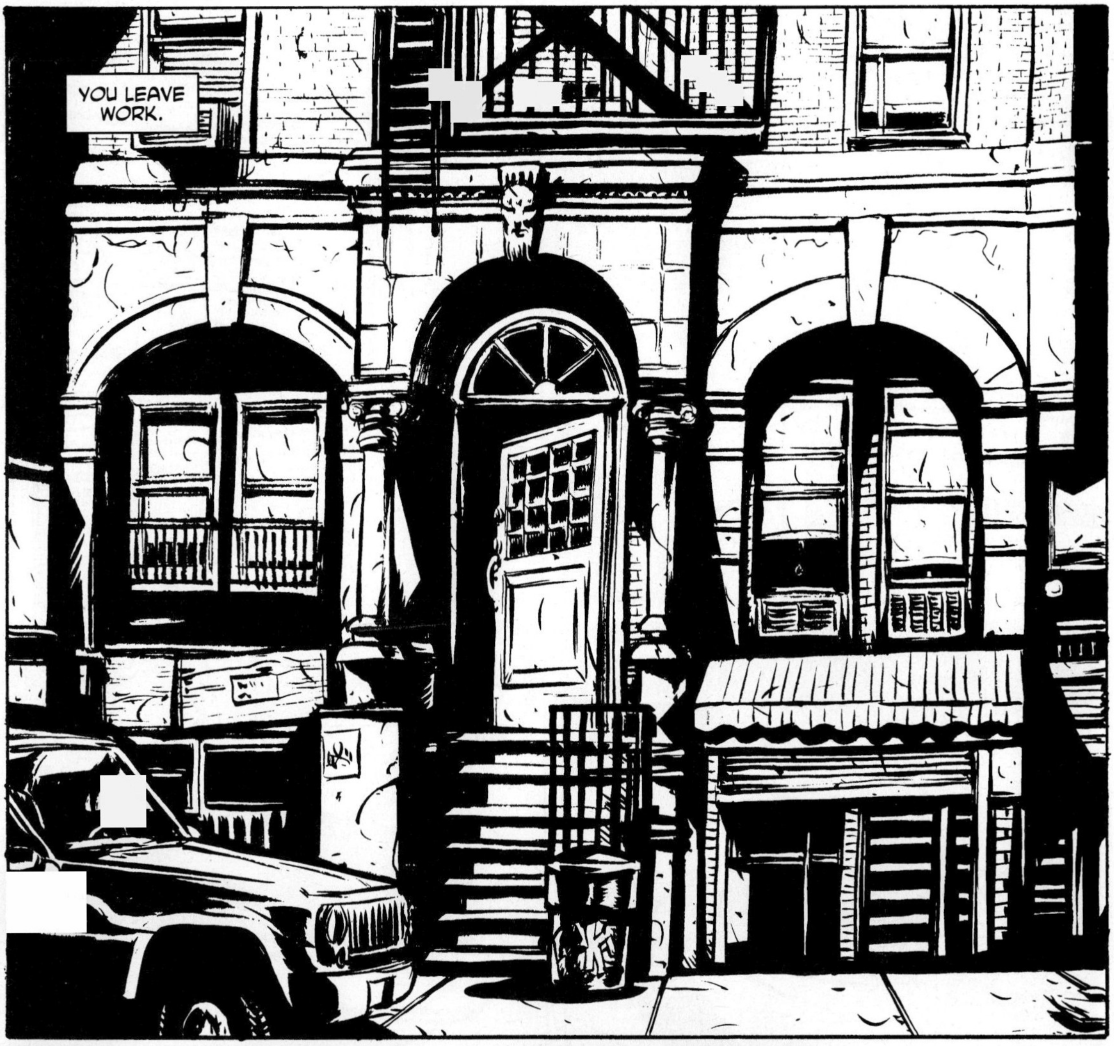
YOU LEAVE WORK.

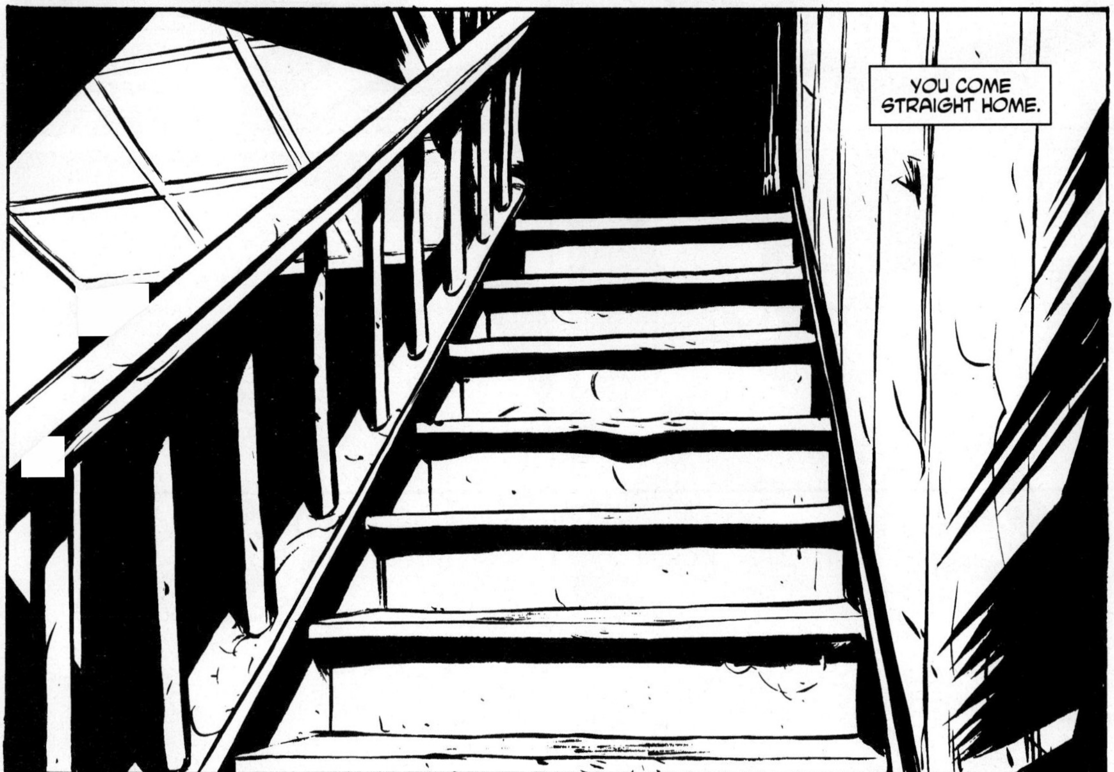
YOU COME STRAIGHT HOME.

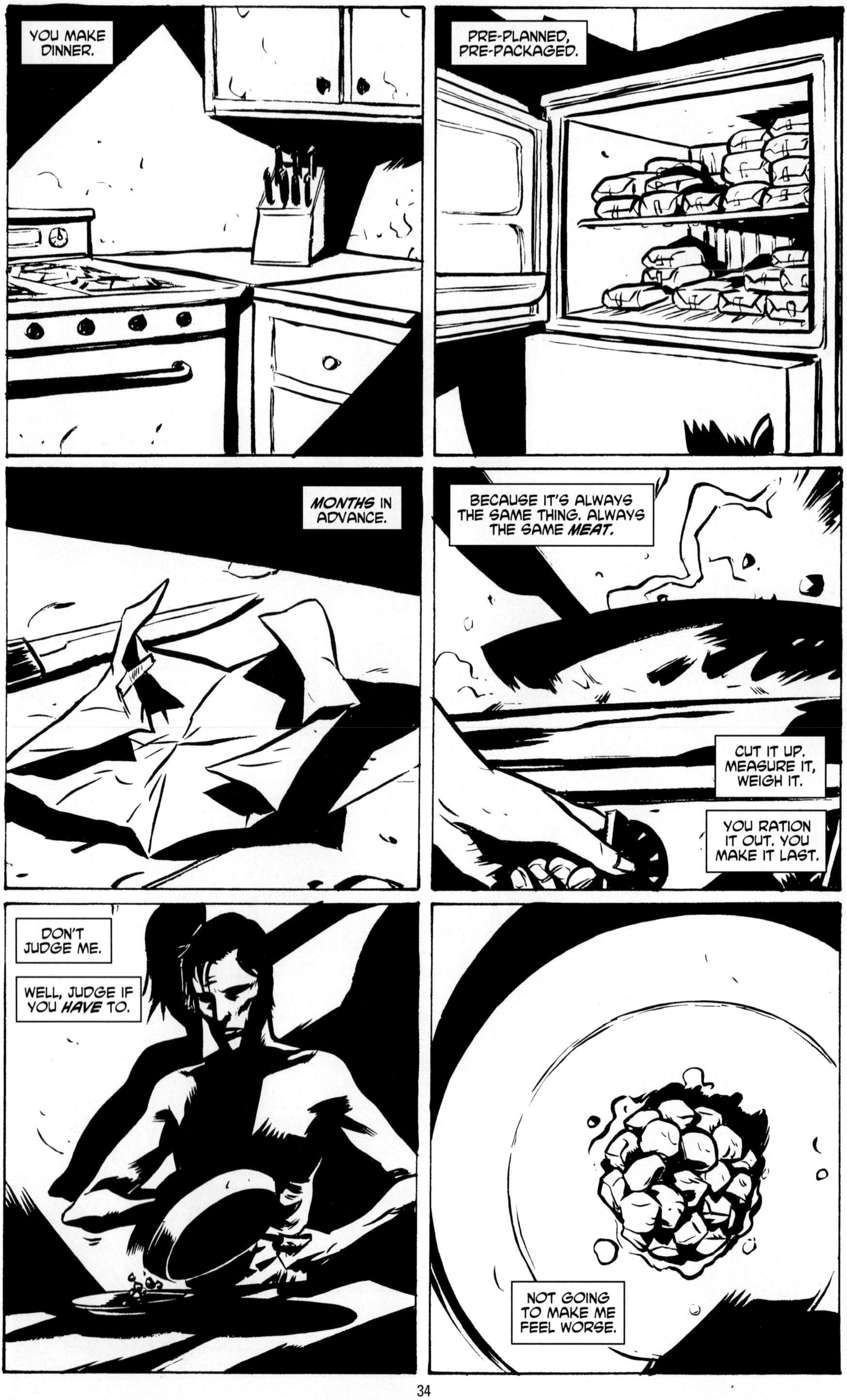
YOU MAKE DINNER.
PRE-PLANNED, PRE-PACKAGED.
MONTHS IN ADVANCE.
BECAUSE IT'S ALWAYS THE SAME THING. ALWAYS THE SAME MEAT.
CUT IT UP. MEASURE IT, WEIGH IT.
YOU RATION IT OUT. YOU MAKE IT LAST.
DON'T JUDGE ME.
WELL, JUDGE IF YOU HAVE TO.
NOT GOING TO MAKE ME FEEL WORSE.

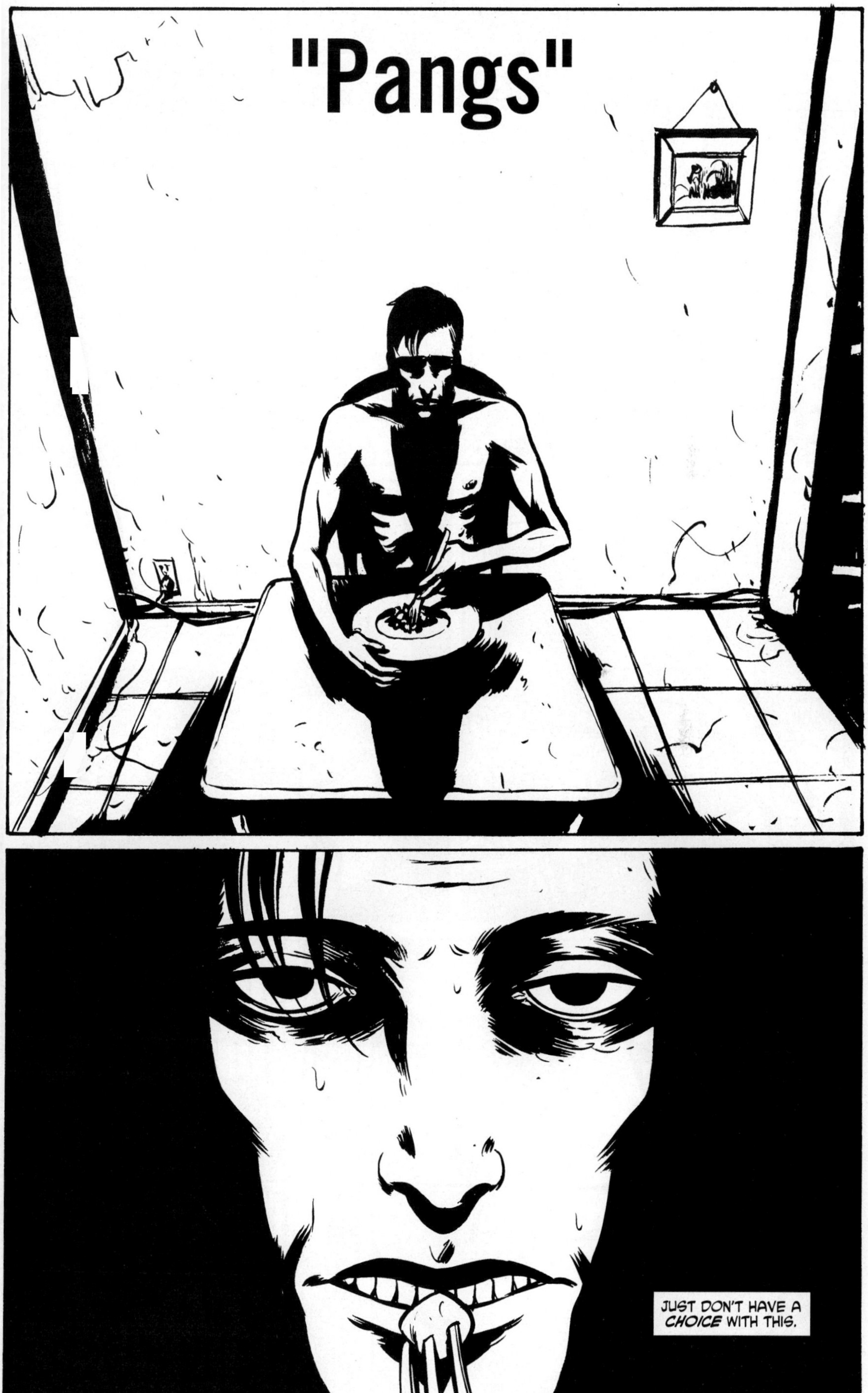
"Pangs"
JUST DON'T HAVE A *CHOICE* WITH THIS.

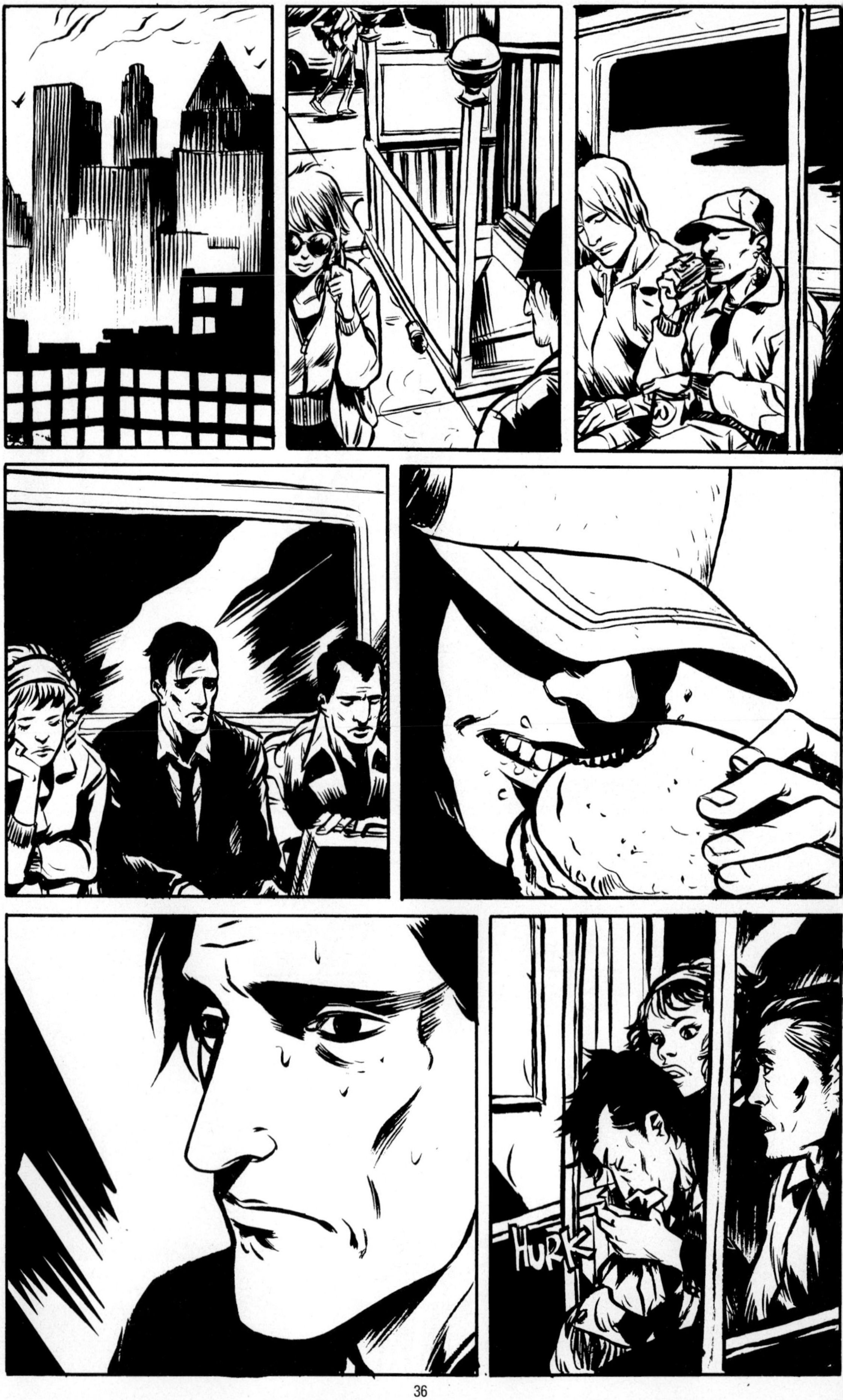
HURK

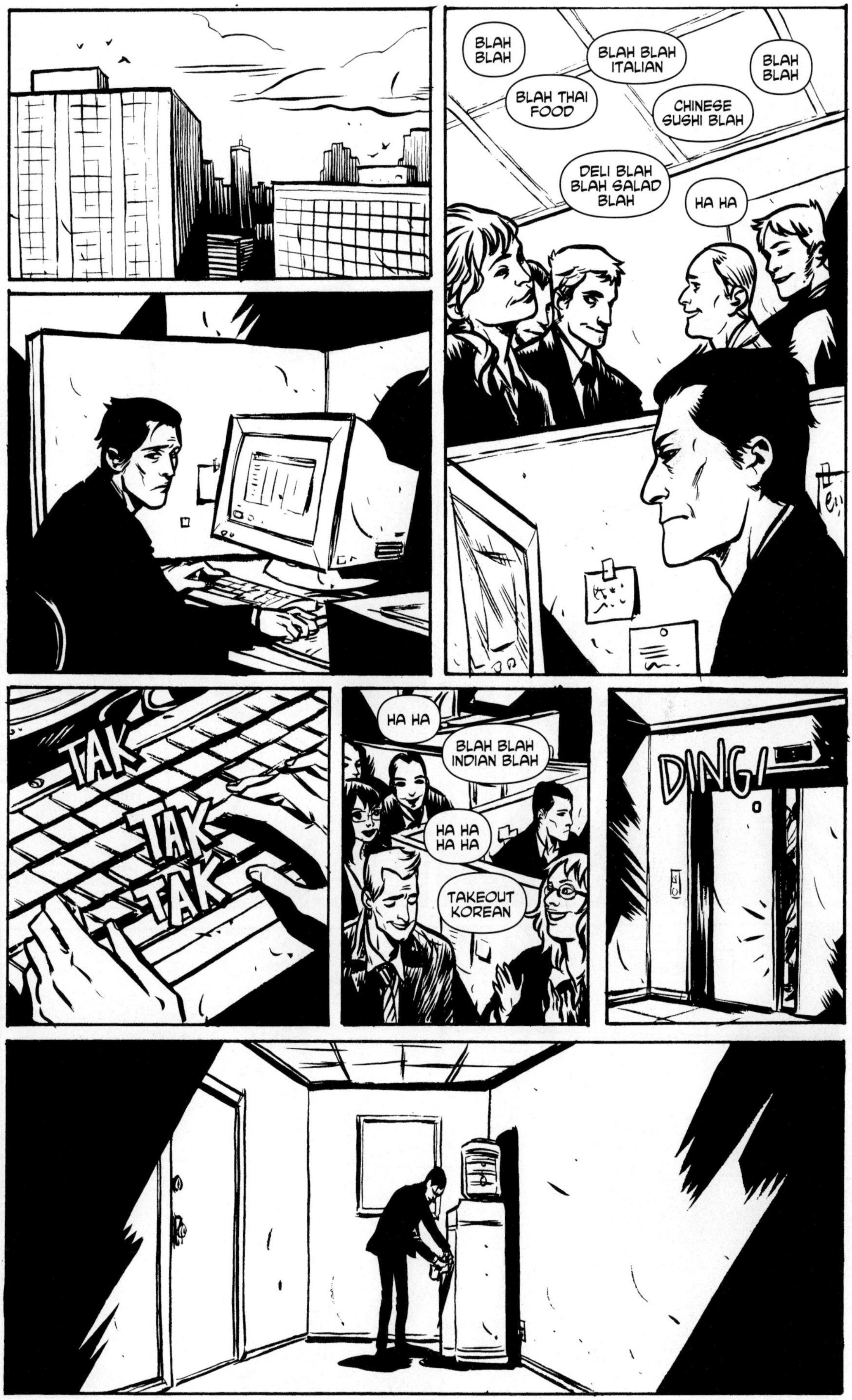
BLAH BLAH
BLAH THAI FOOD
BLAH BLAH ITALIAN
CHINESE SUSHI BLAH
BLAH BLAH
DELI BLAH BLAH SALAD BLAH
HA HA
TAK
TAK
TAK
HA HA
BLAH BLAH INDIAN BLAH
HA HA HA HA
TAKEOUT KOREAN
DING!

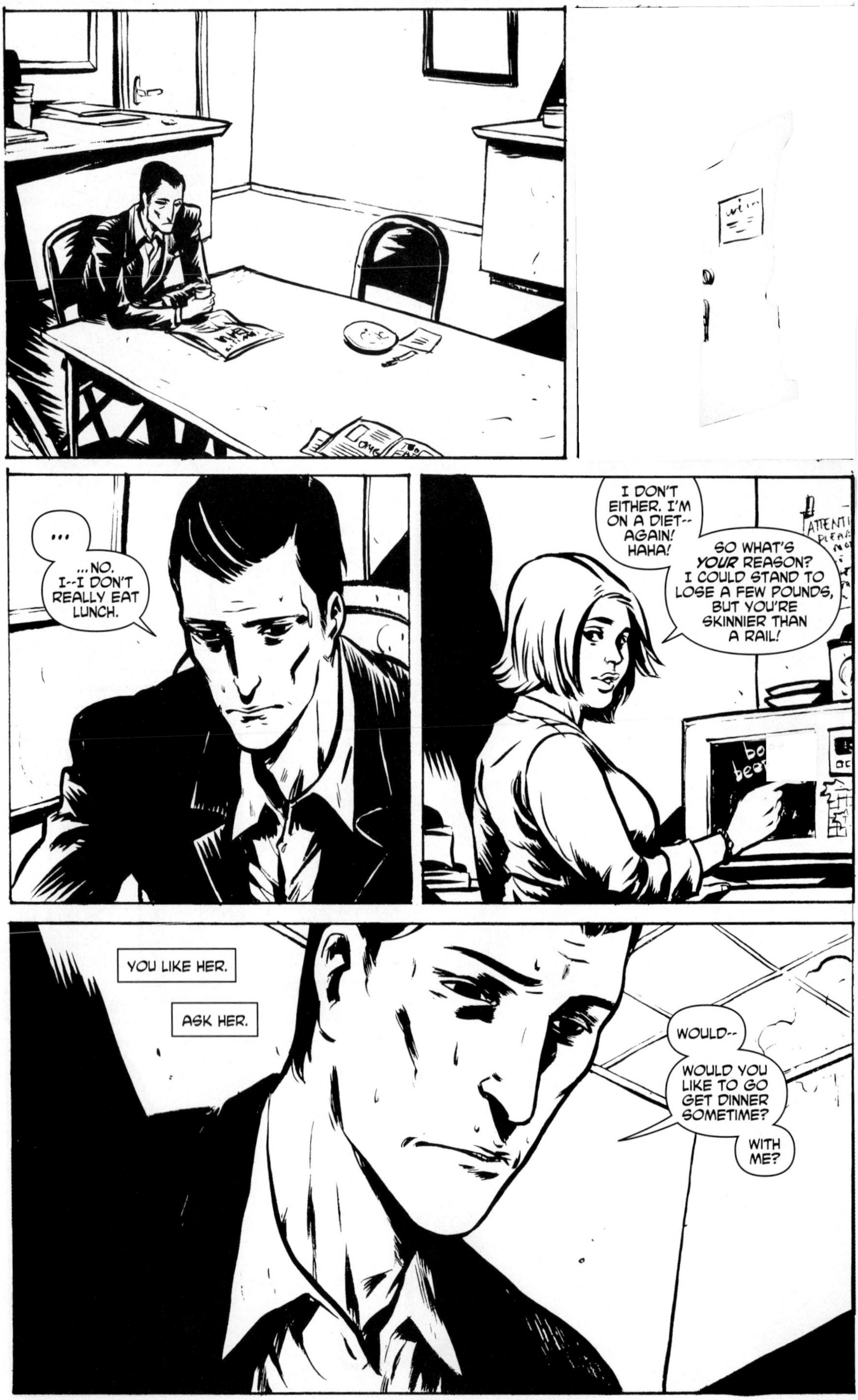
...
...NO. I--I DON'T REALLY EAT LUNCH.
I DON'T EITHER. I'M ON A DIET-- AGAIN! HAHA!
SO WHAT'S *YOUR* REASON? I COULD STAND TO LOSE A FEW POUNDS, BUT YOU'RE SKINNIER THAN A RAIL!
YOU LIKE HER.
ASK HER.
WOULD--
WOULD YOU LIKE TO GO GET DINNER SOMETIME?
WITH ME?

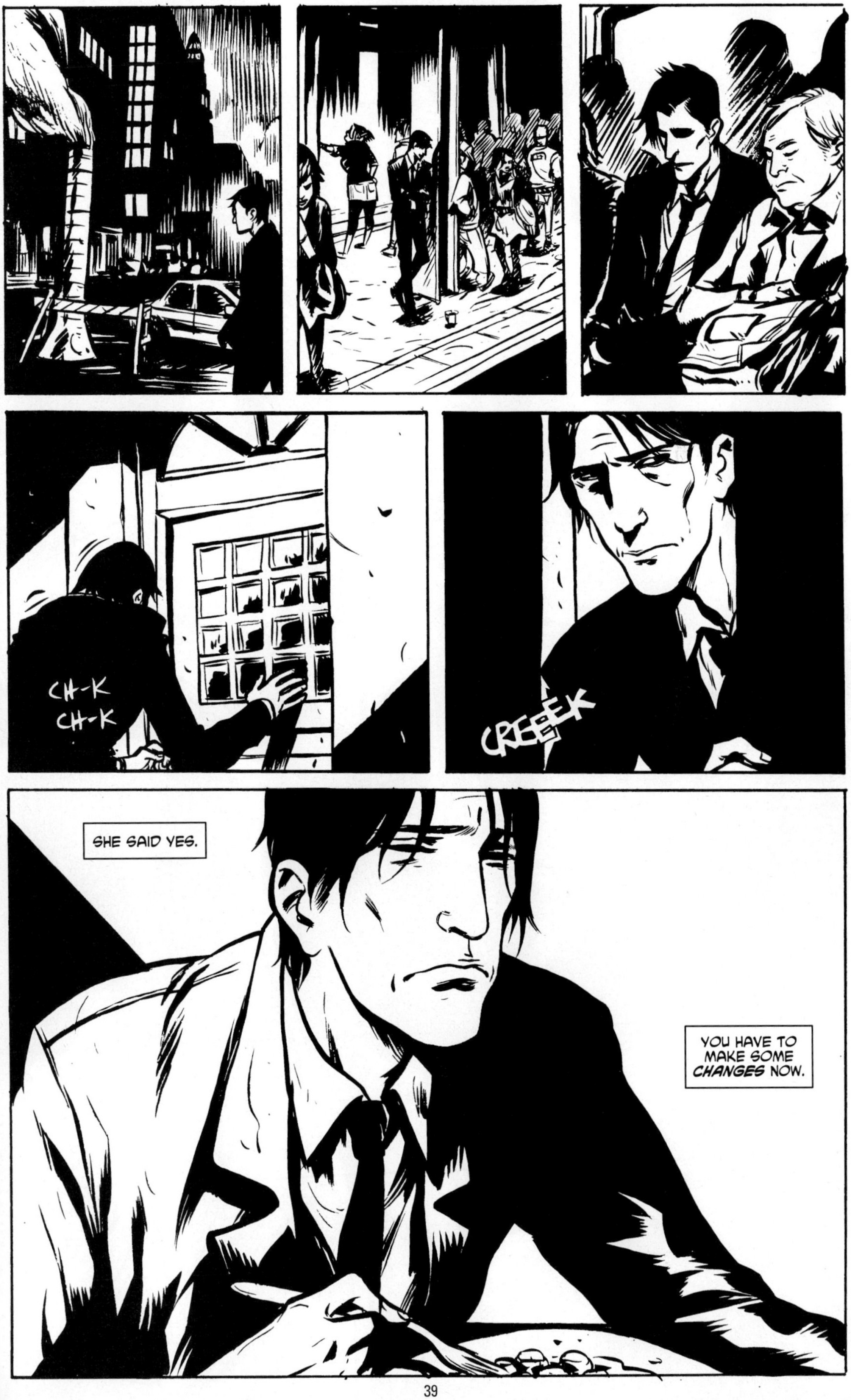
CH-K
CH-K
CREEEEK
SHE SAID YES.
YOU HAVE TO MAKE SOME CHANGES NOW.

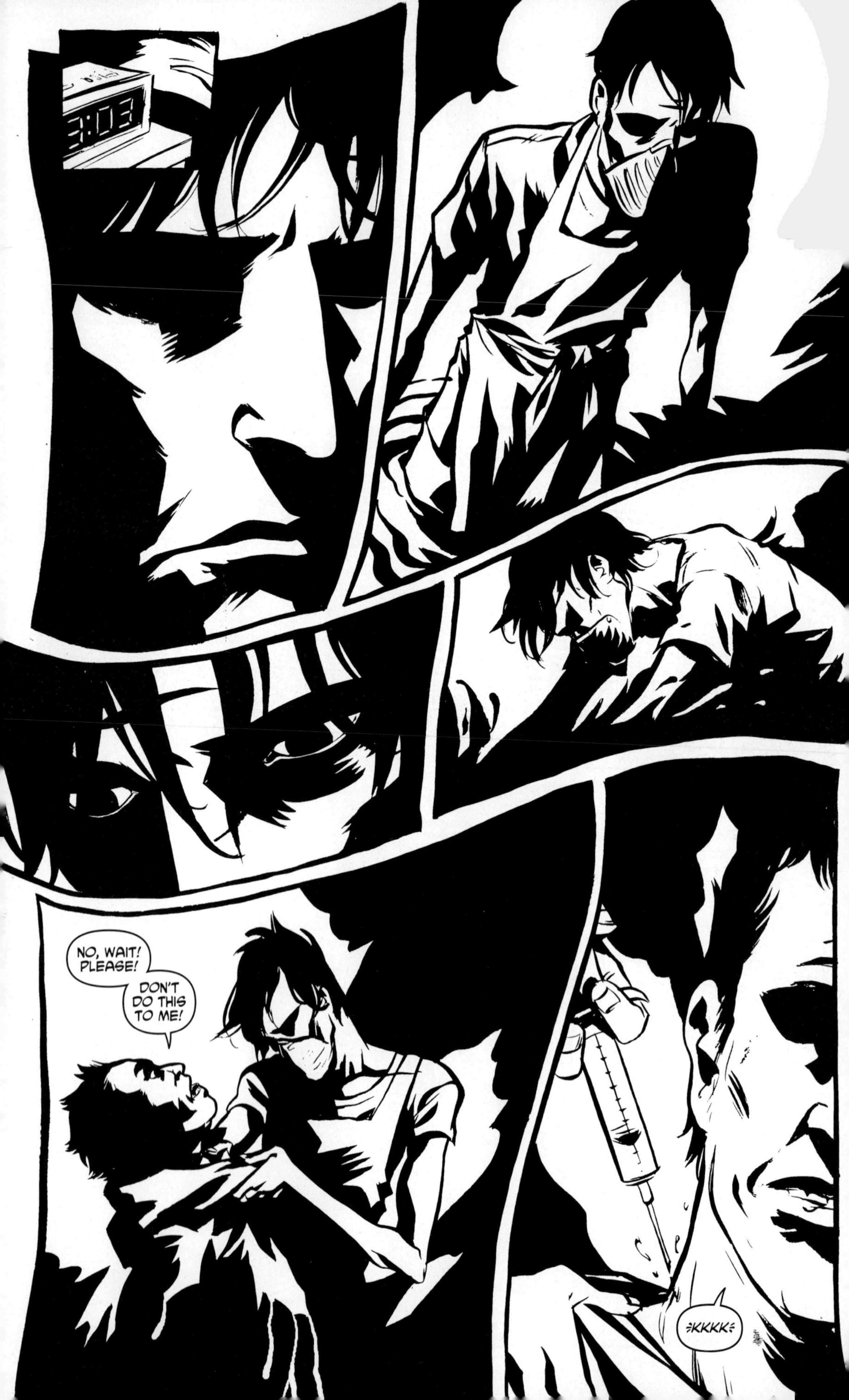
3:03
NO, WAIT! PLEASE!
DON'T DO THIS TO ME!
KKKK

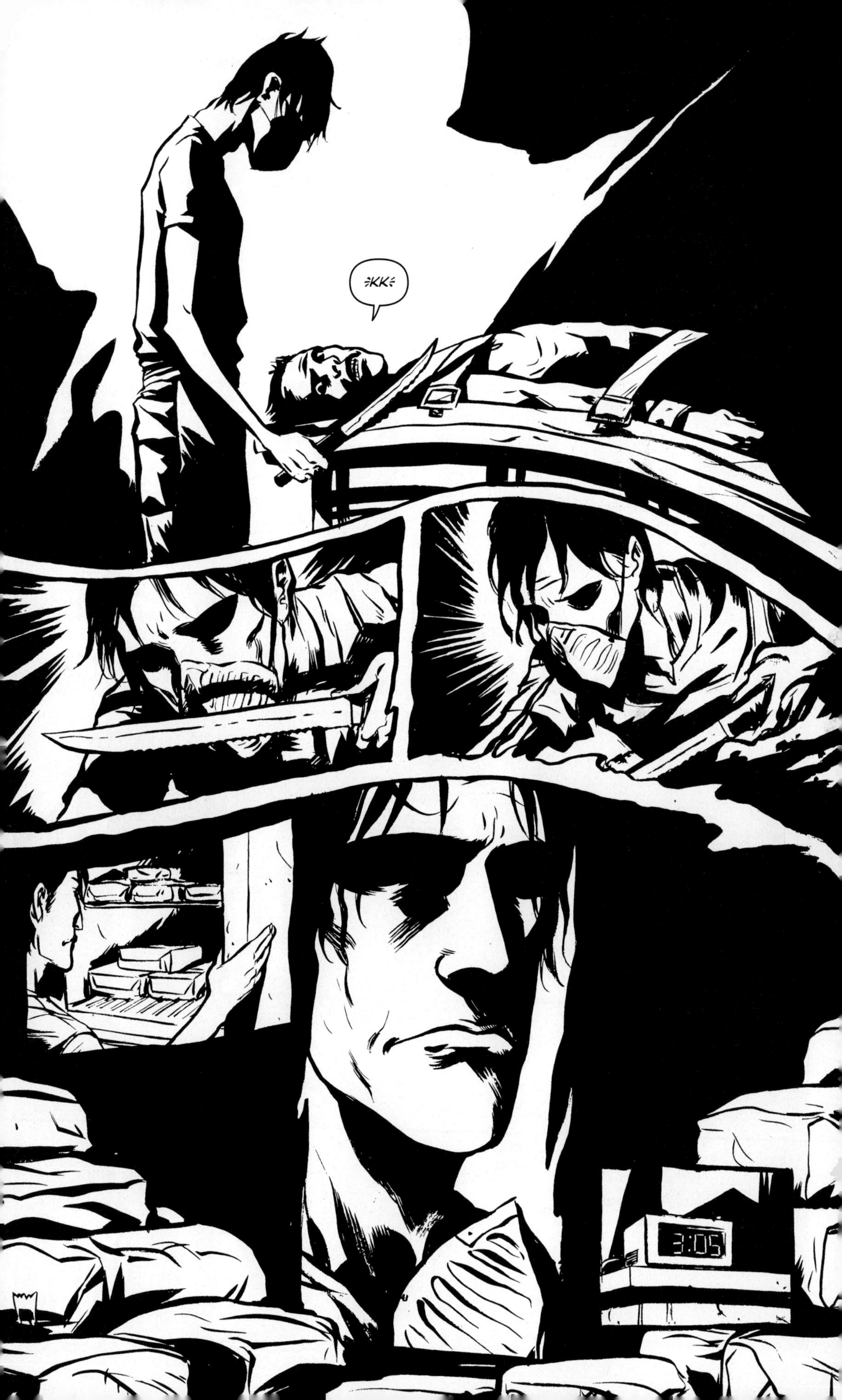
KK
3:05

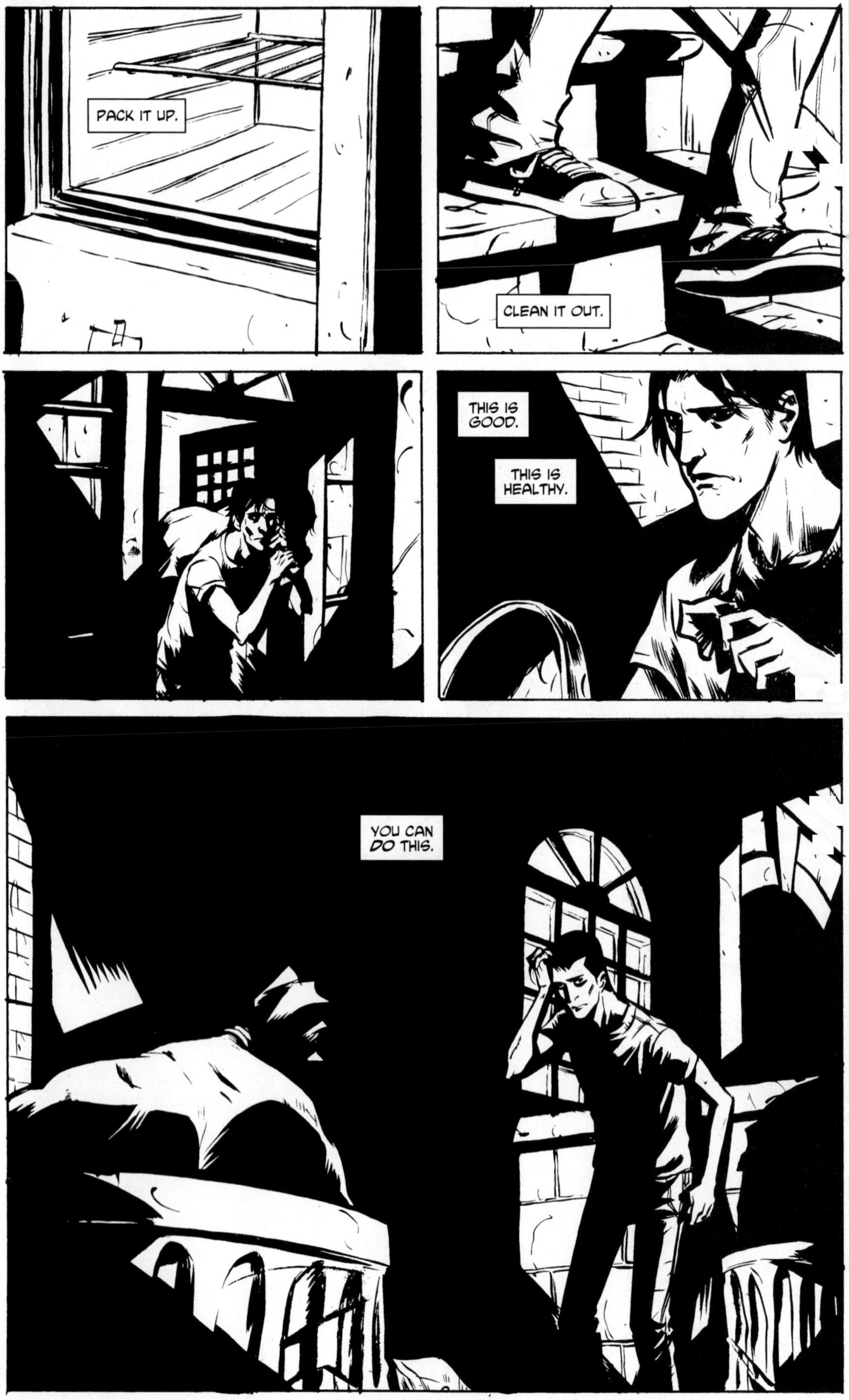
PACK IT UP.
CLEAN IT OUT.
THIS IS GOOD.
THIS IS HEALTHY.
YOU CAN *DO* THIS.

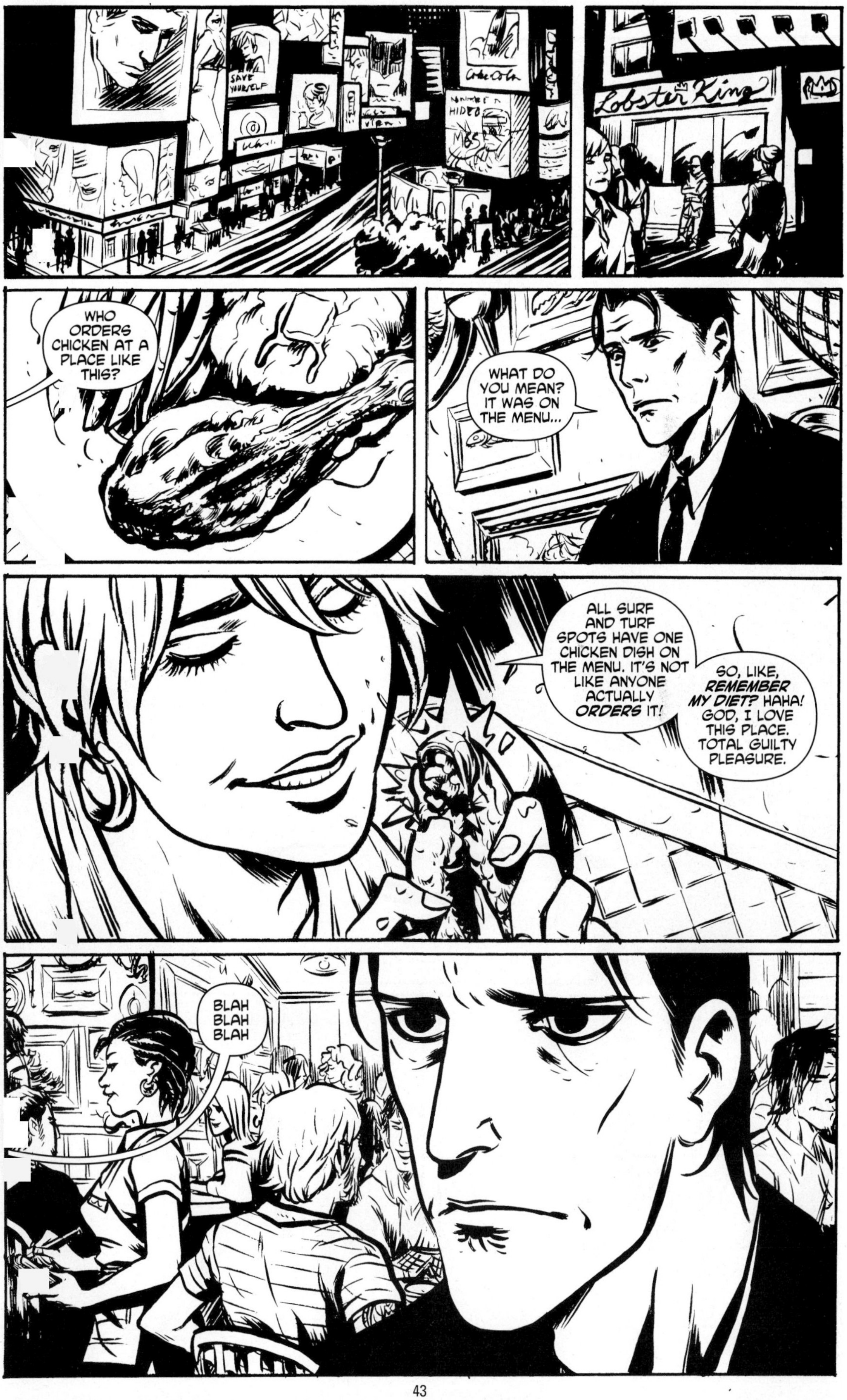
SAVE YOURSELF
Lobster King
WHO ORDERS CHICKEN AT A PLACE LIKE THIS?
WHAT DO YOU MEAN? IT WAS ON THE MENU...
ALL SURF AND TURF SPOTS HAVE ONE CHICKEN DISH ON THE MENU. IT'S NOT LIKE ANYONE ACTUALLY ORDERS IT!
SO, LIKE, REMEMBER MY DIET? HAHA! GOD, I LOVE THIS PLACE. TOTAL GUILTY PLEASURE.
BLAH BLAH BLAH

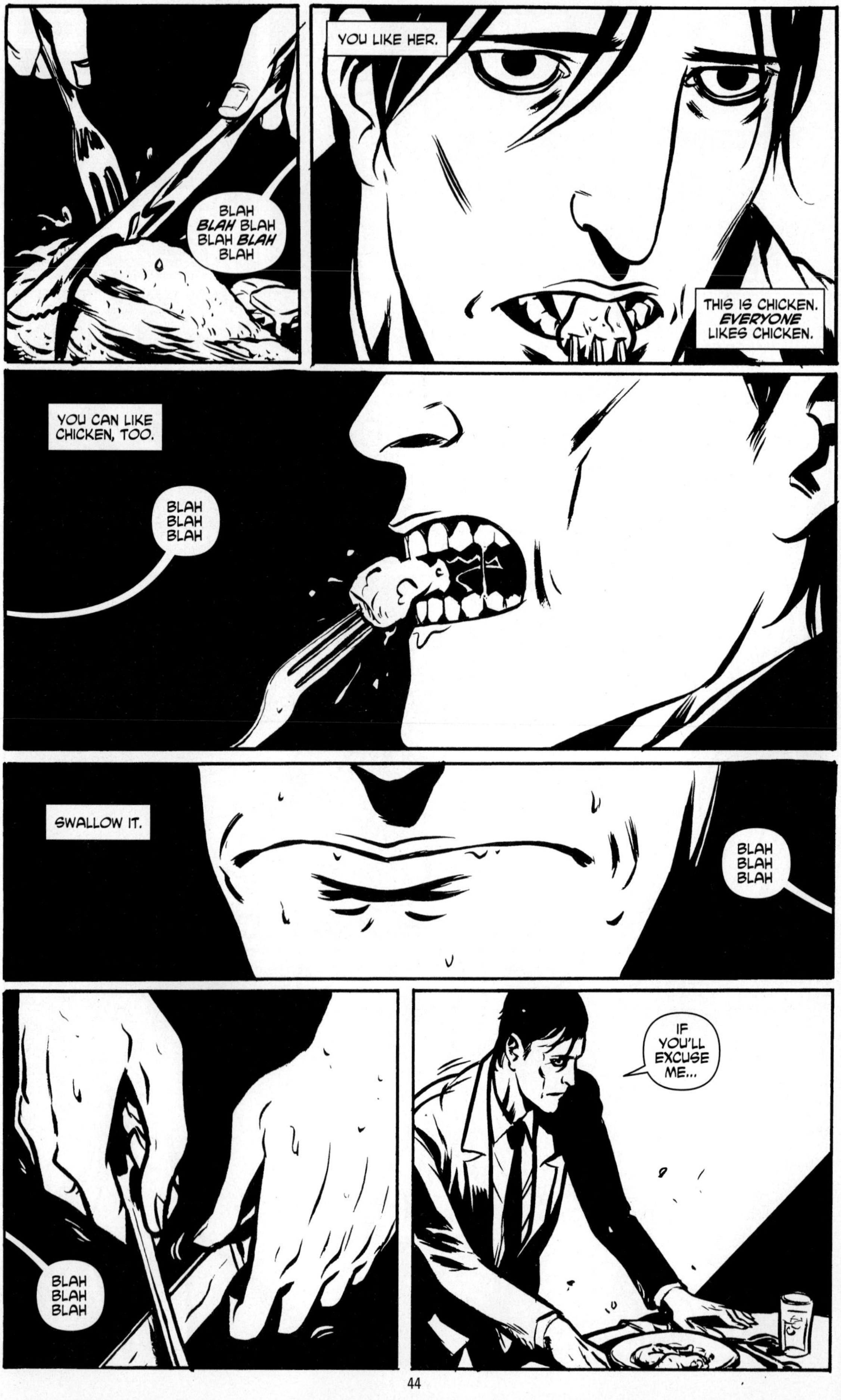
BLAH BLAH BLAH BLAH BLAH BLAH
YOU LIKE HER.
THIS IS CHICKEN. EVERYONE LIKES CHICKEN.
YOU CAN LIKE CHICKEN, TOO.
BLAH BLAH BLAH
SWALLOW IT.
BLAH BLAH BLAH
BLAH BLAH BLAH
IF YOU'LL EXCUSE ME...

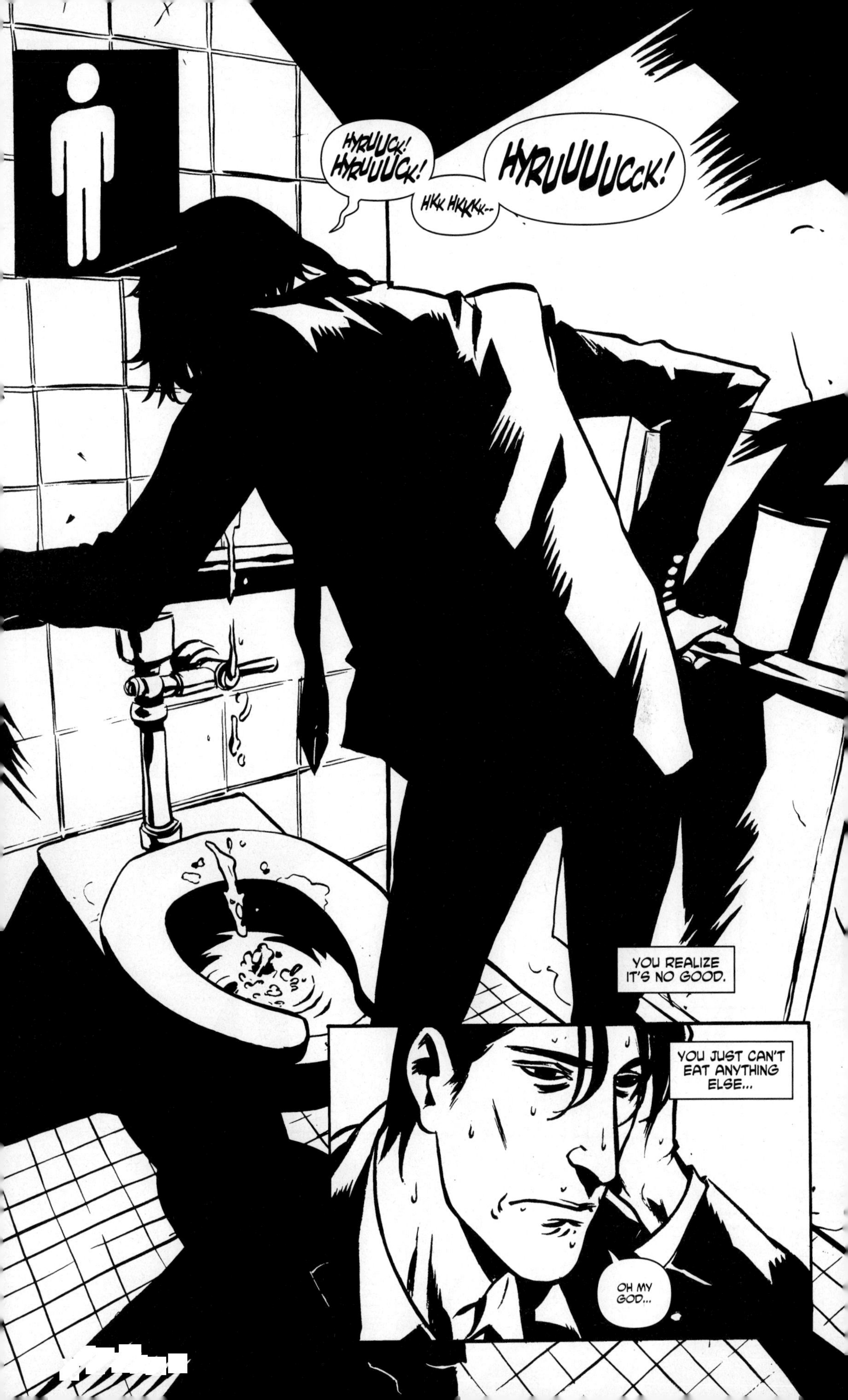
HYRUUCK! HYRUUUCK!
HKK HKKKK--
HYRUUUUCCK!
YOU REALIZE IT'S NO GOOD.
YOU JUST CAN'T EAT ANYTHING ELSE...
OH MY GOD...

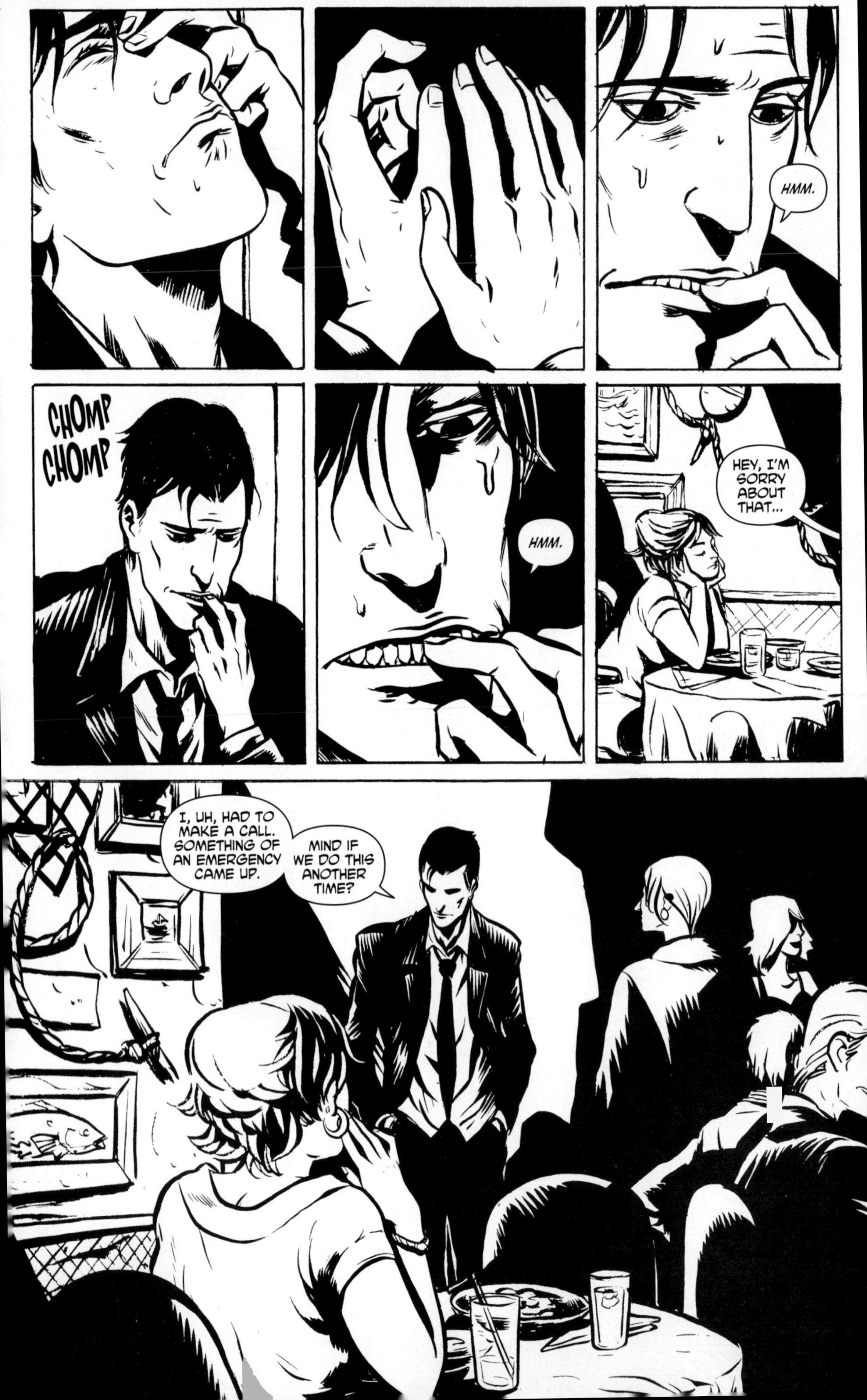
HMM.
CHOMP
CHOMP
HMM.
HEY, I'M SORRY ABOUT THAT...
I, UH, HAD TO MAKE A CALL. SOMETHING OF AN EMERGENCY CAME UP.
MIND IF WE DO THIS ANOTHER TIME?

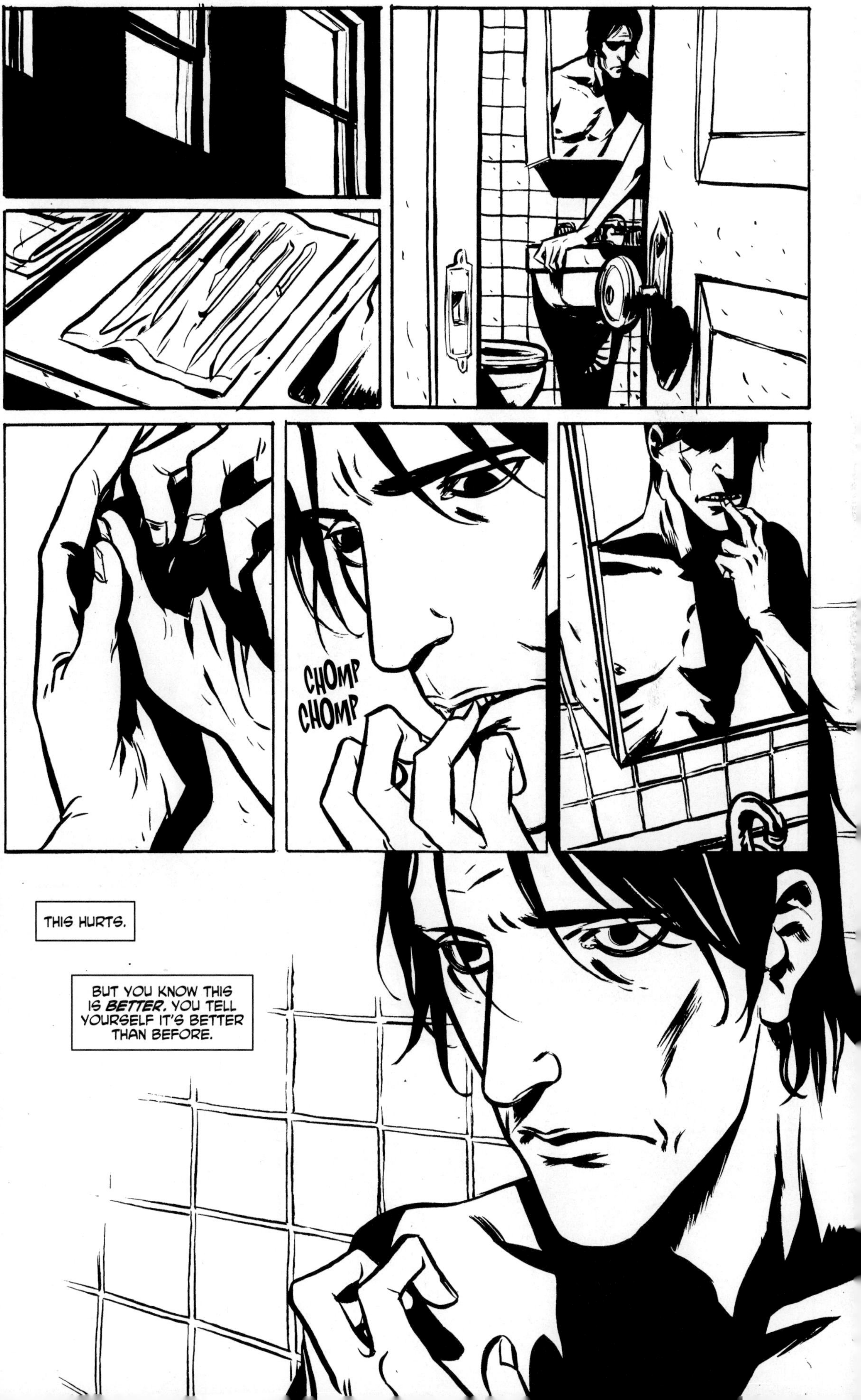
CHOMP
CHOMP
THIS HURTS.
BUT YOU KNOW THIS IS *BETTER.* YOU TELL YOURSELF IT'S BETTER THAN BEFORE.

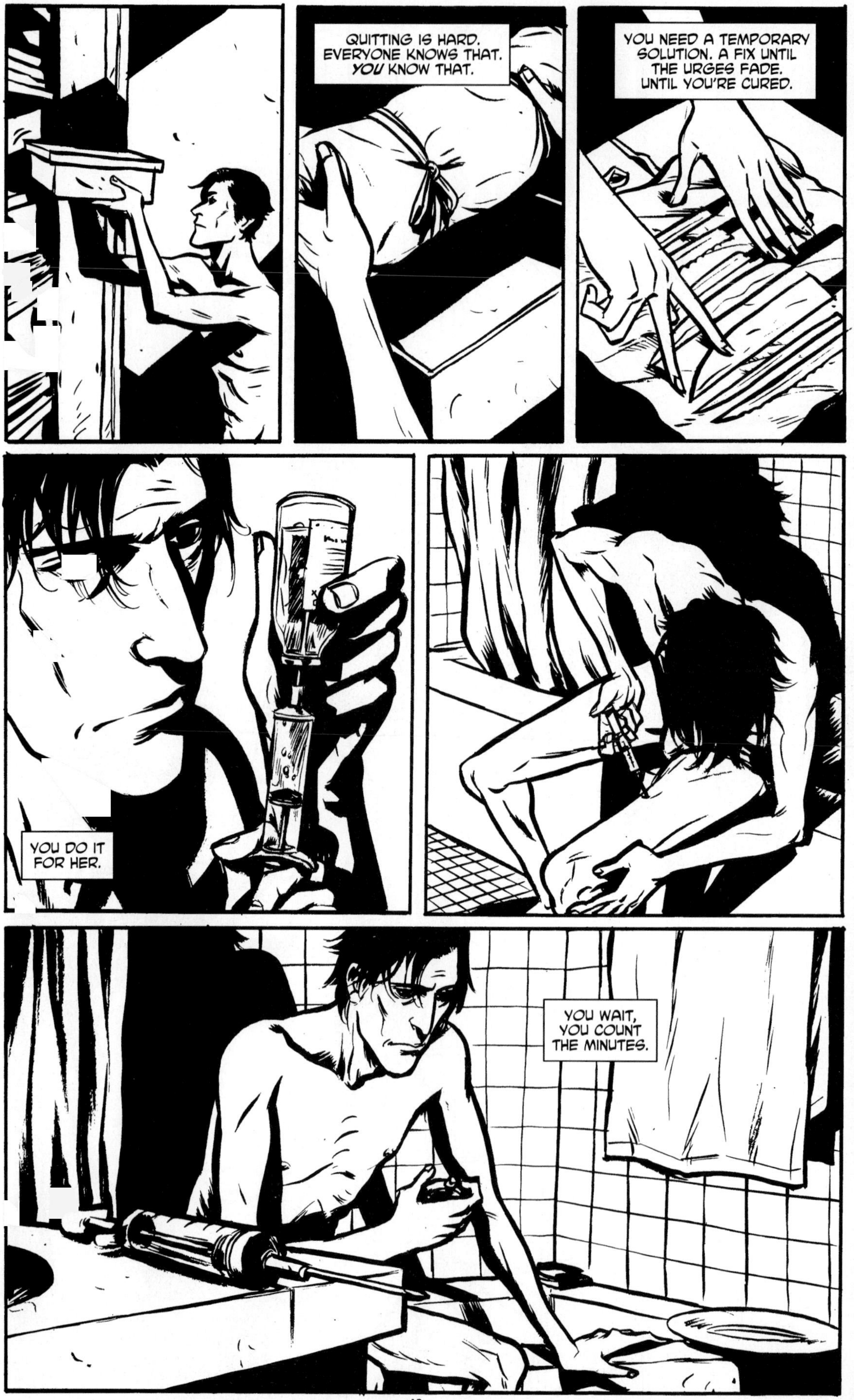
QUITTING IS HARD. EVERYONE KNOWS THAT. *YOU* KNOW THAT.
YOU NEED A TEMPORARY SOLUTION. A FIX UNTIL THE URGES FADE. UNTIL YOU'RE CURED.
YOU DO IT FOR HER.
YOU WAIT, YOU COUNT THE MINUTES.

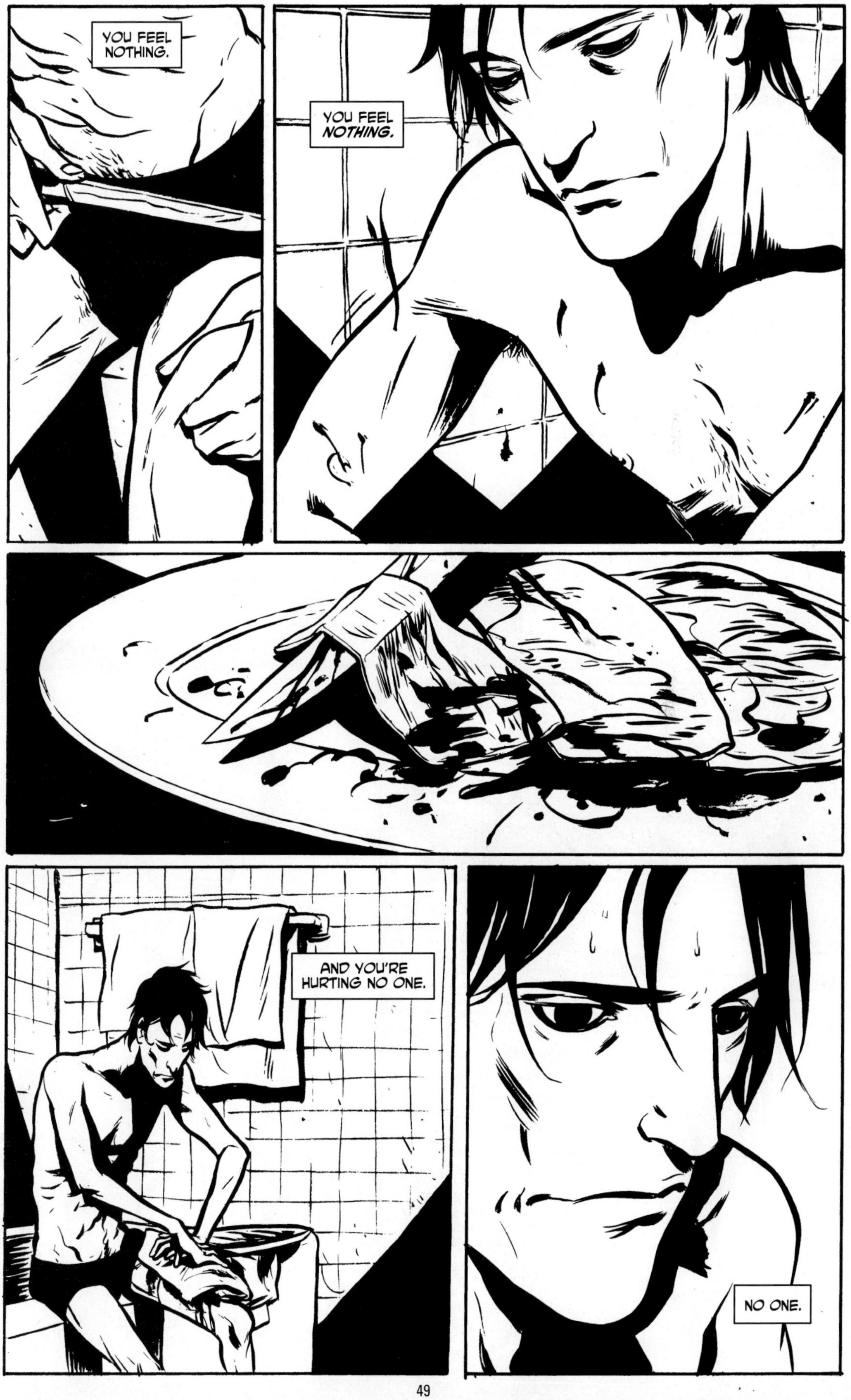
YOU FEEL NOTHING.
YOU FEEL *NOTHING.*
AND YOU'RE HURTING NO ONE.
NO ONE.

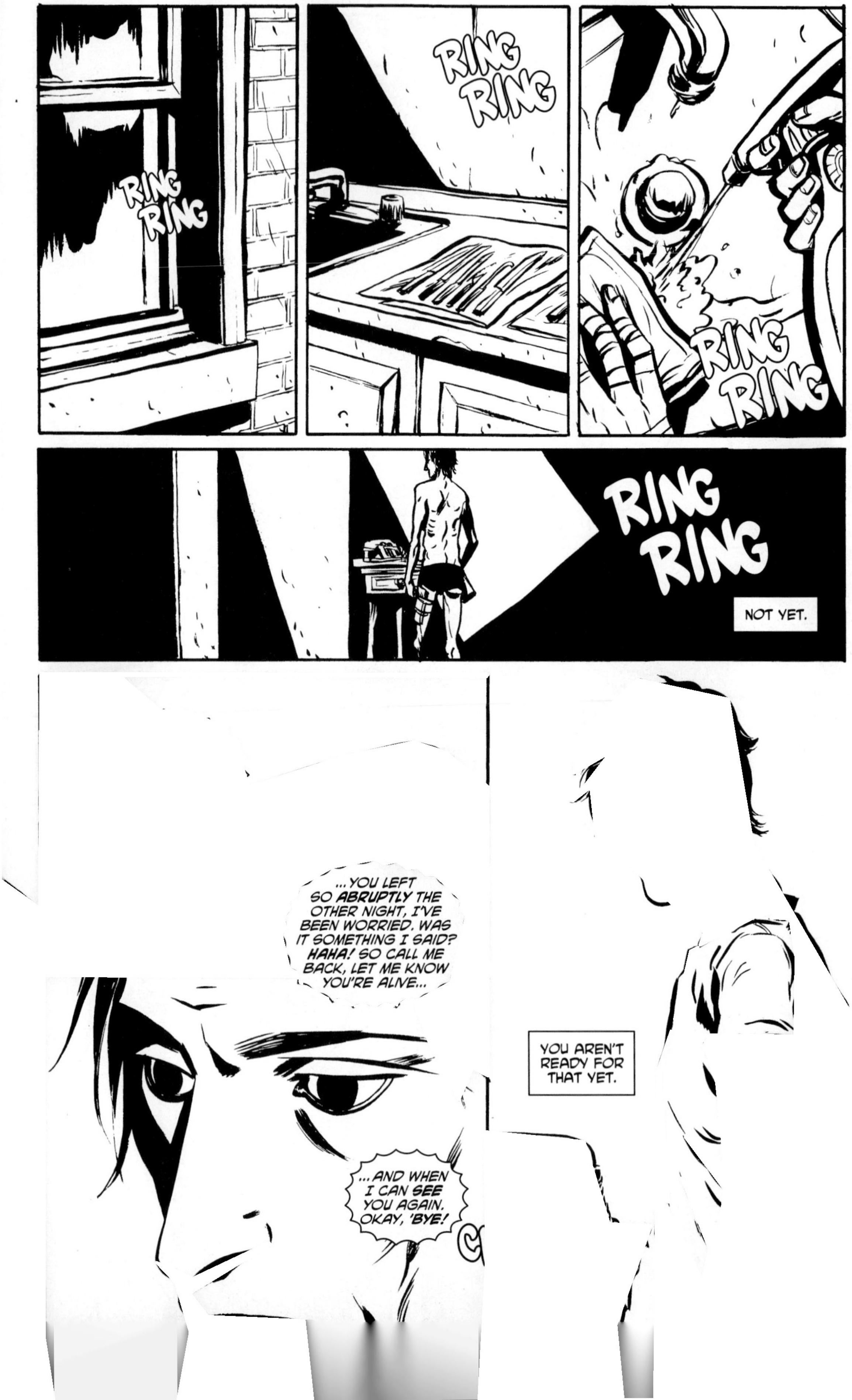
RING RING
RING RING
RING RING
RING RING
NOT YET.
...YOU LEFT SO ABRUPTLY THE OTHER NIGHT, I'VE BEEN WORRIED. WAS IT SOMETHING I SAID? HAHA! SO CALL ME BACK, LET ME KNOW YOU'RE ALIVE...
...AND WHEN I CAN SEE YOU AGAIN. OKAY, 'BYE!
YOU AREN'T READY FOR THAT YET.

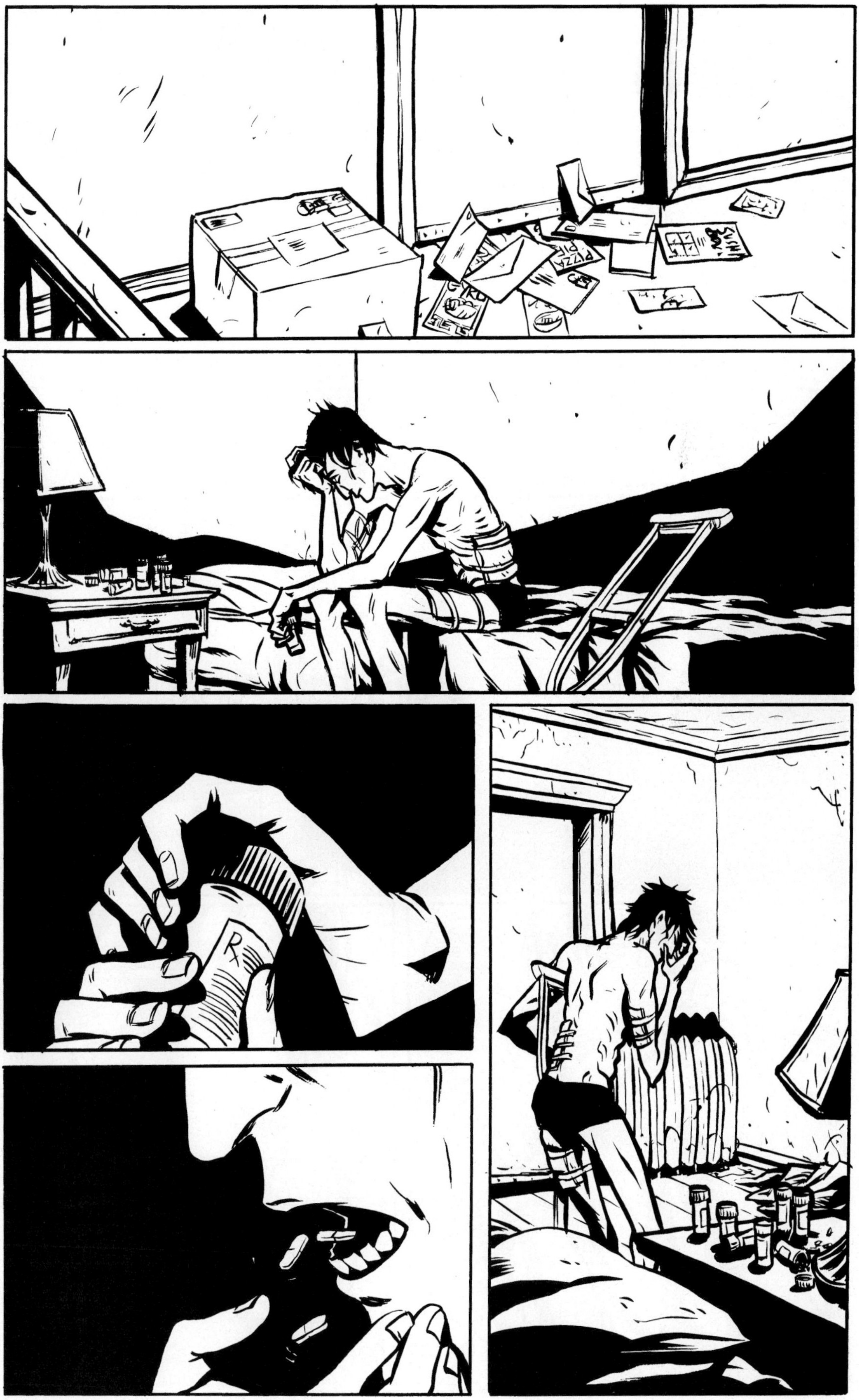
PIZZA PIE
SUSHI BOY

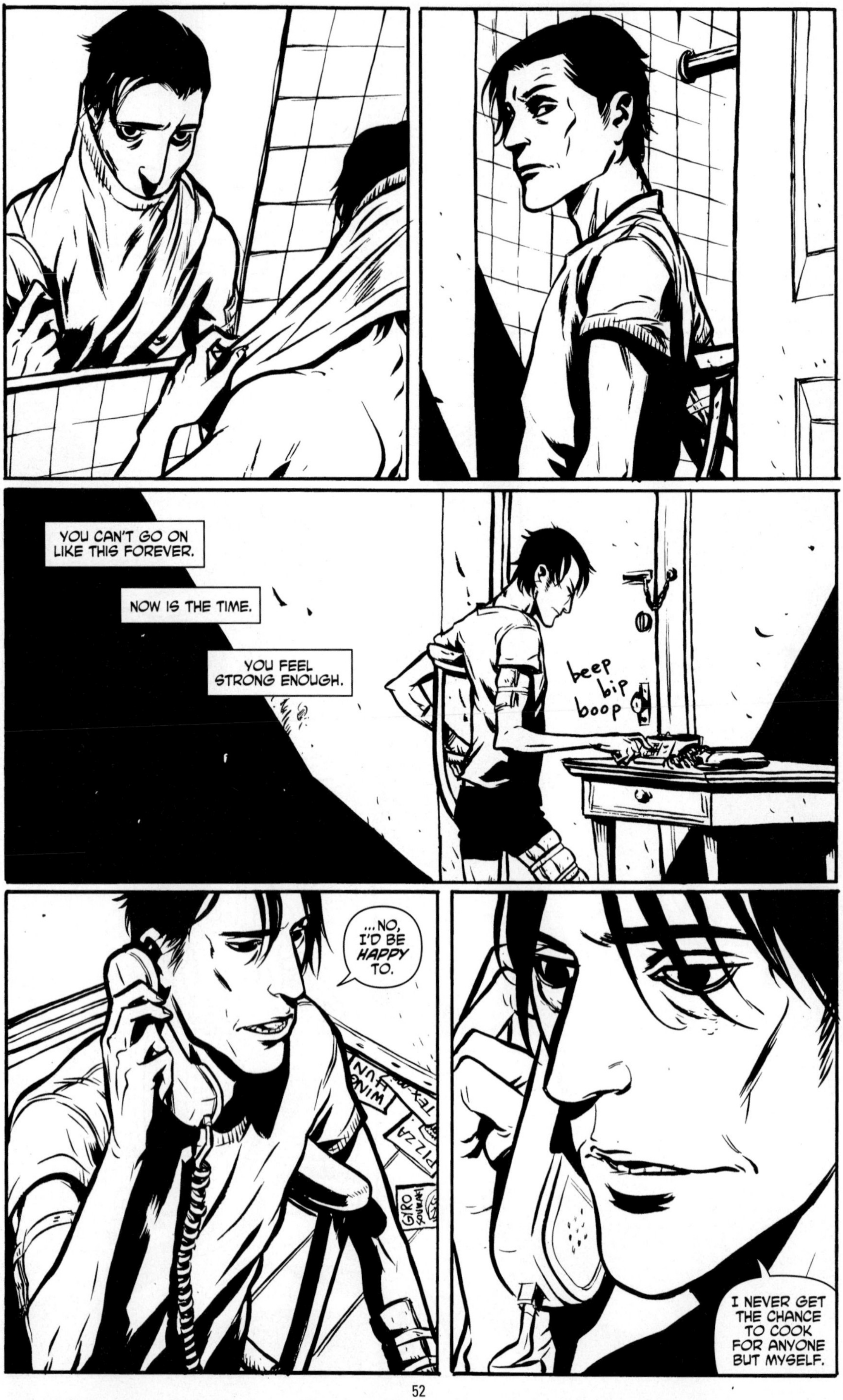
YOU CAN'T GO ON LIKE THIS FOREVER.
NOW IS THE TIME.
YOU FEEL STRONG ENOUGH.
beep bip boop
...NO, I'D BE *HAPPY* TO.
WING
TEX-N-FUN
PIZZA
GYRO SOUVLAKI
I NEVER GET THE CHANCE TO COOK FOR ANYONE BUT MYSELF.

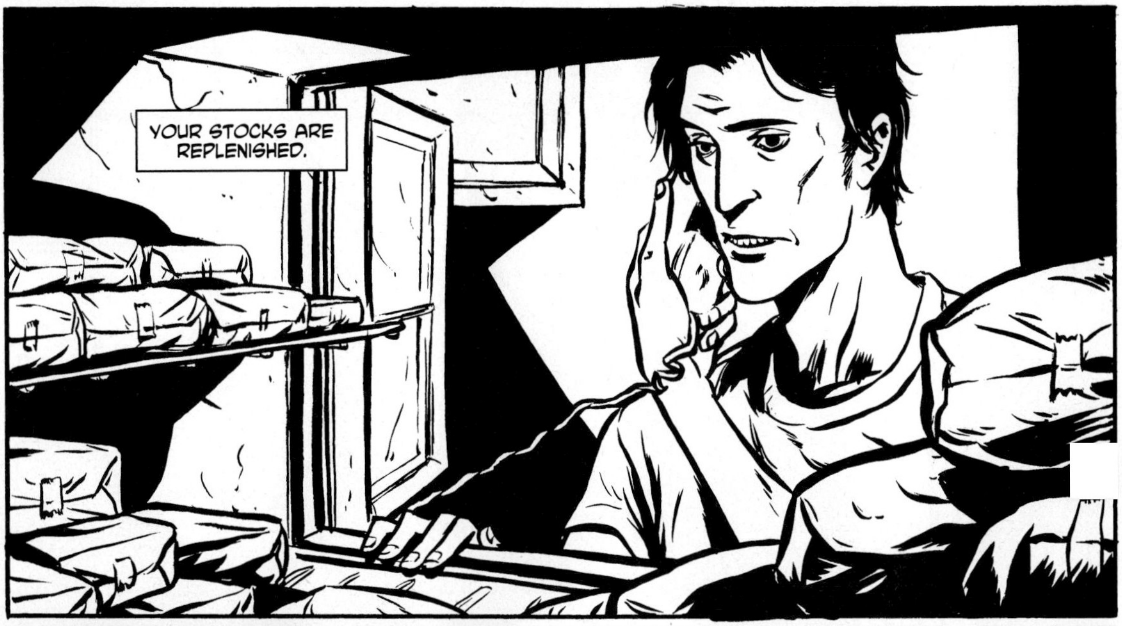
YOUR STOCKS ARE REPLENISHED.

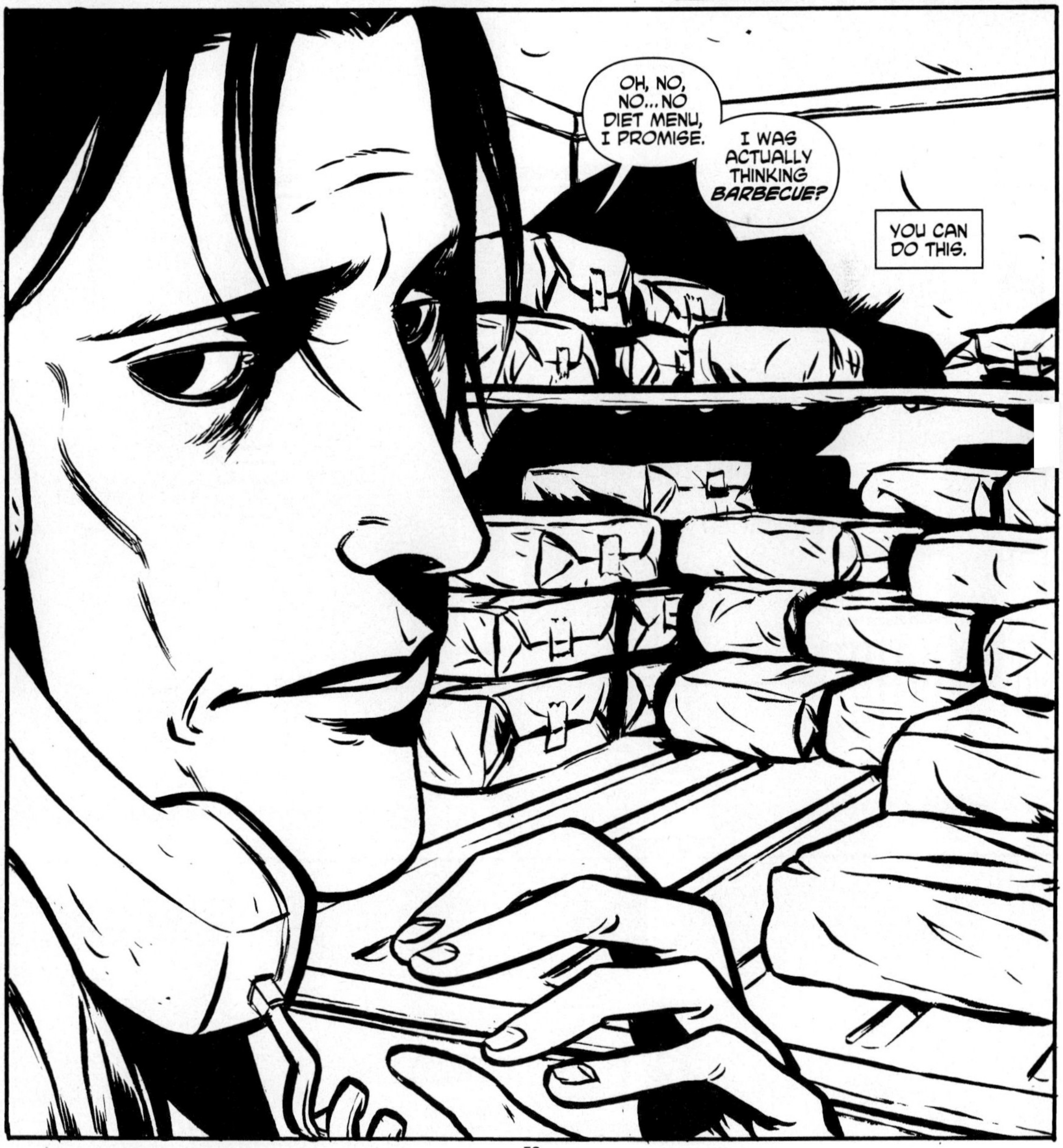
OH, NO, NO... NO DIET MENU, I PROMISE.
I WAS ACTUALLY THINKING *BARBECUE?*
YOU CAN DO THIS.

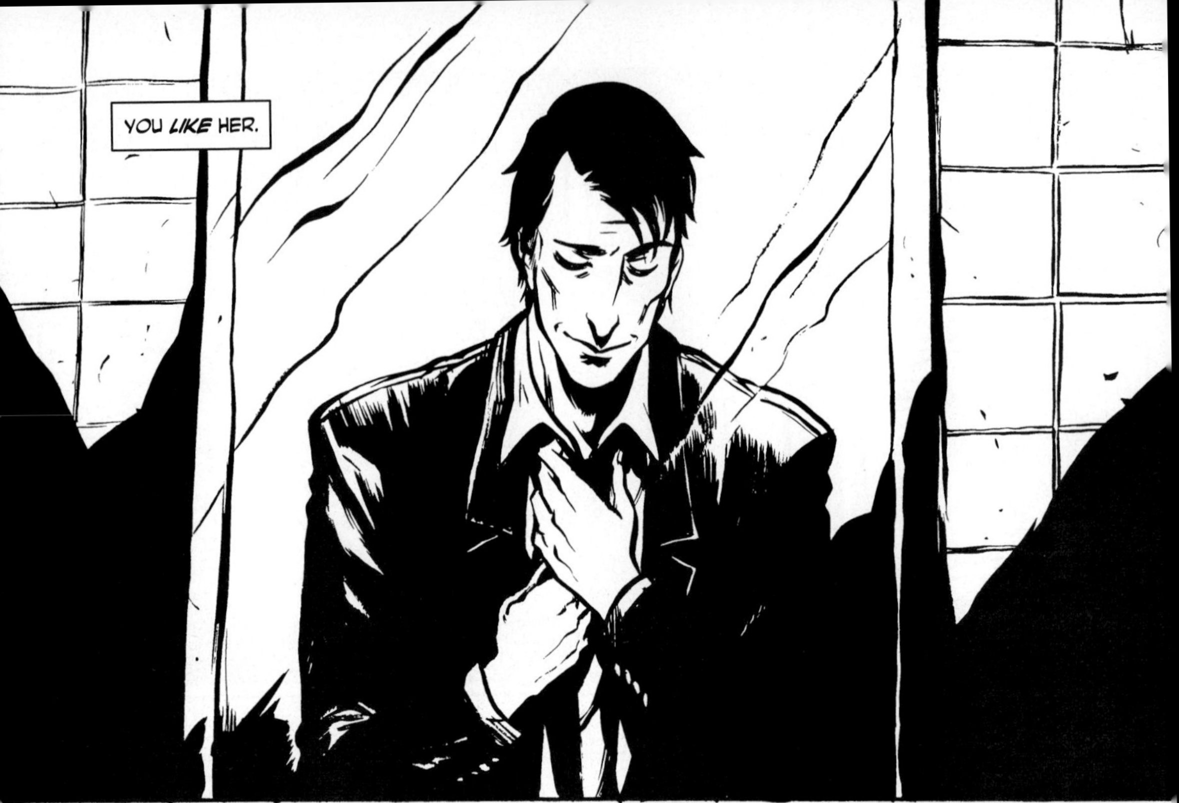
YOU *LIKE* HER.

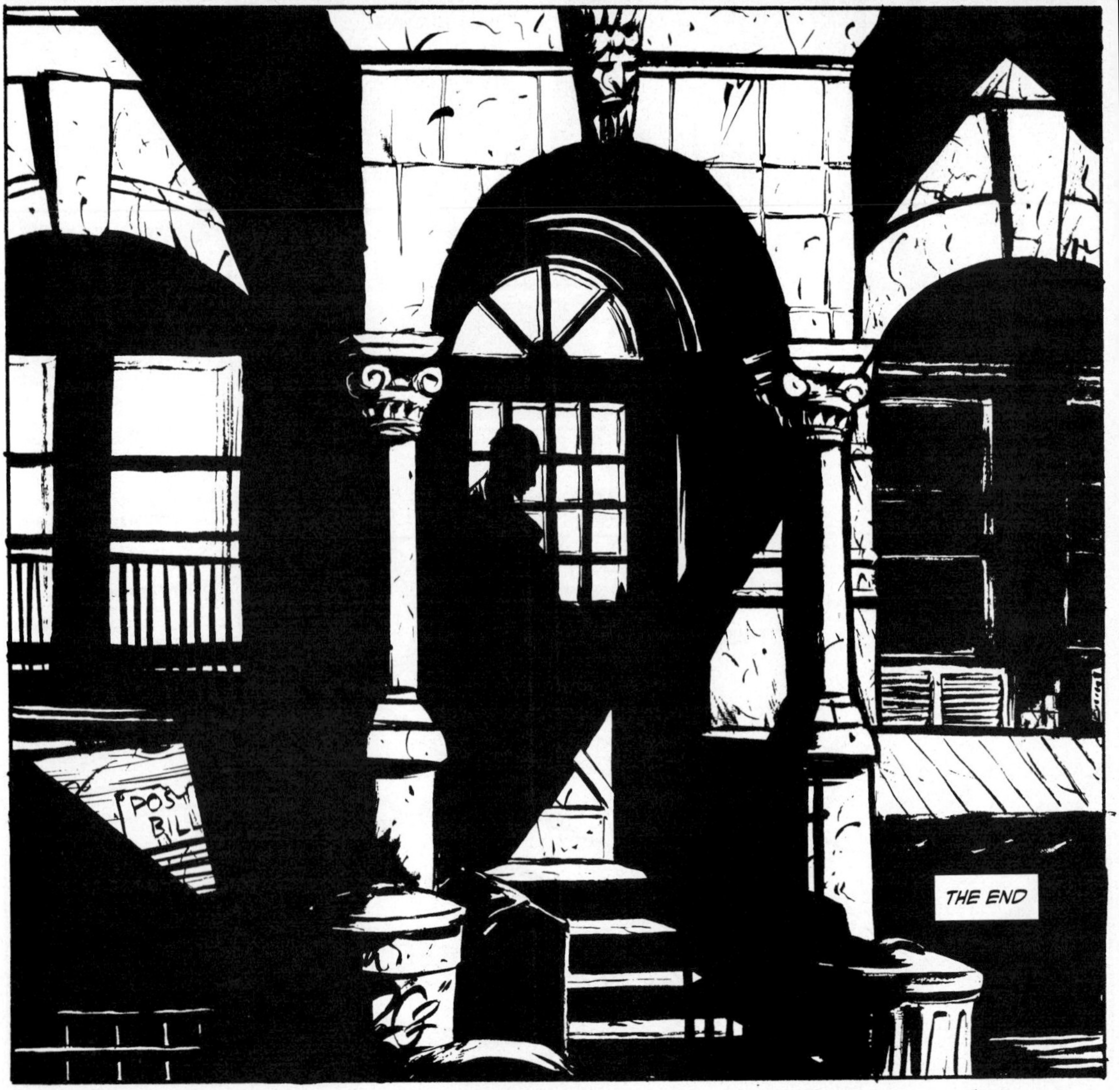
THE END

3

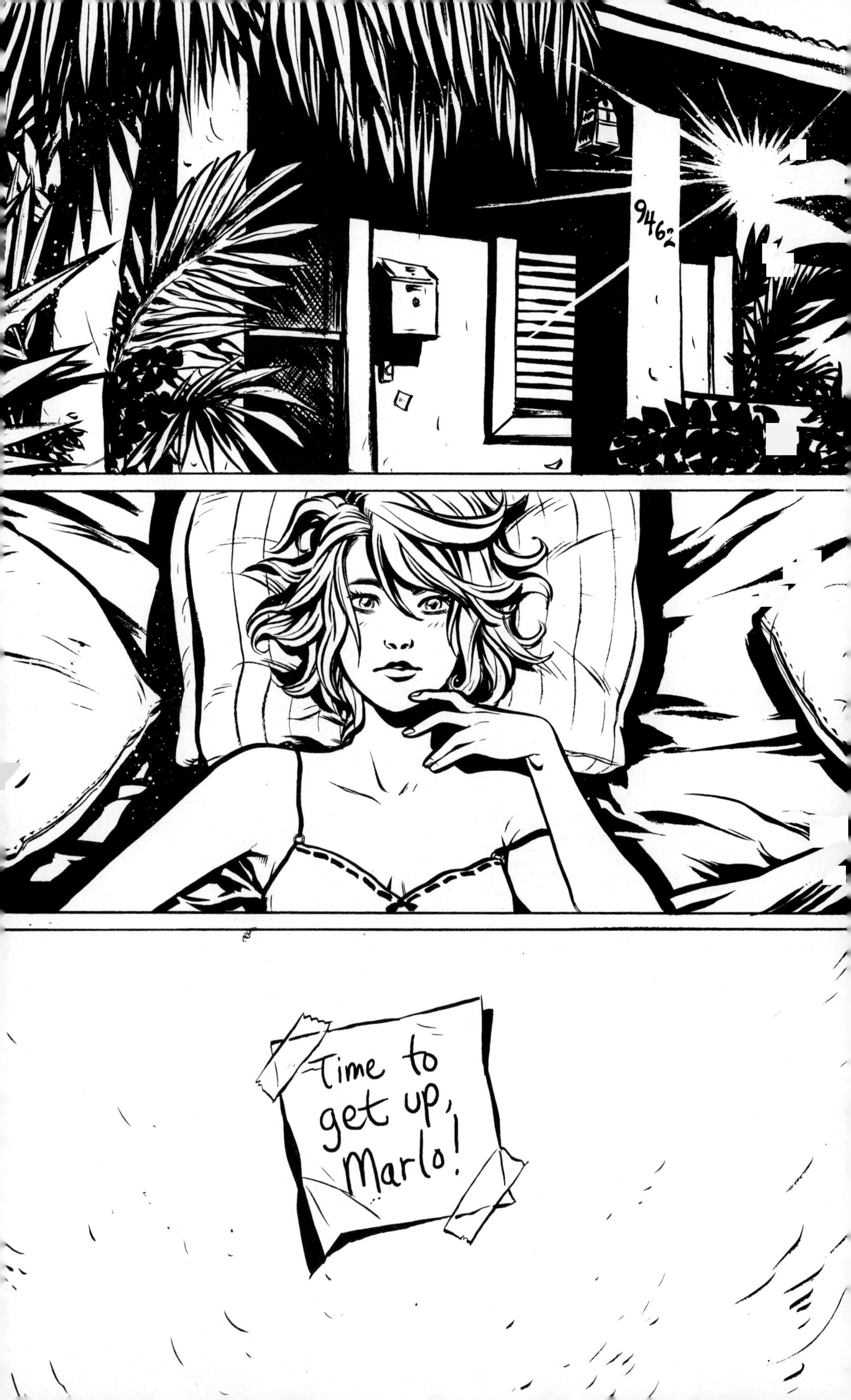
9462
Time to get up, Marlo!

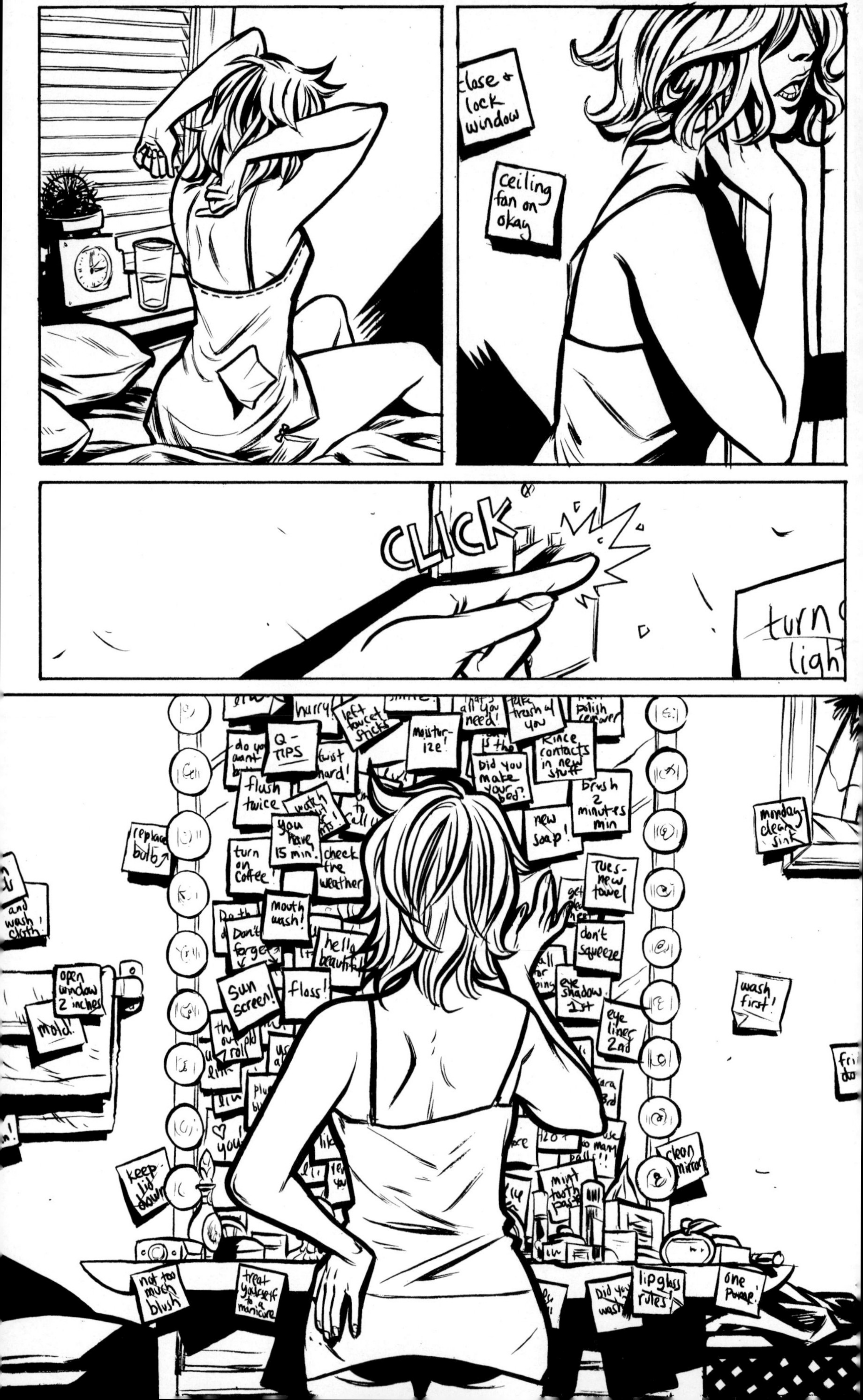

close & lock window
ceiling fan on okay
CLICK
turn
hurry
left faucet sticks
moisturize!
all you need!
take trash w/ you
polish remover
Q-TIPS
twist hard!
Rince contacts in new stuff
Did you make your bed?
flush twice
brush 2 minutes min
you have 15 min.
new soap!
monday-clean sink
replace bulb
turn on coffee
check the weather
Tues-new towel
mouth wash!
don't squeeze
hello beautiful
open window 2 inches
mold.
Sun screen!
floss!
eye shadow 1st
eye liner 2nd
wash first!
keep lid down
clean mirror
mint tooth paste
not too much blush
treat yourself to a manicure
Did you wash
lipgloss rules!
one pump!

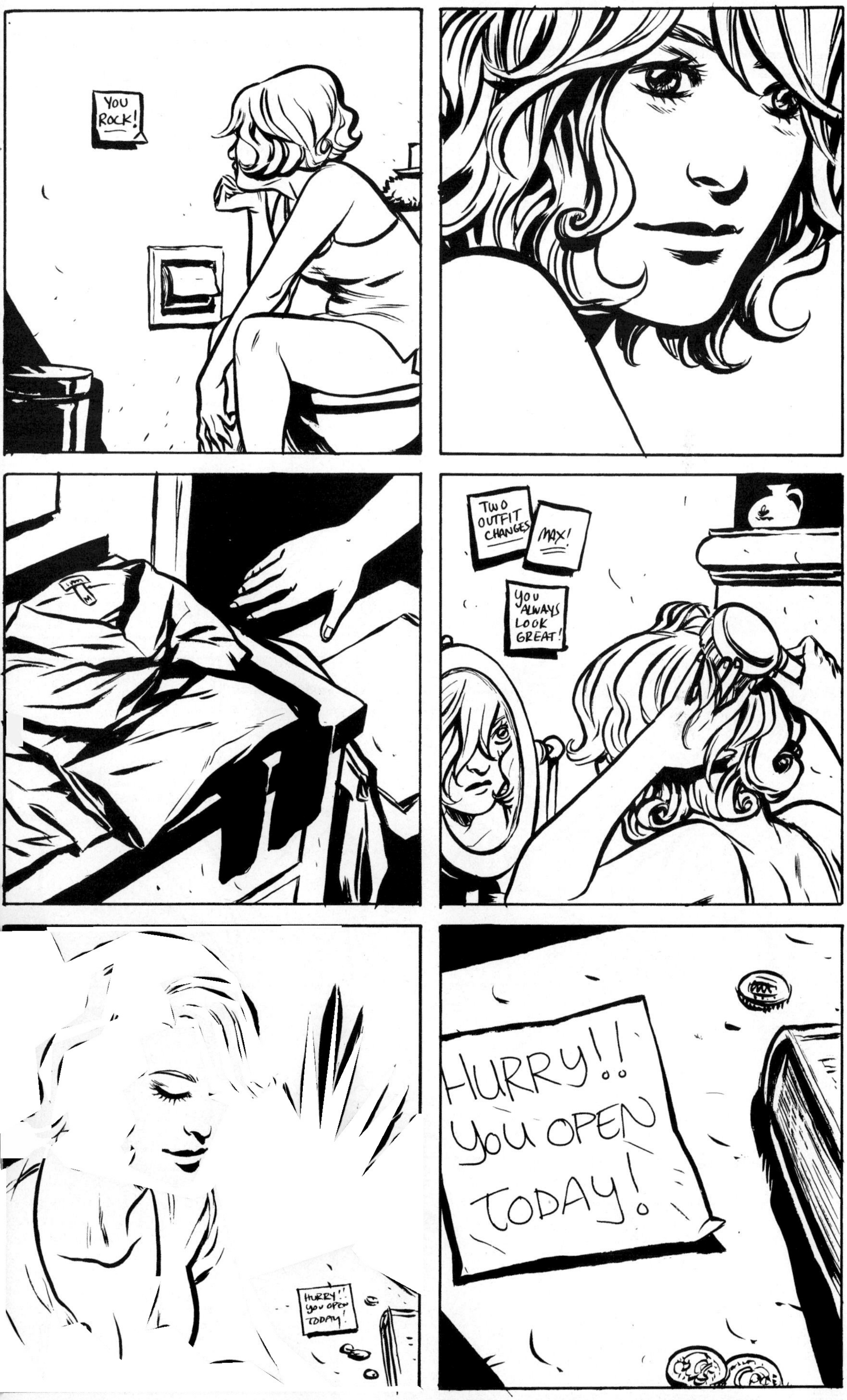
YOU ROCK!
TWO OUTFIT CHANGES
MAX!
YOU ALWAYS LOOK GREAT!
HURRY!! YOU OPEN TODAY!
HURRY!! YOU OPEN TODAY!

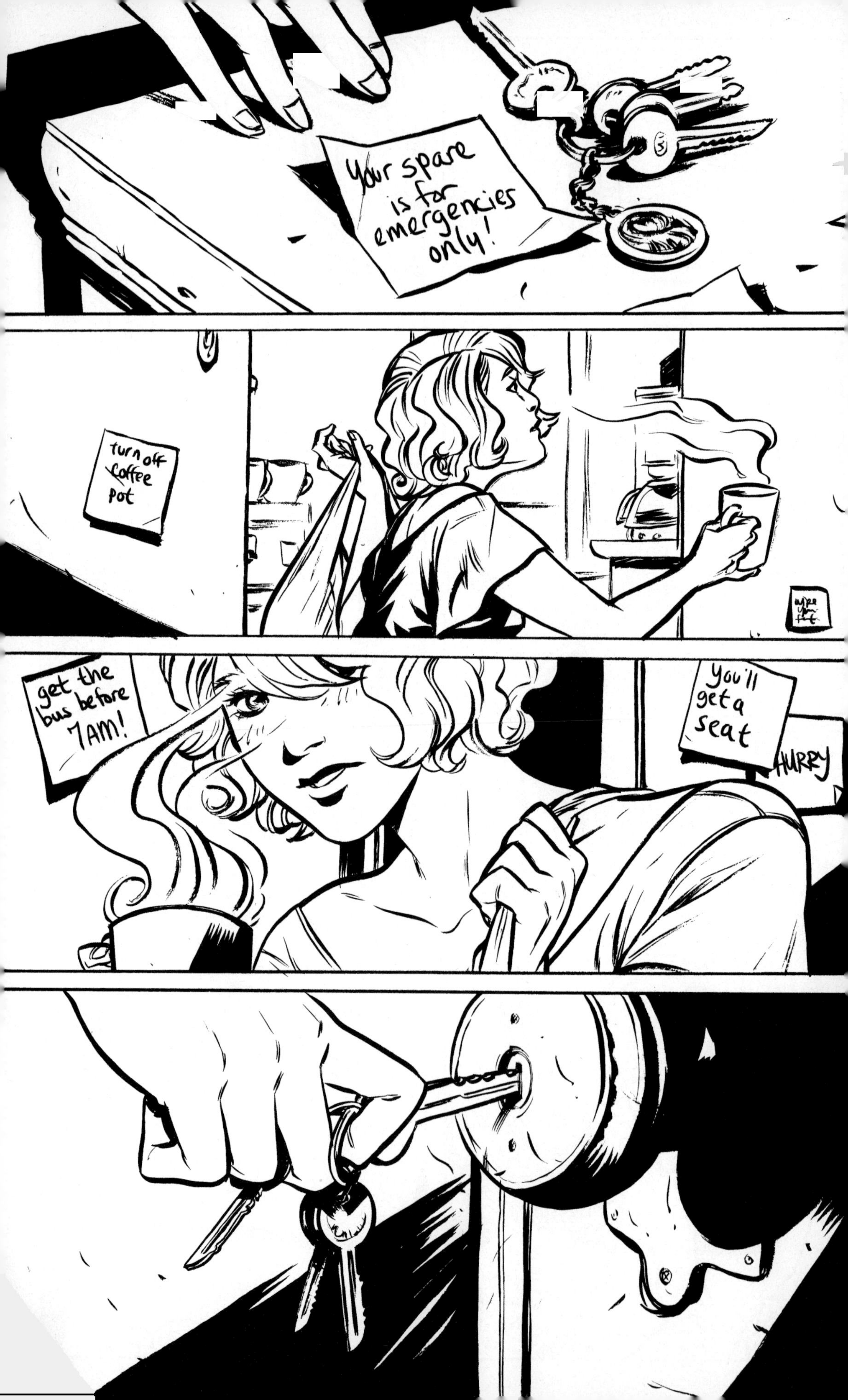
Your spare is for emergencies only!
turn off coffee pot
get the bus before 7AM!
You'll get a seat
HURRY

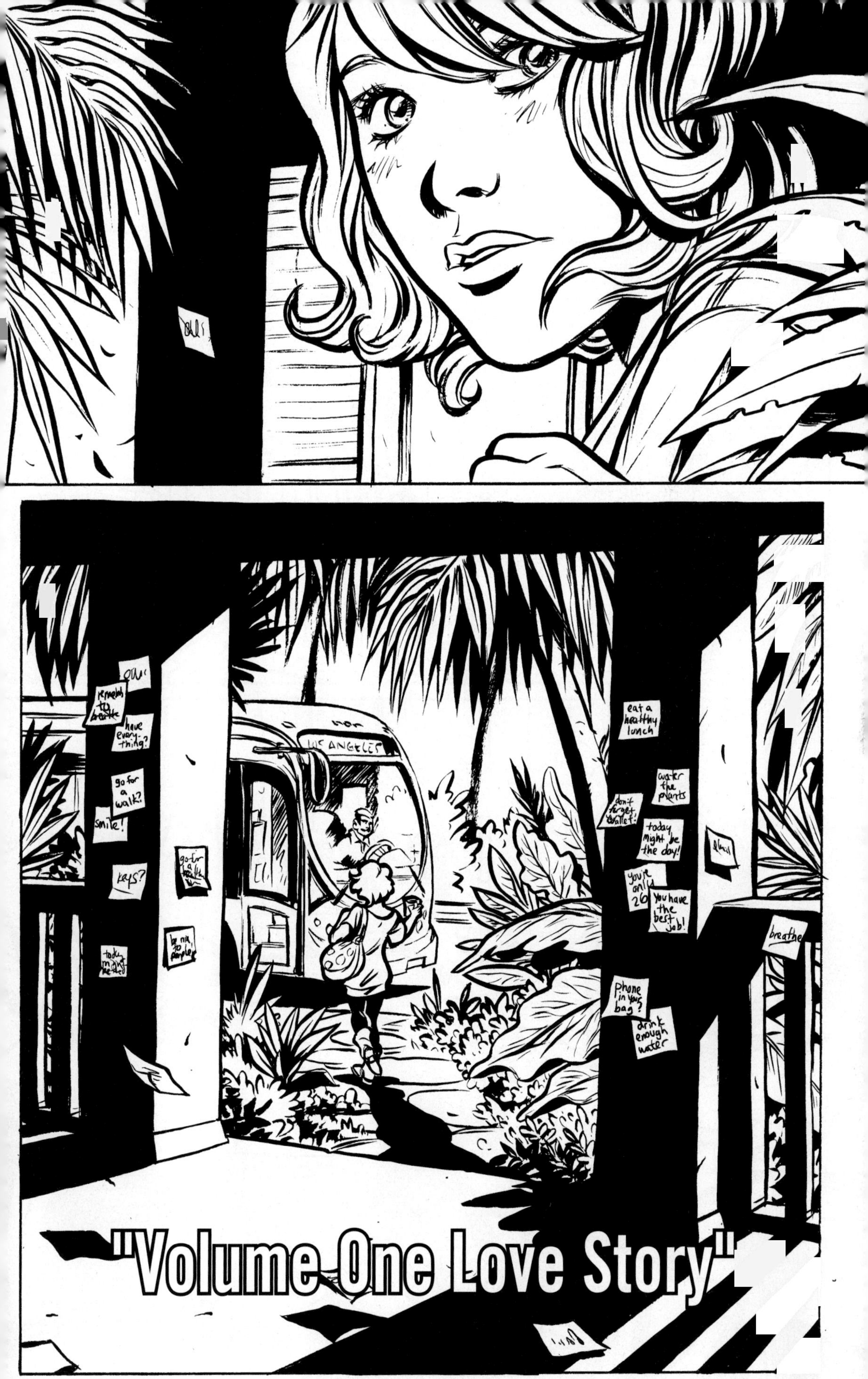
LOS ANGELES
have every-thing?
go for a walk?
smile!
keys?
be nice to people!
eat a healthy lunch
water the plants
don't forget wallet!
today might be the day!
you're only 26
You have the best job!
breathe
Phone in your bag?
drink enough water
"Volume One Love Story"

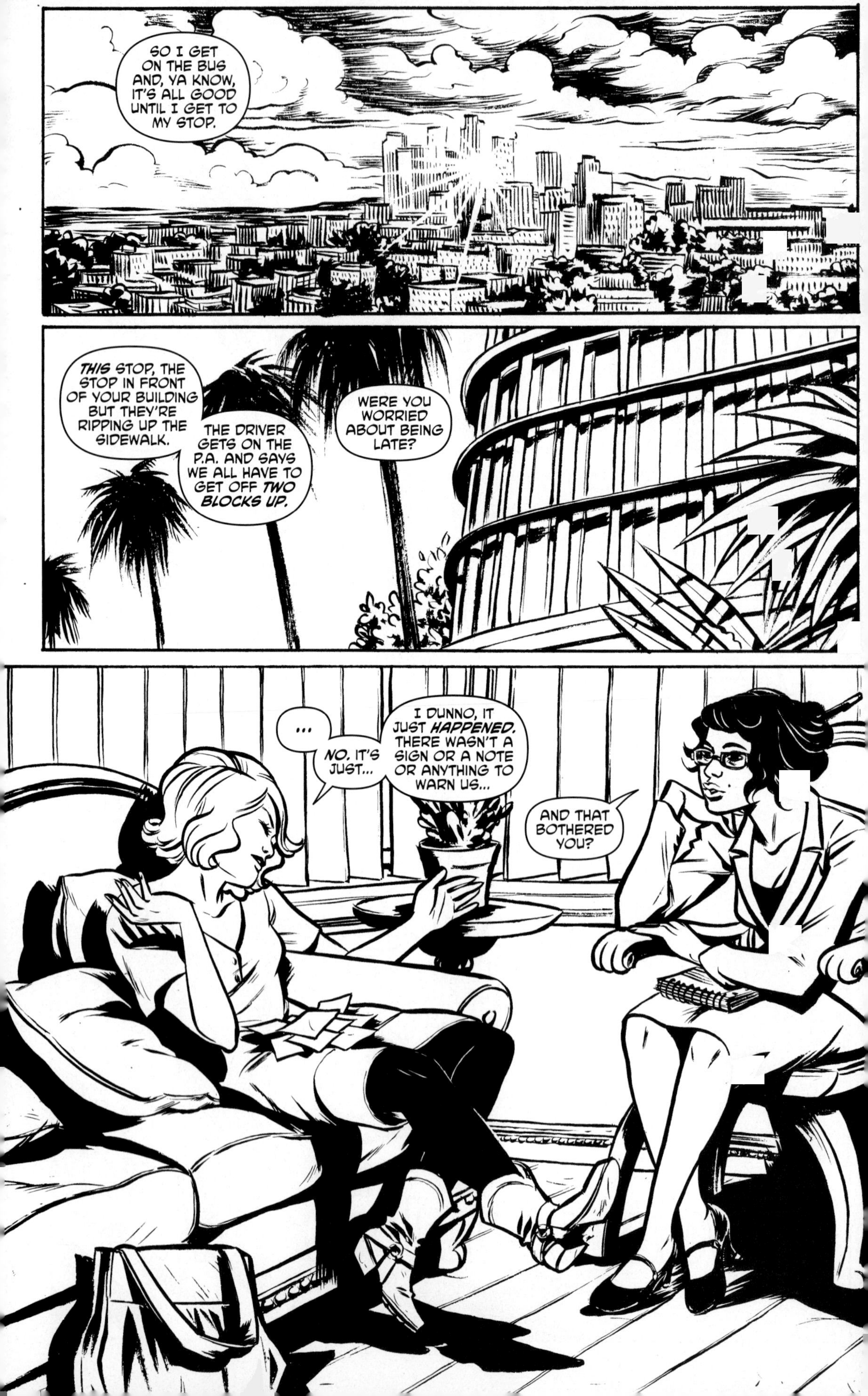
SO I GET ON THE BUS AND, YA KNOW, IT'S ALL GOOD UNTIL I GET TO MY STOP.
THIS STOP, THE STOP IN FRONT OF YOUR BUILDING BUT THEY'RE RIPPING UP THE SIDEWALK.
THE DRIVER GETS ON THE P.A. AND SAYS WE ALL HAVE TO GET OFF TWO BLOCKS UP.
WERE YOU WORRIED ABOUT BEING LATE?
...
NO. IT'S JUST...
I DUNNO, IT JUST HAPPENED. THERE WASN'T A SIGN OR A NOTE OR ANYTHING TO WARN US...
AND THAT BOTHERED YOU?

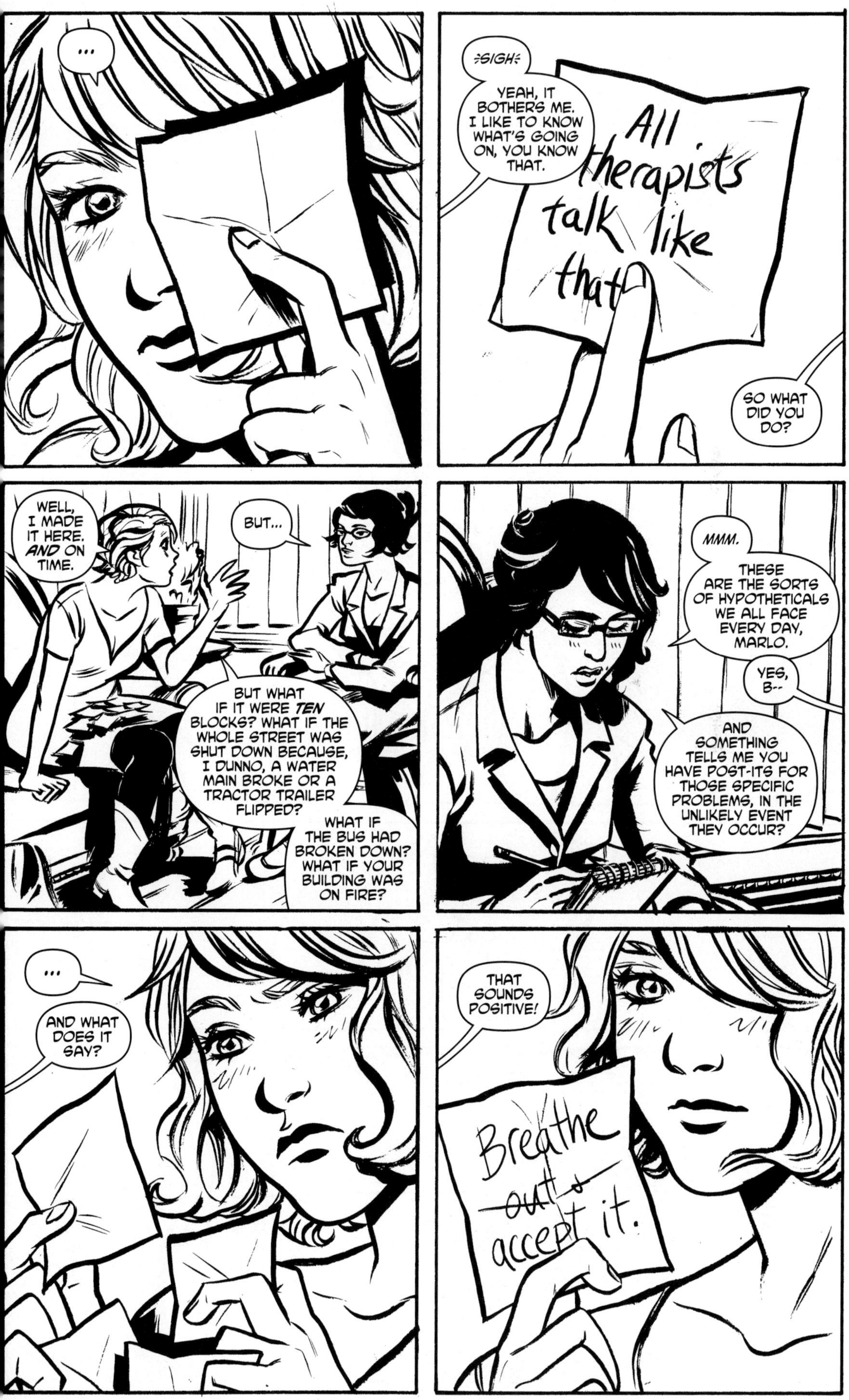
...
SIGH
YEAH, IT BOTHERS ME. I LIKE TO KNOW WHAT'S GOING ON, YOU KNOW THAT.
All therapists talk like that
SO WHAT DID YOU DO?
WELL, I MADE IT HERE. AND ON TIME.
BUT...
BUT WHAT IF IT WERE TEN BLOCKS? WHAT IF THE WHOLE STREET WAS SHUT DOWN BECAUSE, I DUNNO, A WATER MAIN BROKE OR A TRACTOR TRAILER FLIPPED?
WHAT IF THE BUS HAD BROKEN DOWN? WHAT IF YOUR BUILDING WAS ON FIRE?
MMM.
THESE ARE THE SORTS OF HYPOTHETICALS WE ALL FACE EVERY DAY, MARLO.
YES, B--
AND SOMETHING TELLS ME YOU HAVE POST-ITS FOR THOSE SPECIFIC PROBLEMS, IN THE UNLIKELY EVENT THEY OCCUR?
...
AND WHAT DOES IT SAY?
THAT SOUNDS POSITIVE!
Breathe out & accept it.

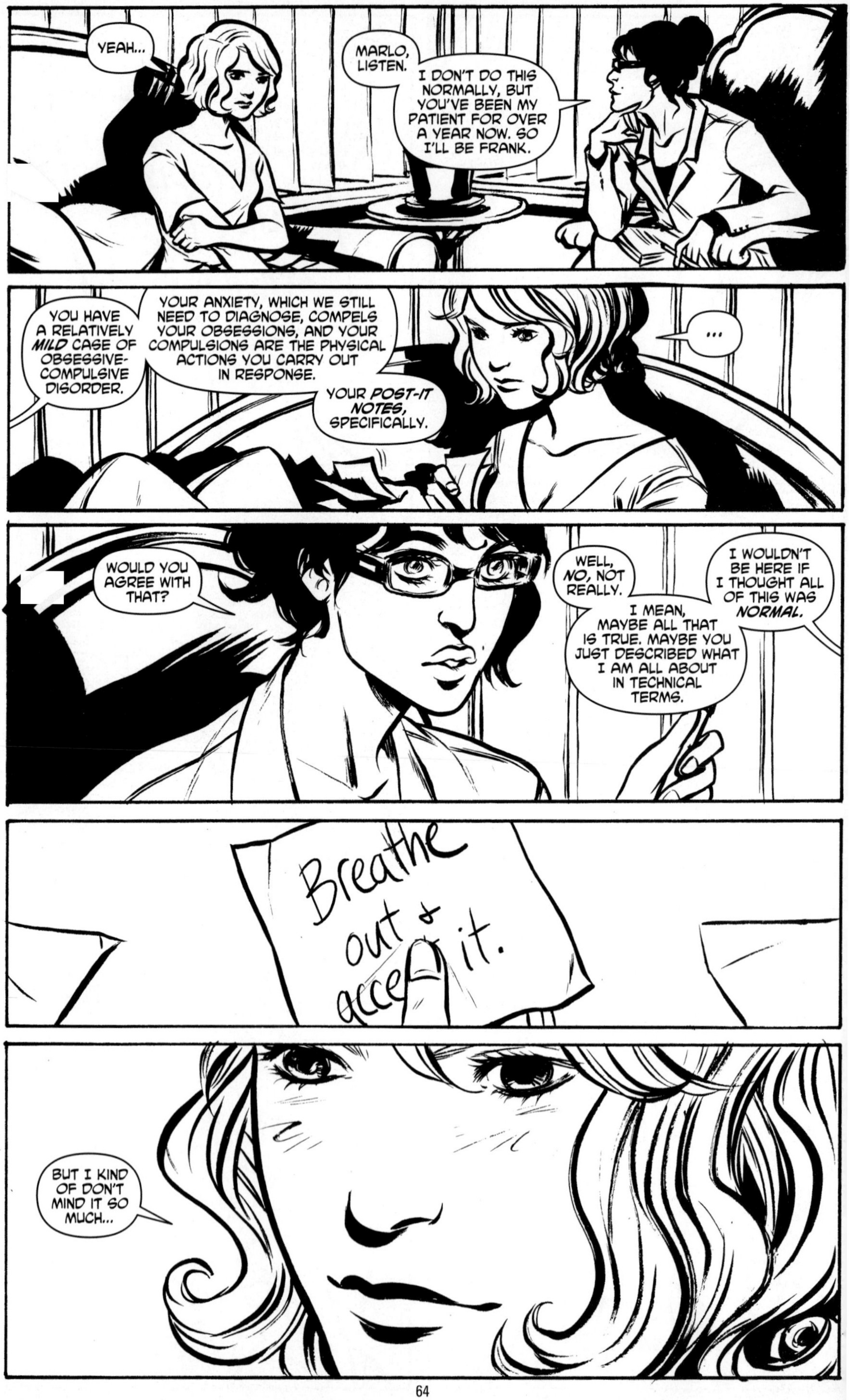
YEAH...
MARLO, LISTEN.
I DON'T DO THIS NORMALLY, BUT YOU'VE BEEN MY PATIENT FOR OVER A YEAR NOW. SO I'LL BE FRANK.
YOU HAVE A RELATIVELY MILD CASE OF OBSESSIVE-COMPULSIVE DISORDER.
YOUR ANXIETY, WHICH WE STILL NEED TO DIAGNOSE, COMPELS YOUR OBSESSIONS, AND YOUR COMPULSIONS ARE THE PHYSICAL ACTIONS YOU CARRY OUT IN RESPONSE.
YOUR POST-IT NOTES, SPECIFICALLY.
...
WOULD YOU AGREE WITH THAT?
WELL, NO, NOT REALLY.
I MEAN, MAYBE ALL THAT IS TRUE. MAYBE YOU JUST DESCRIBED WHAT I AM ALL ABOUT IN TECHNICAL TERMS.
I WOULDN'T BE HERE IF I THOUGHT ALL OF THIS WAS NORMAL.
Breathe out &
it.
BUT I KIND OF DON'T MIND IT SO MUCH...

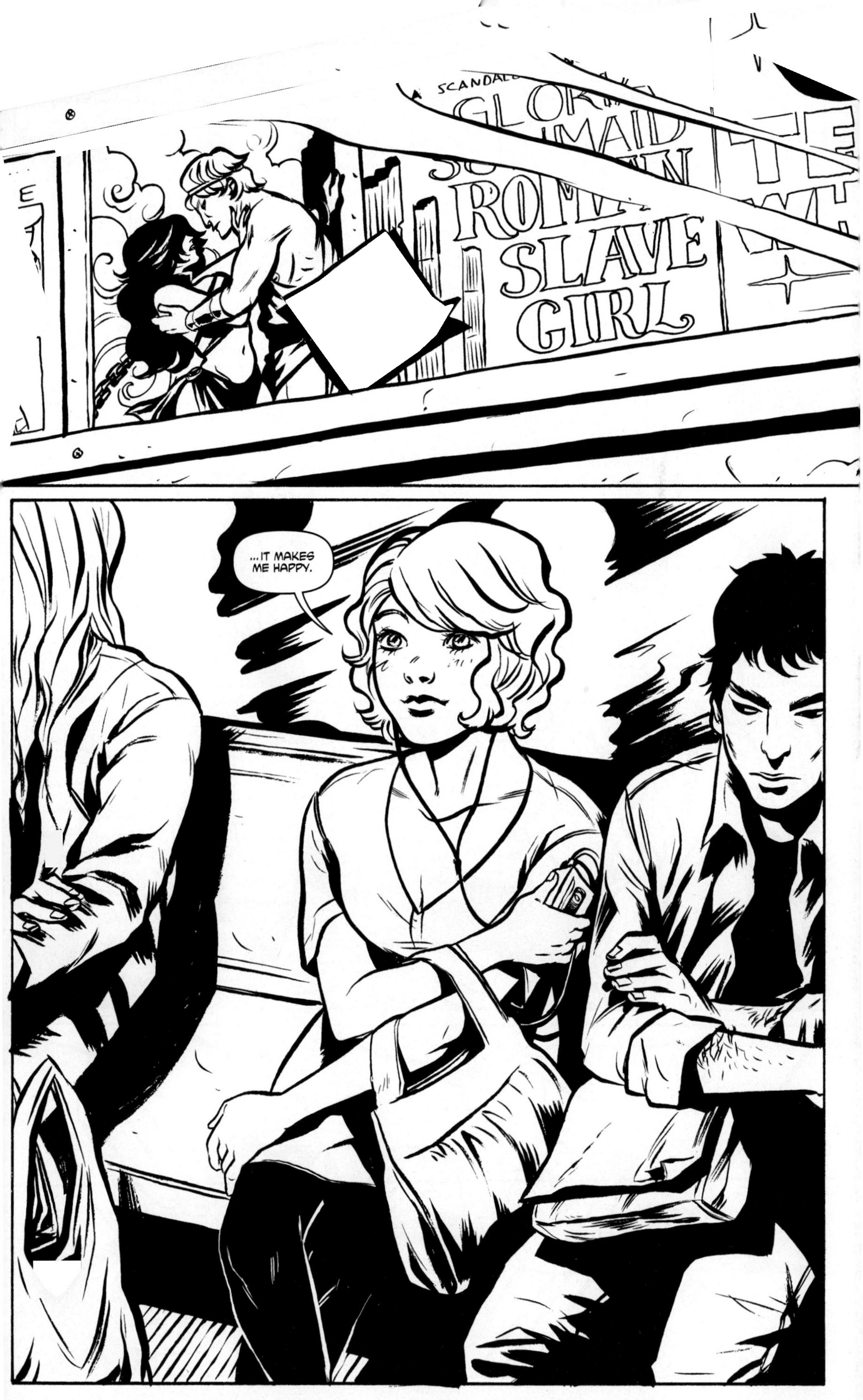
SCANDAL
SLAVE GIRL
...IT MAKES ME HAPPY.

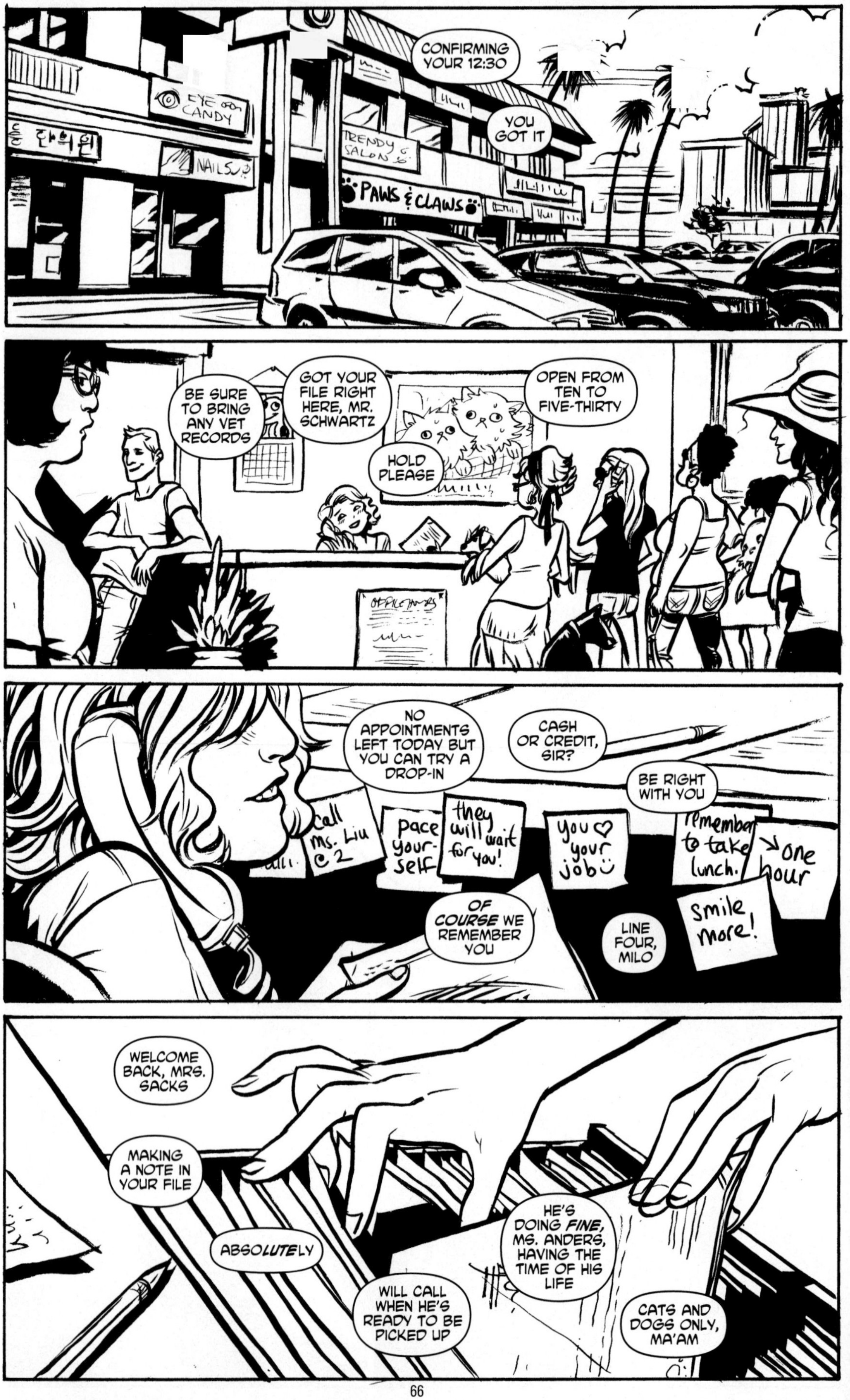
EYE CANDY
NAILS
TRENDY SALON
PAWS & CLAWS
CONFIRMING YOUR 12:30
YOU GOT IT
BE SURE TO BRING ANY VET RECORDS
GOT YOUR FILE RIGHT HERE, MR. SCHWARTZ
HOLD PLEASE
OPEN FROM TEN TO FIVE-THIRTY
NO APPOINTMENTS LEFT TODAY BUT YOU CAN TRY A DROP-IN
CASH OR CREDIT, SIR?
BE RIGHT WITH YOU
call Ms. Liu @ 2
pace yourself
they will wait for you!
you ♥ your job
remember to take lunch.
→ one hour
smile more!
OF *COURSE* WE REMEMBER YOU
LINE FOUR, MILO
WELCOME BACK, MRS. SACKS
MAKING A NOTE IN YOUR FILE
ABSO*LUTE*LY
WILL CALL WHEN HE'S READY TO BE PICKED UP
HE'S DOING *FINE*, MS. ANDERS, HAVING THE TIME OF HIS LIFE
CATS AND DOGS ONLY, MA'AM

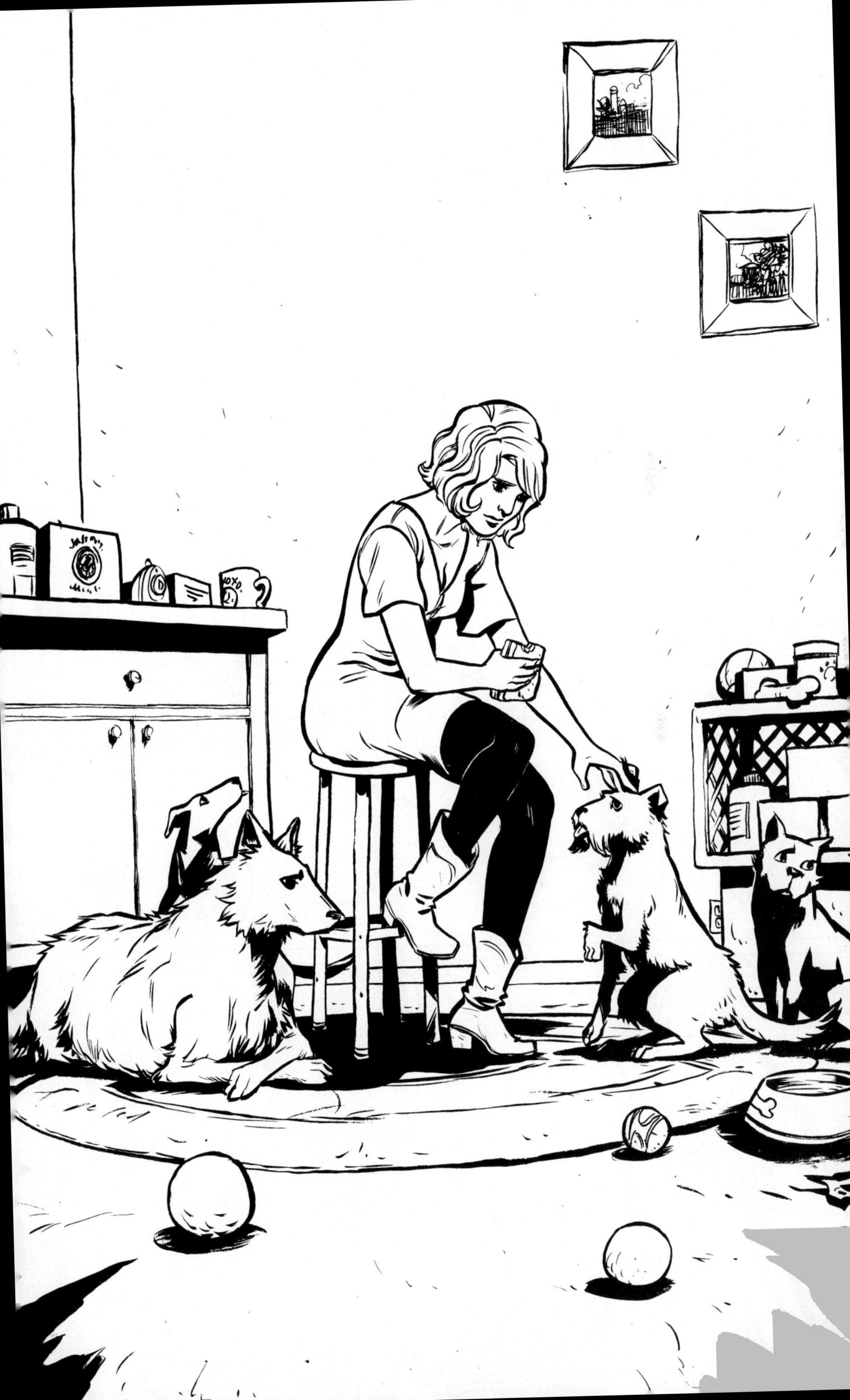

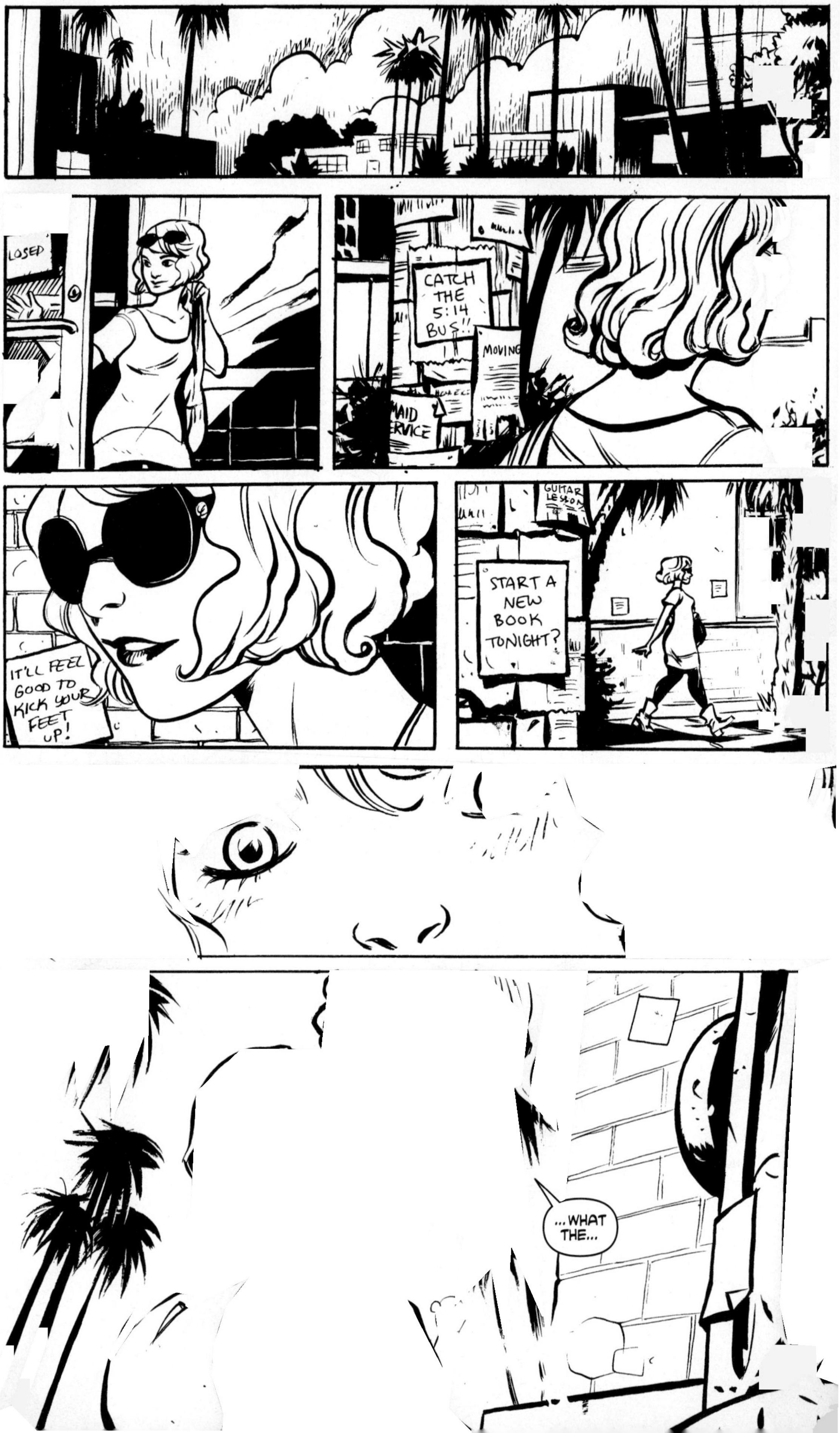
LOSED
CATCH THE 5:14 BUS!!
MOVING
MAID SERVICE
IT'LL FEEL GOOD TO KICK YOUR FEET UP!
GUITAR LESSON
START A NEW BOOK TONIGHT?
...WHAT THE...

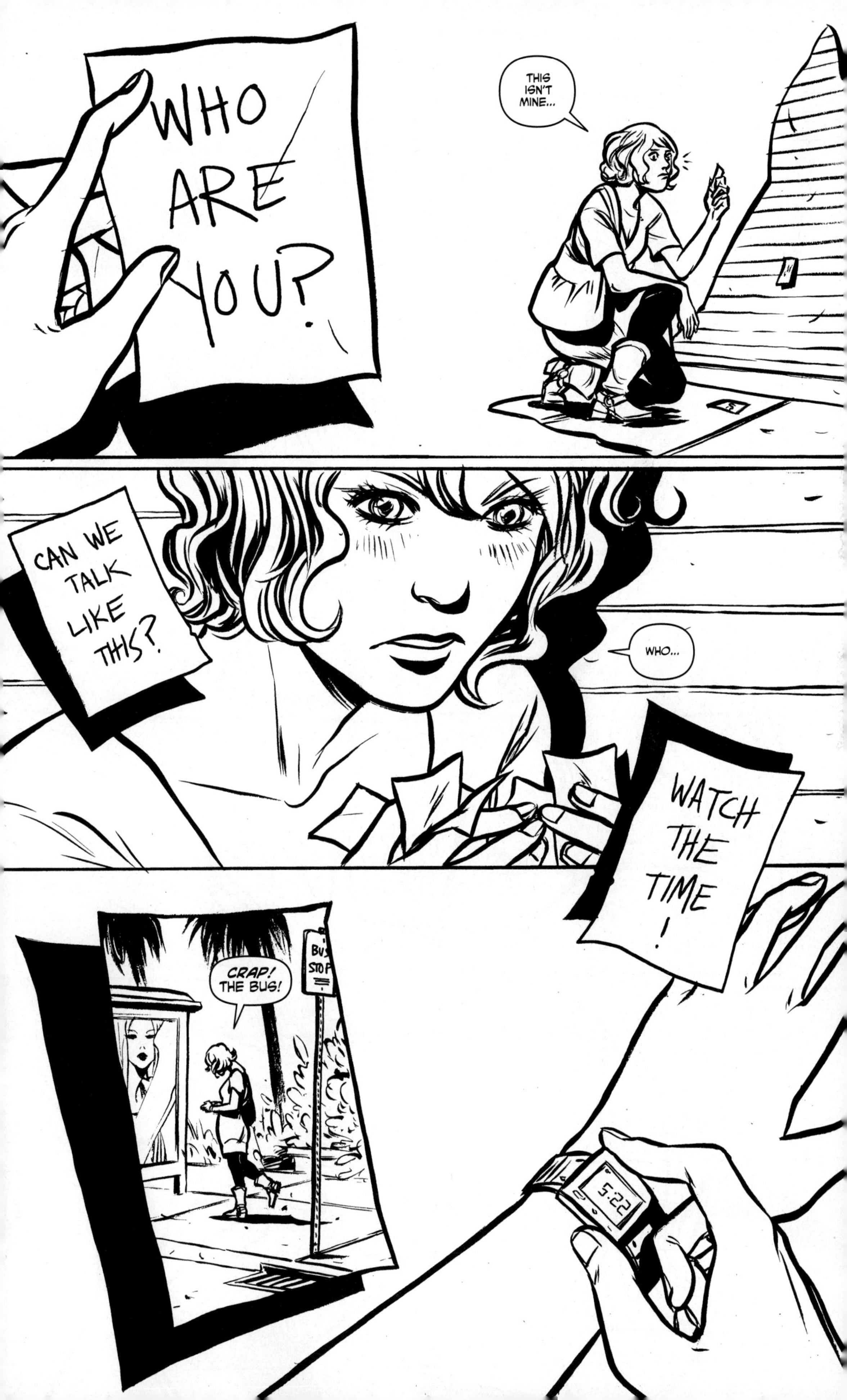

WHO ARE YOU?
THIS ISN'T MINE...
CAN WE TALK LIKE THIS?
WHO...
WATCH THE TIME!
CRAP! THE BUS!
BUS STOP
5:22

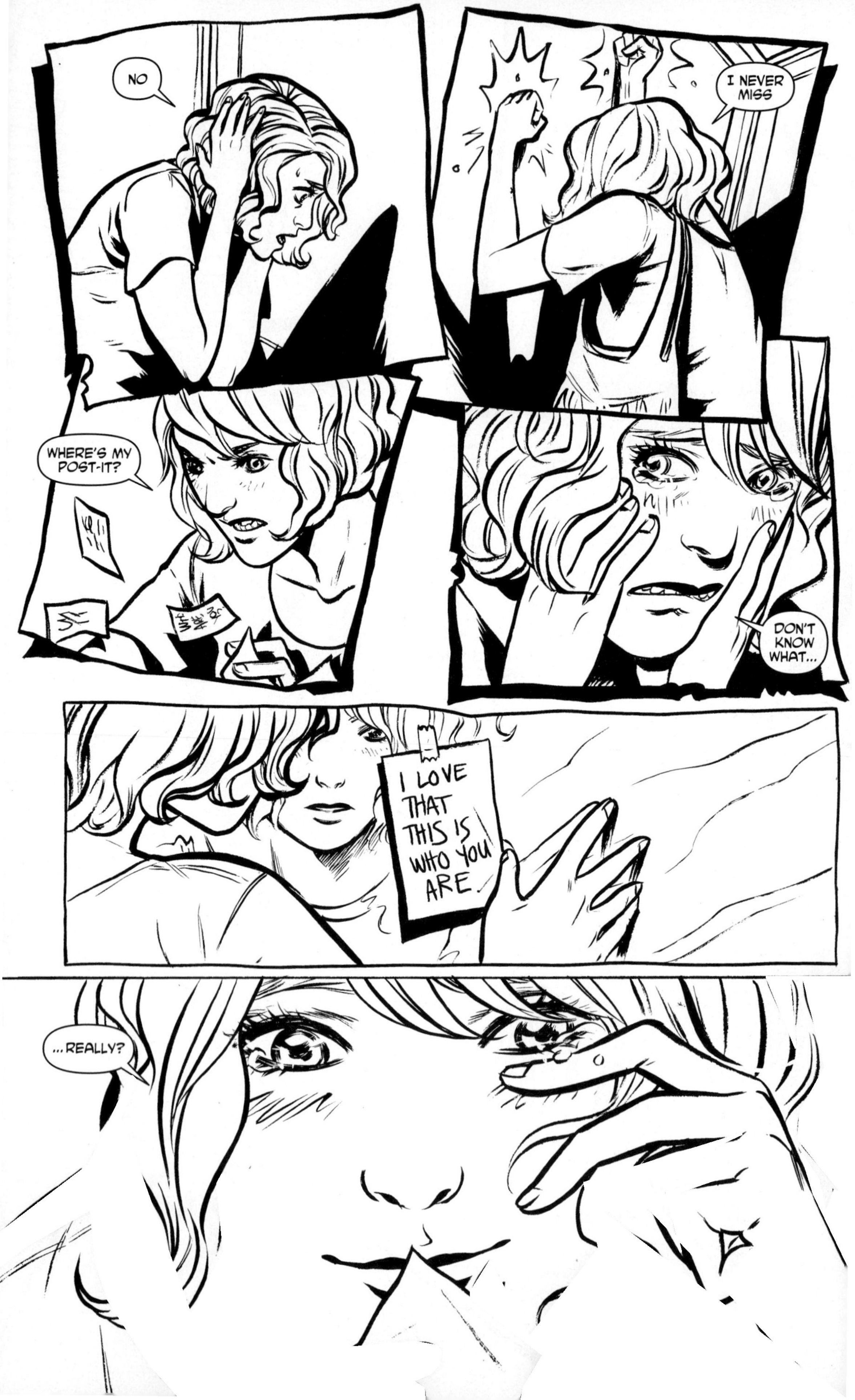
NO
I NEVER MISS
WHERE'S MY POST-IT?
DON'T KNOW WHAT...
I LOVE THAT THIS IS WHO YOU ARE.
...REALLY?

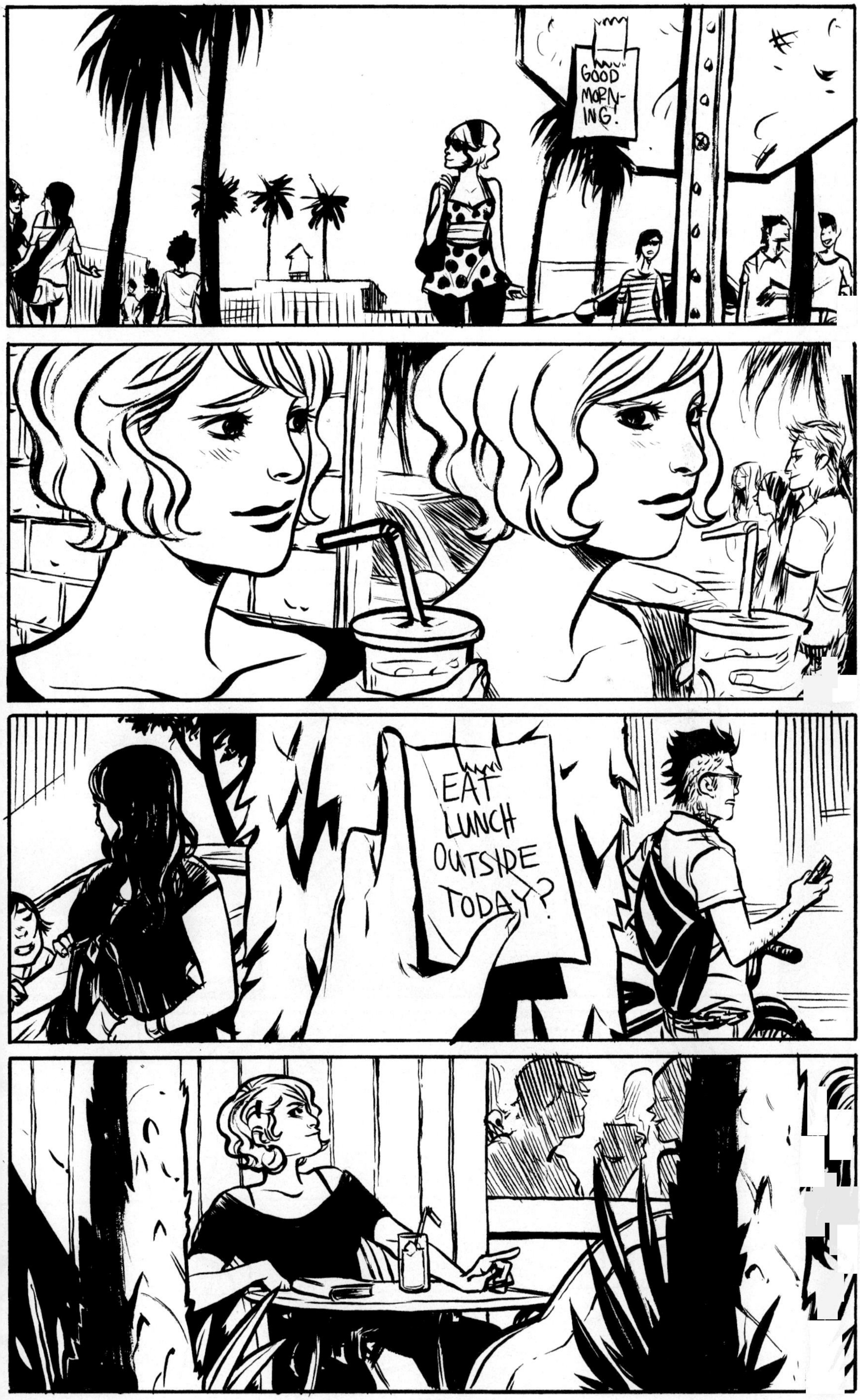
GOOD MORN-ING!
EAT LUNCH OUTSIDE TODAY?

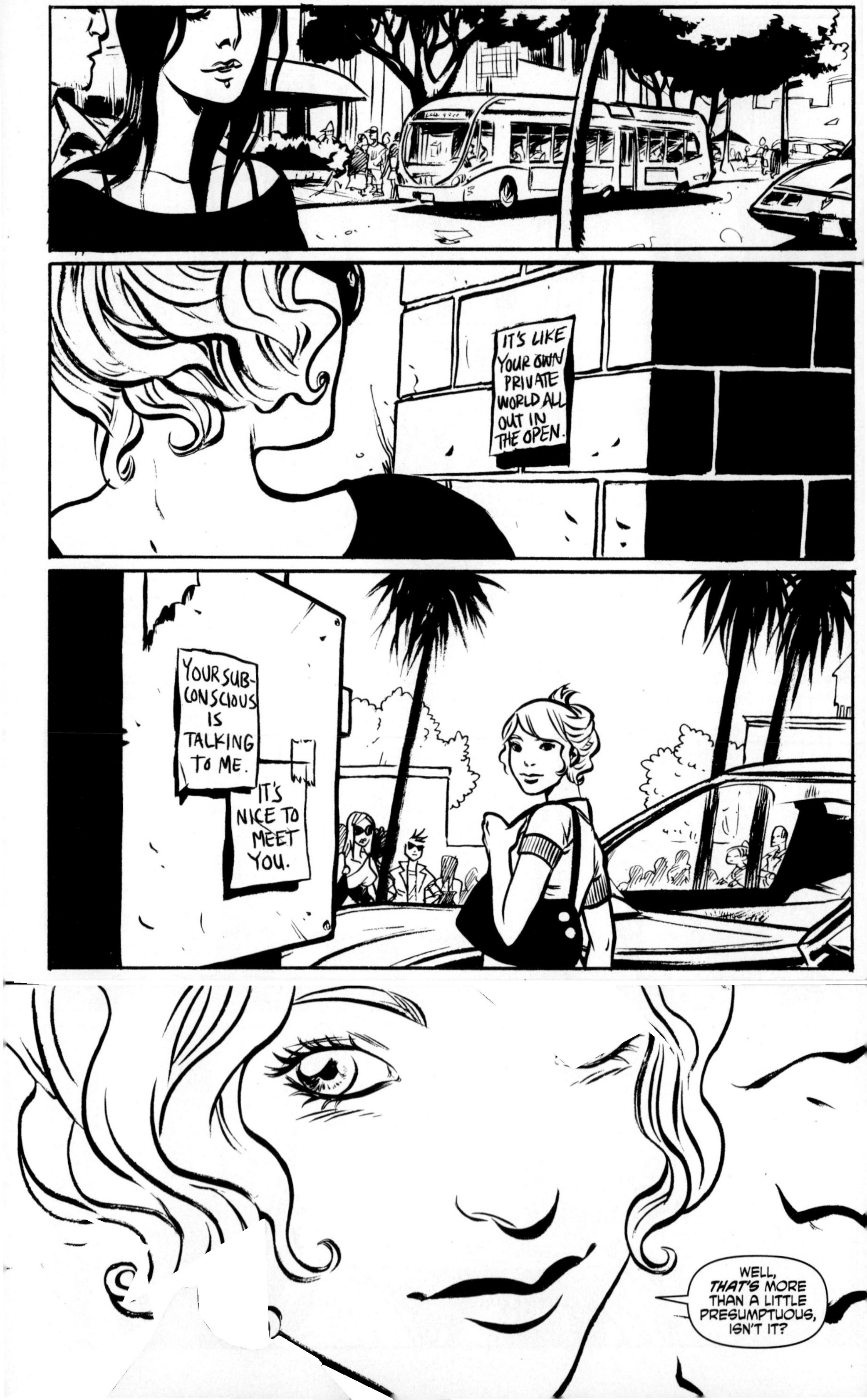
IT'S LIKE YOUR OWN PRIVATE WORLD ALL OUT IN THE OPEN.
YOUR SUB-CONSCIOUS IS TALKING TO ME.
IT'S NICE TO MEET YOU.
WELL, *THAT'S* MORE THAN A LITTLE PRESUMPTUOUS, ISN'T IT?

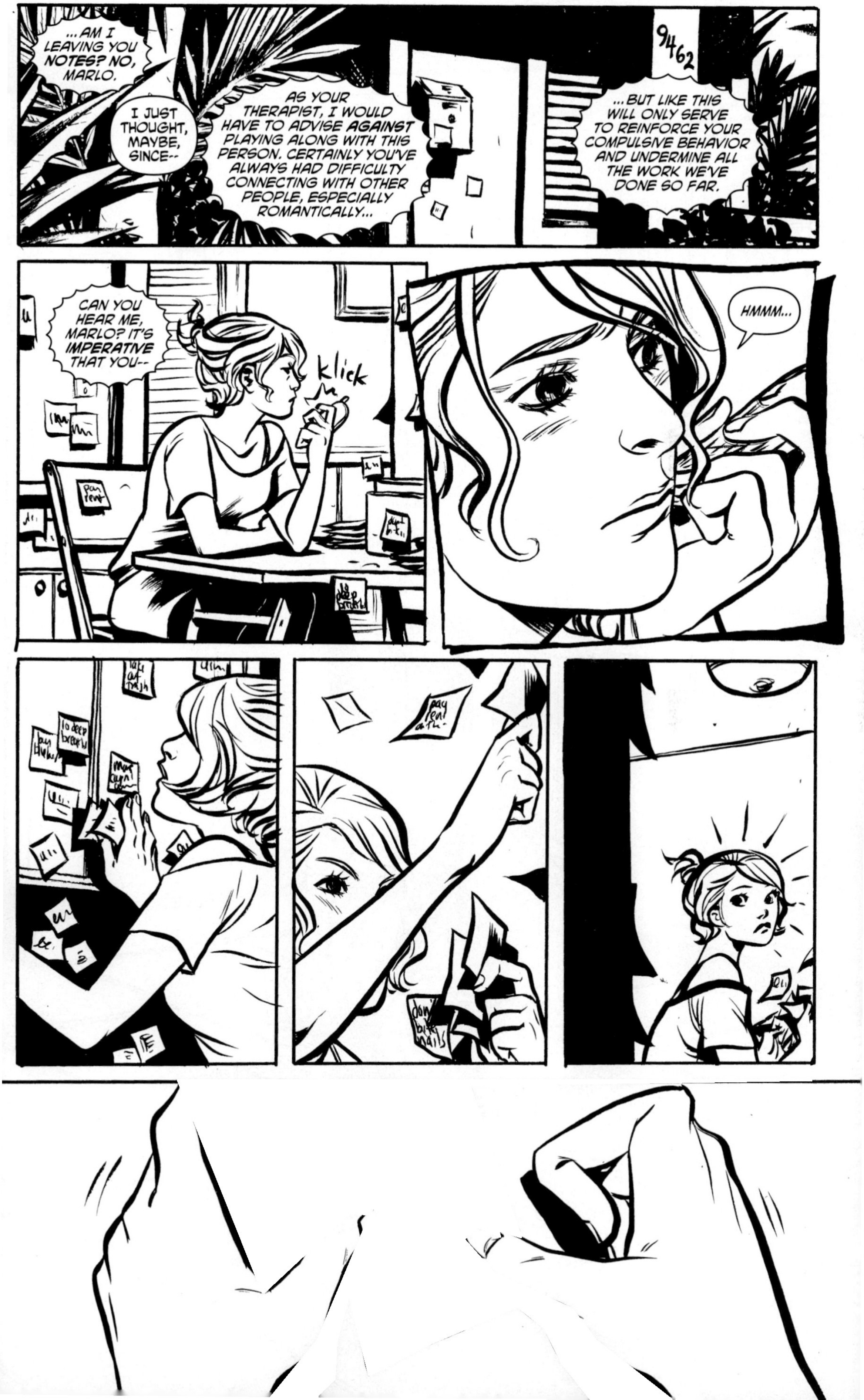
...AM I LEAVING YOU NOTES? NO, MARLO.
I JUST THOUGHT, MAYBE, SINCE--
AS YOUR THERAPIST, I WOULD HAVE TO ADVISE AGAINST PLAYING ALONG WITH THIS PERSON. CERTAINLY YOU'VE ALWAYS HAD DIFFICULTY CONNECTING WITH OTHER PEOPLE, ESPECIALLY ROMANTICALLY...
...BUT LIKE THIS WILL ONLY SERVE TO REINFORCE YOUR COMPULSIVE BEHAVIOR AND UNDERMINE ALL THE WORK WE'VE DONE SO FAR.
9462
CAN YOU HEAR ME, MARLO? IT'S IMPERATIVE THAT YOU--
klick
HMMM...

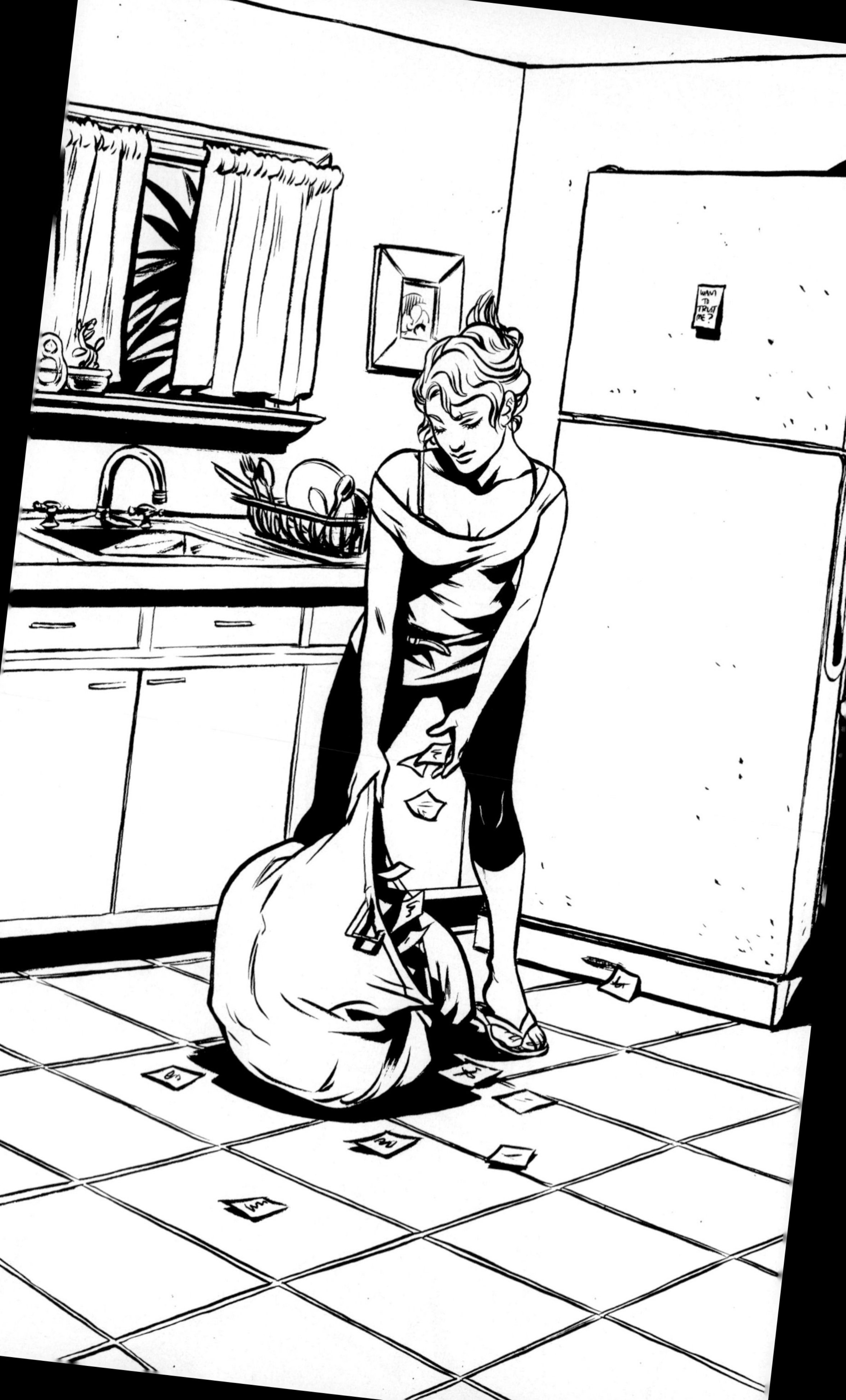
WANT TO TRUST ME?

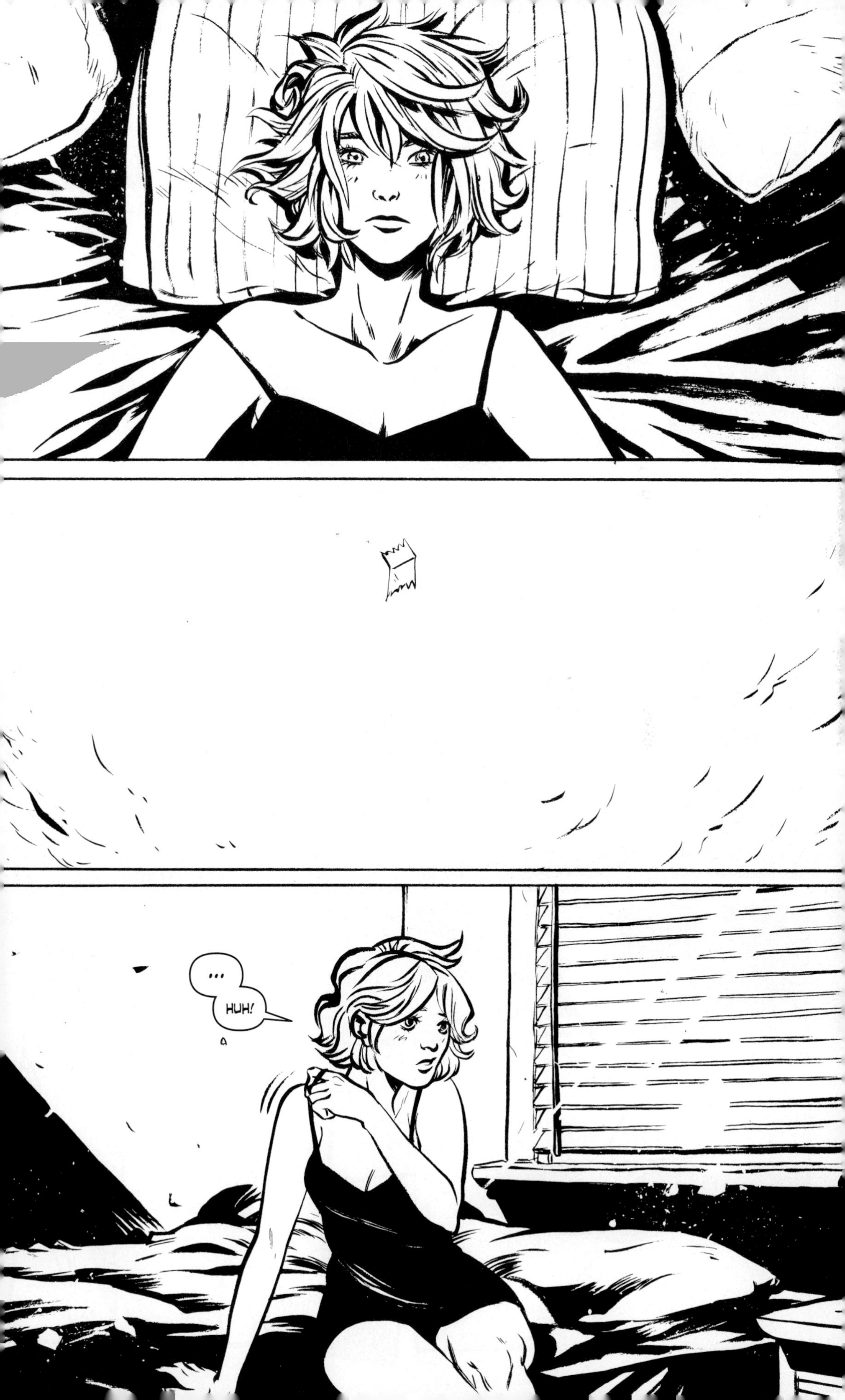
...
HUH!

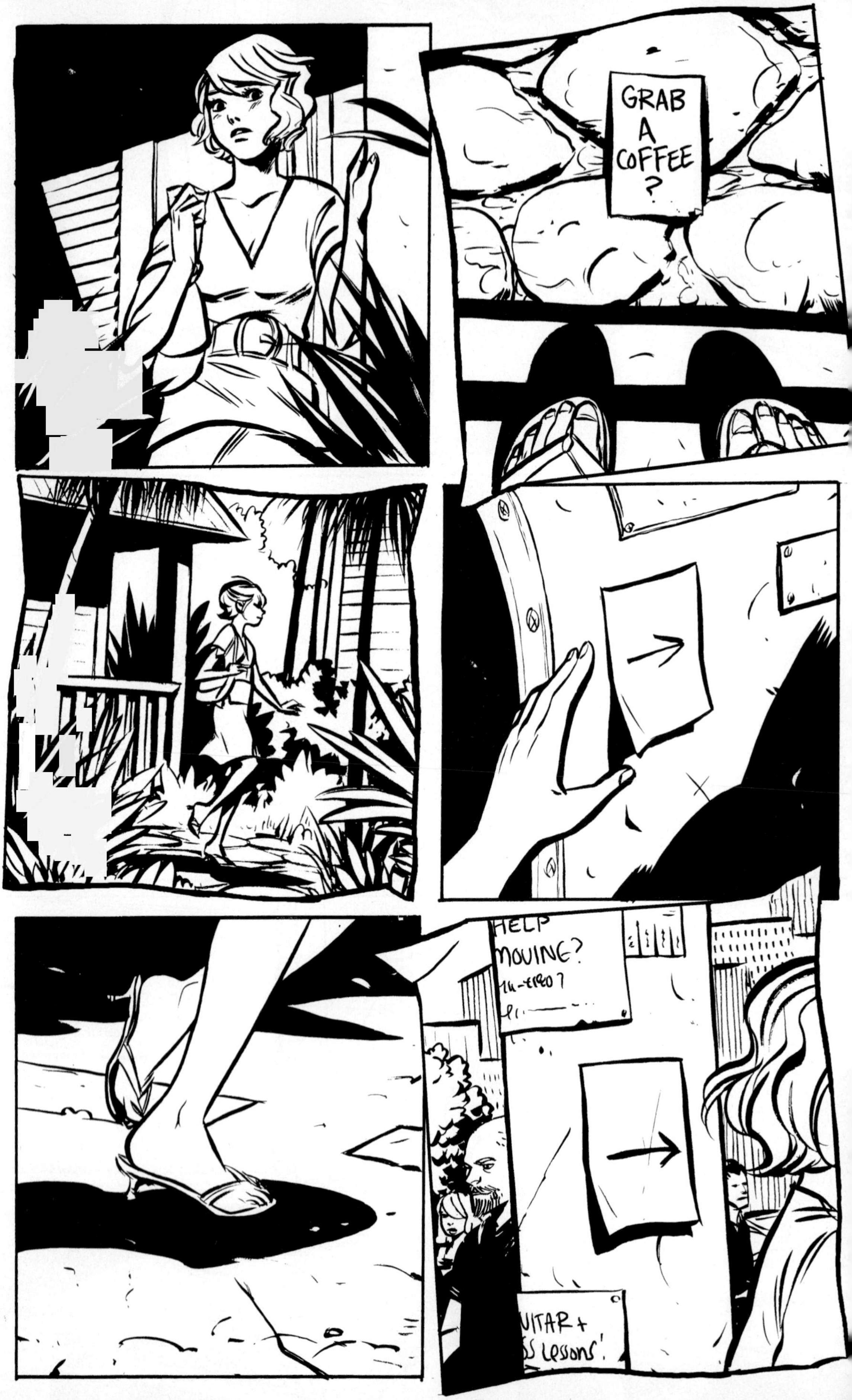
GRAB A COFFEE ?

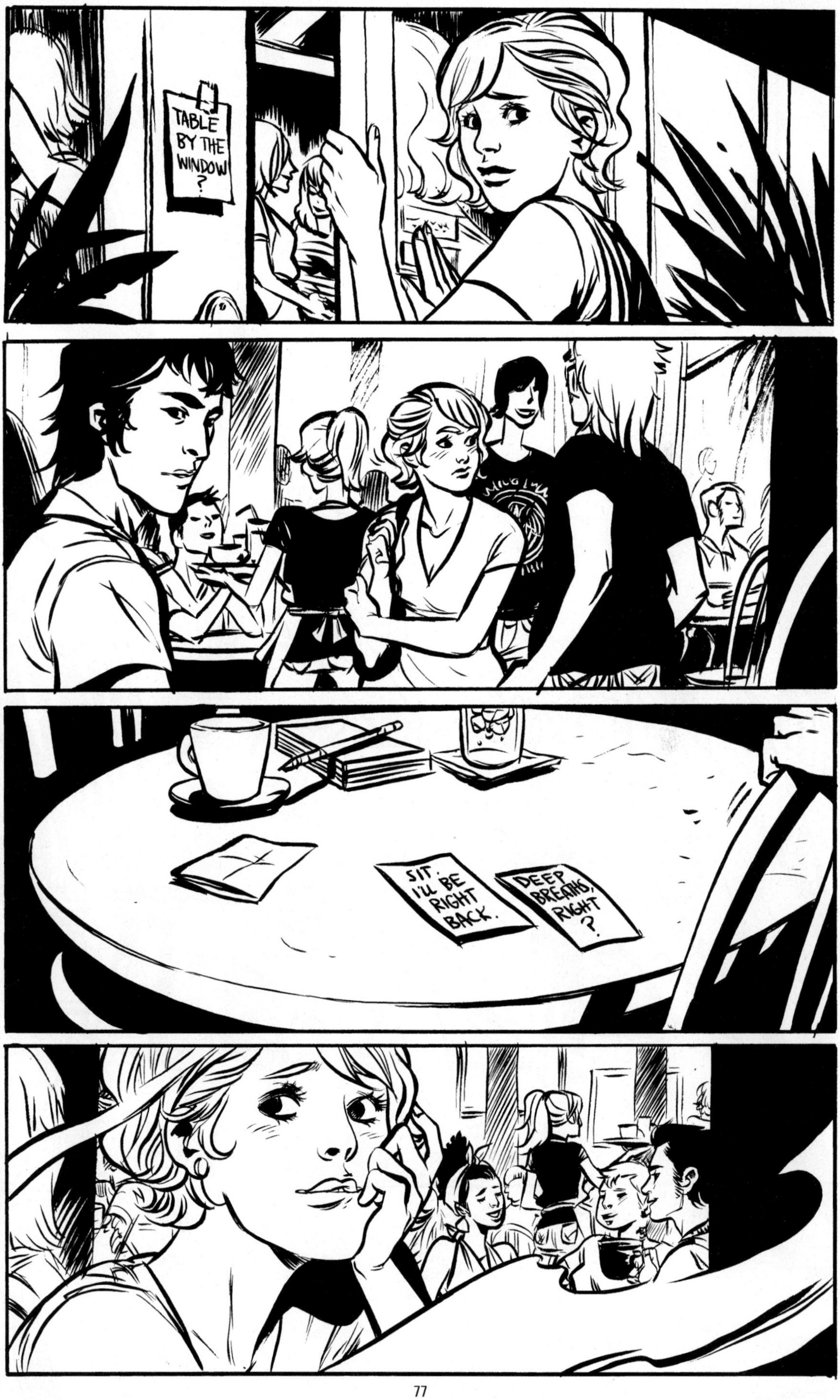
TABLE BY THE WINDOW ?
SIT. I'LL BE RIGHT BACK.
DEEP BREATHS, RIGHT ?

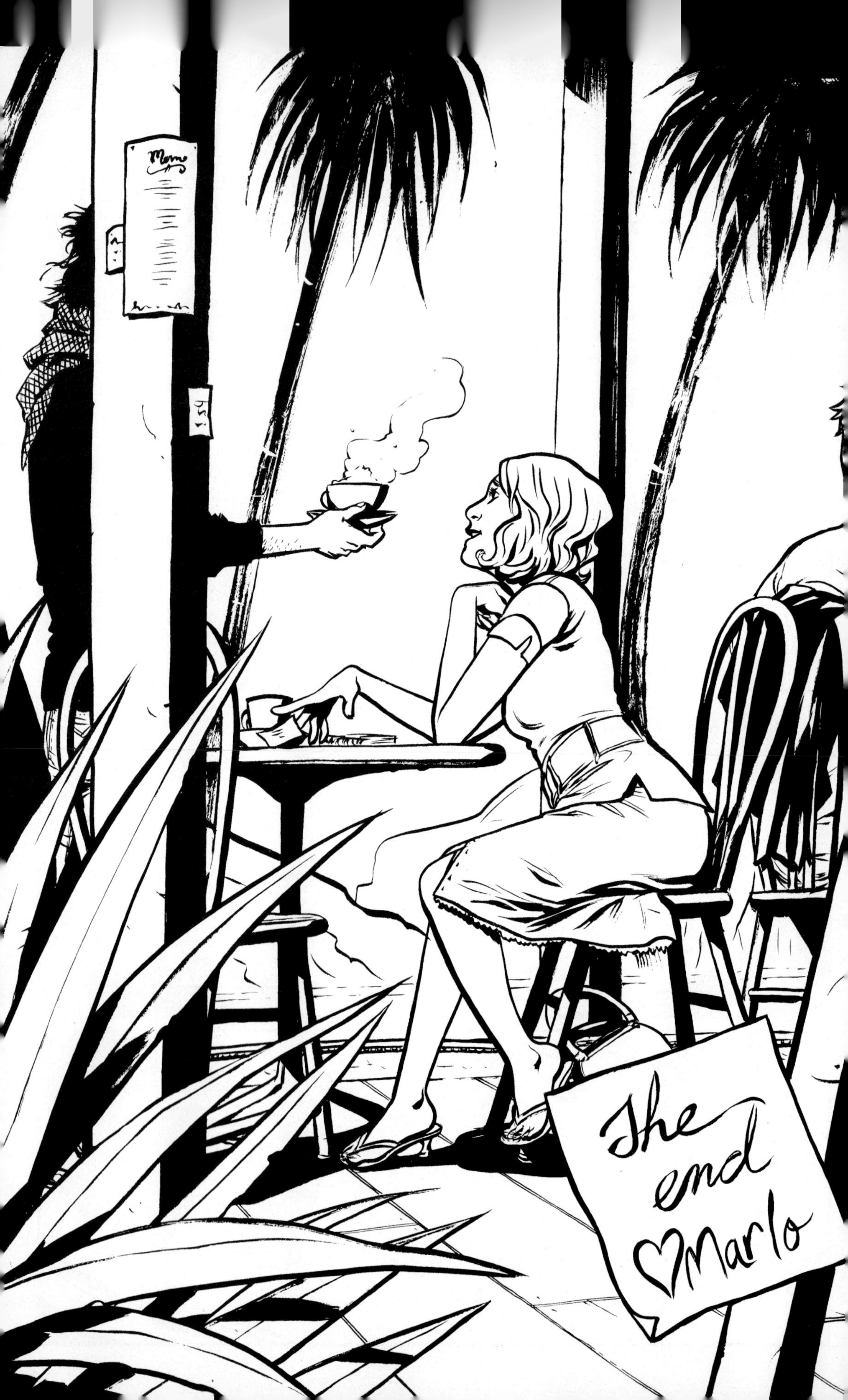
Menu
The end
♥Marlo

4

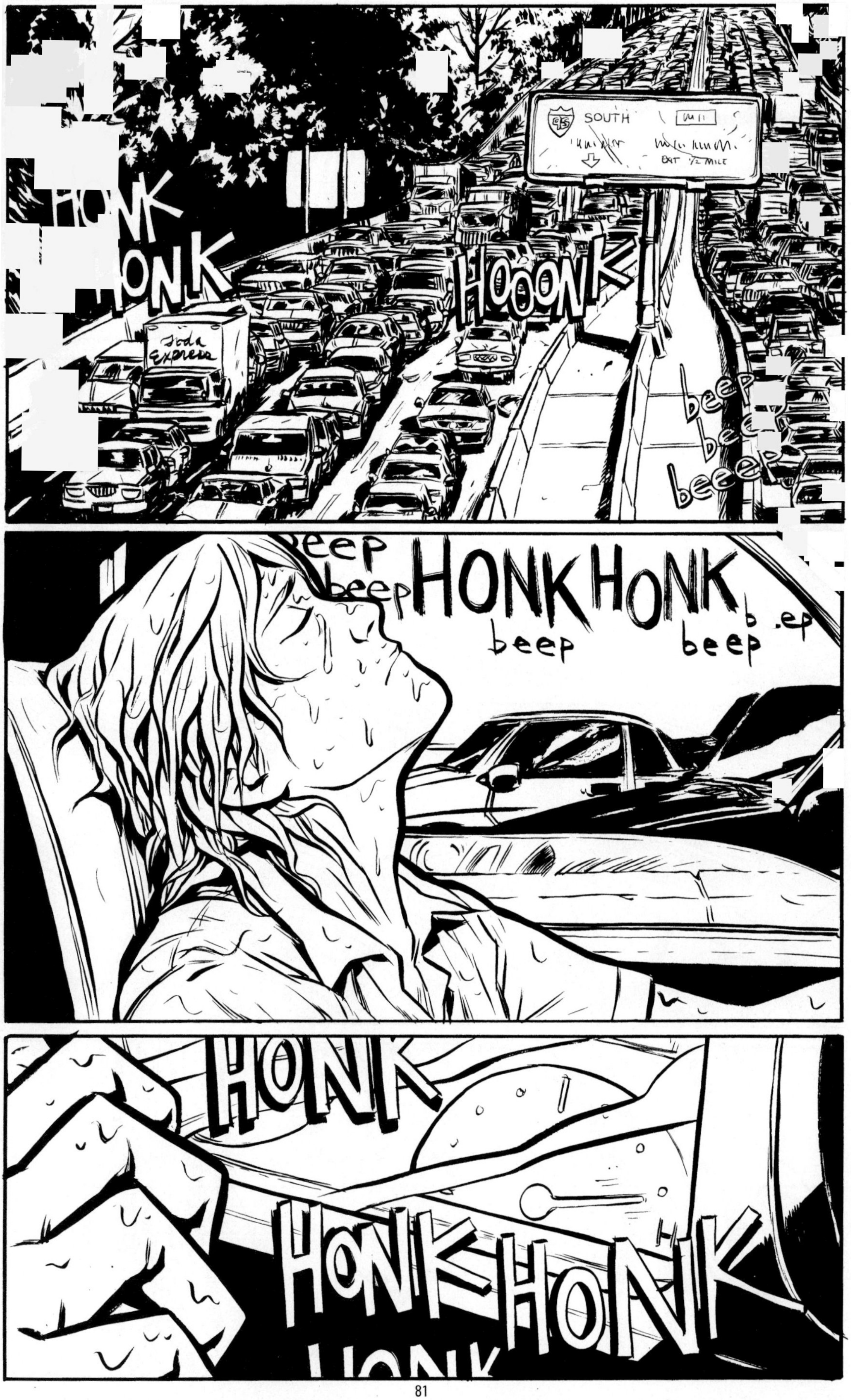
HONK
HOOONK
95 SOUTH
EXIT 1/2 MILE
Soda Express
beep
beeep
beep
HONK HONK
beep beep
HONK
HONK HONK

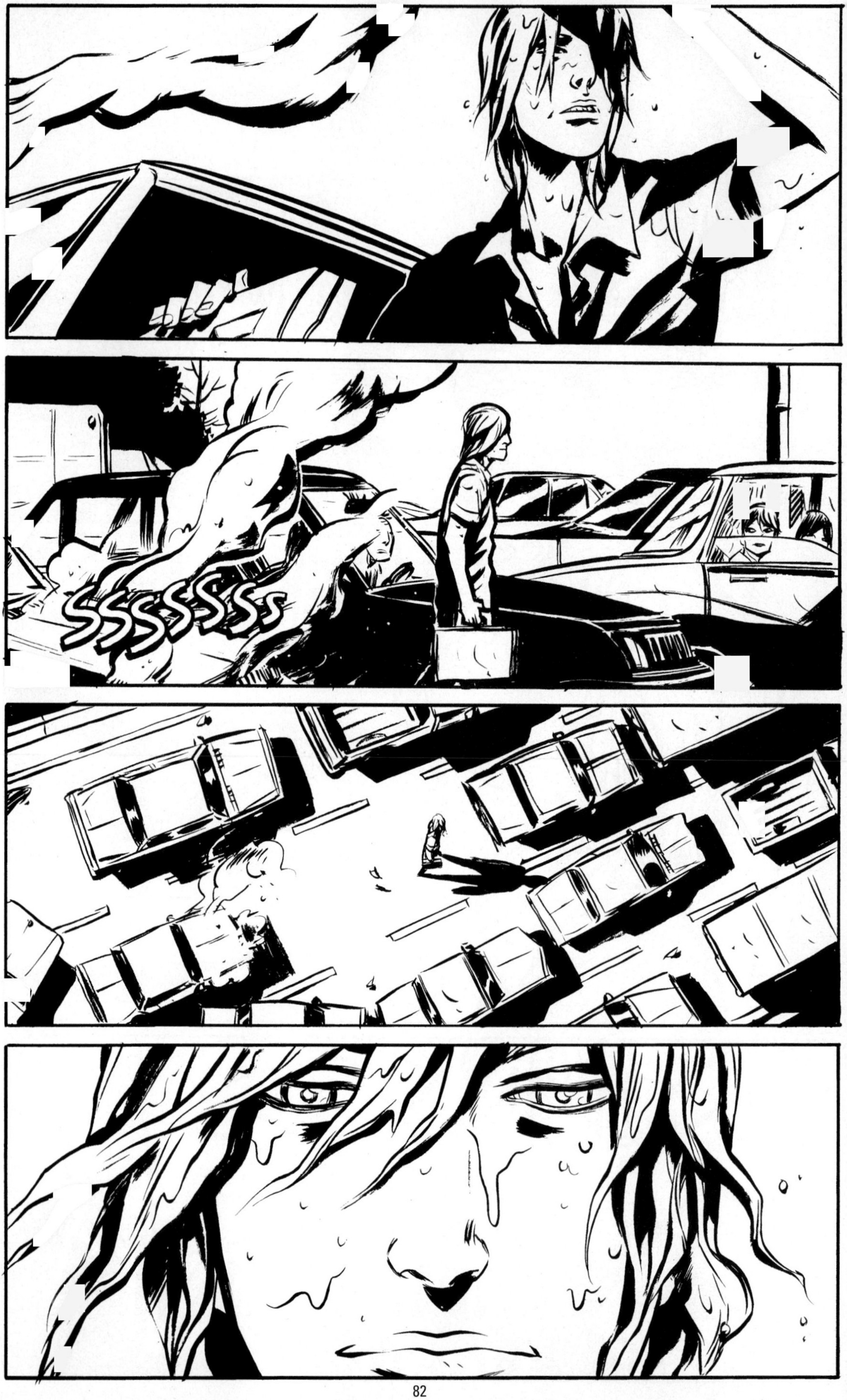
SSSSSSs

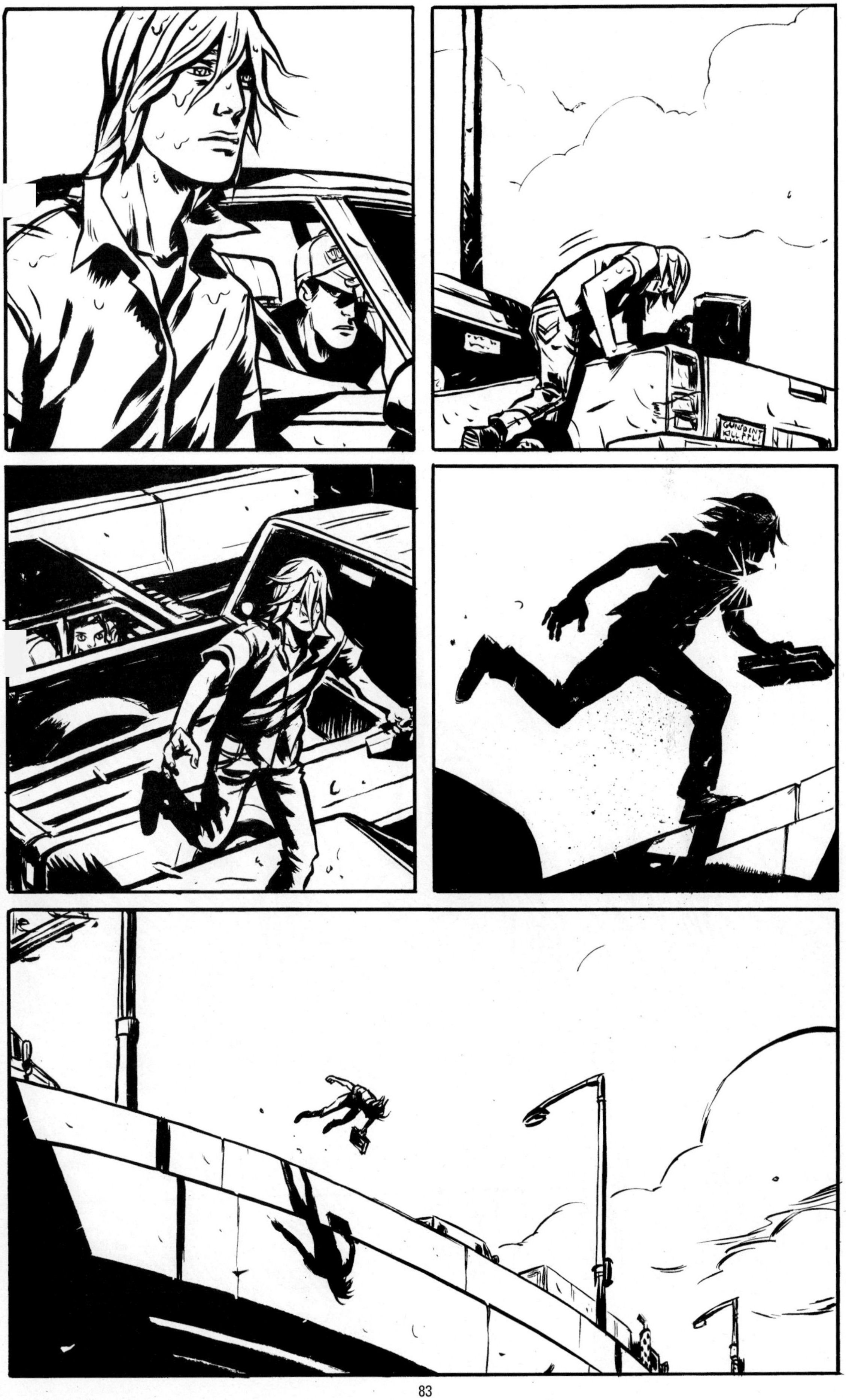

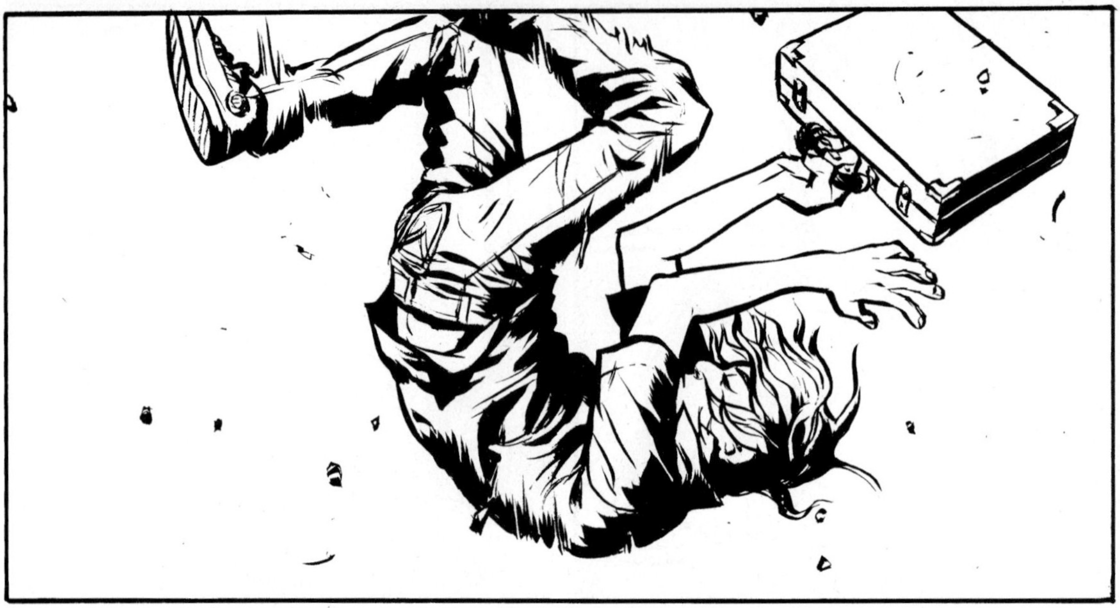

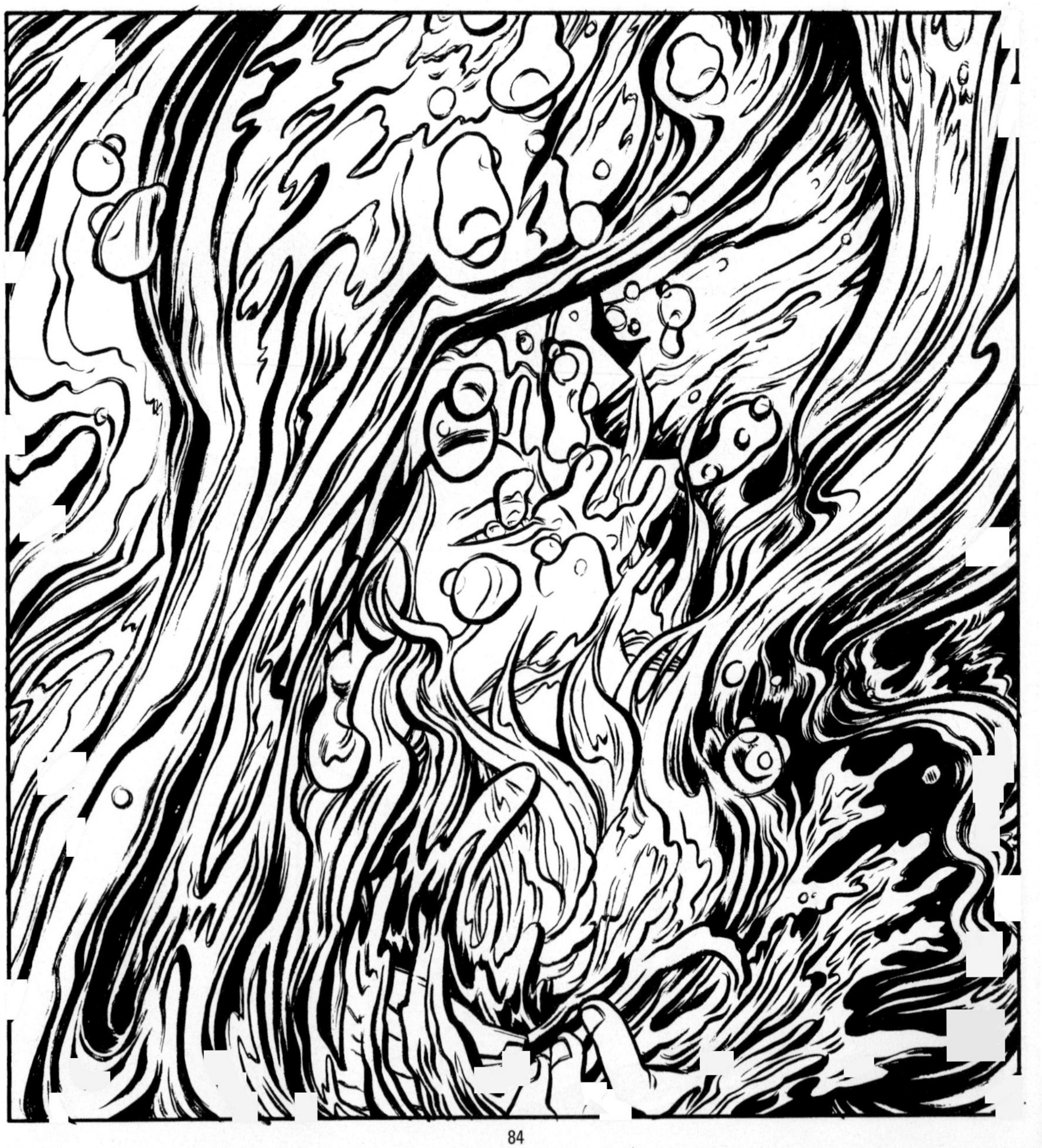

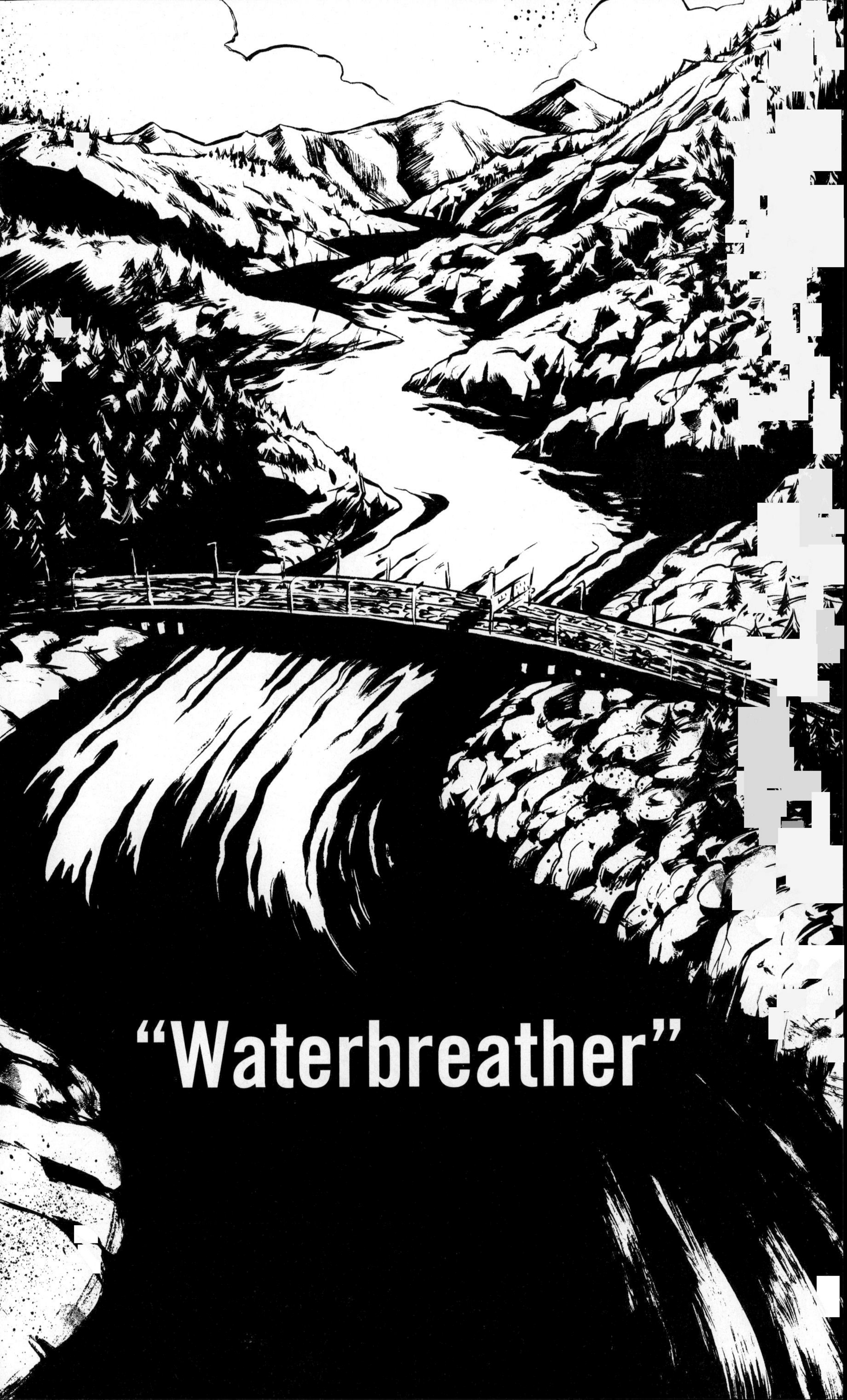
"Waterbreather"

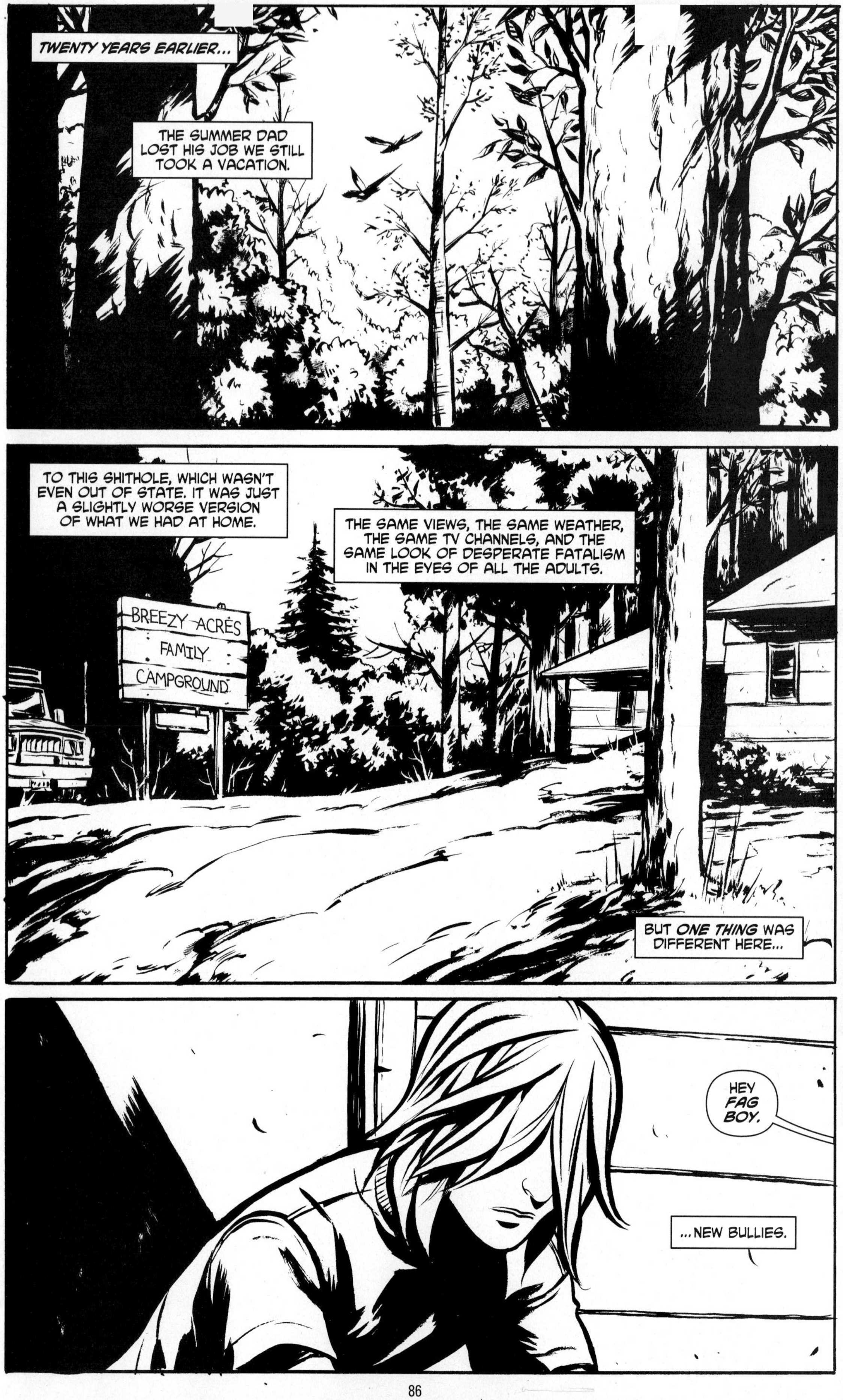
TWENTY YEARS EARLIER...
THE SUMMER DAD LOST HIS JOB WE STILL TOOK A VACATION.
TO THIS SHITHOLE, WHICH WASN'T EVEN OUT OF STATE. IT WAS JUST A SLIGHTLY WORSE VERSION OF WHAT WE HAD AT HOME.
THE SAME VIEWS, THE SAME WEATHER, THE SAME TV CHANNELS, AND THE SAME LOOK OF DESPERATE FATALISM IN THE EYES OF ALL THE ADULTS.
BREEZY ACRES
FAMILY
CAMPGROUND
BUT *ONE THING* WAS DIFFERENT HERE...
HEY *FAG* BOY.
...NEW BULLIES.

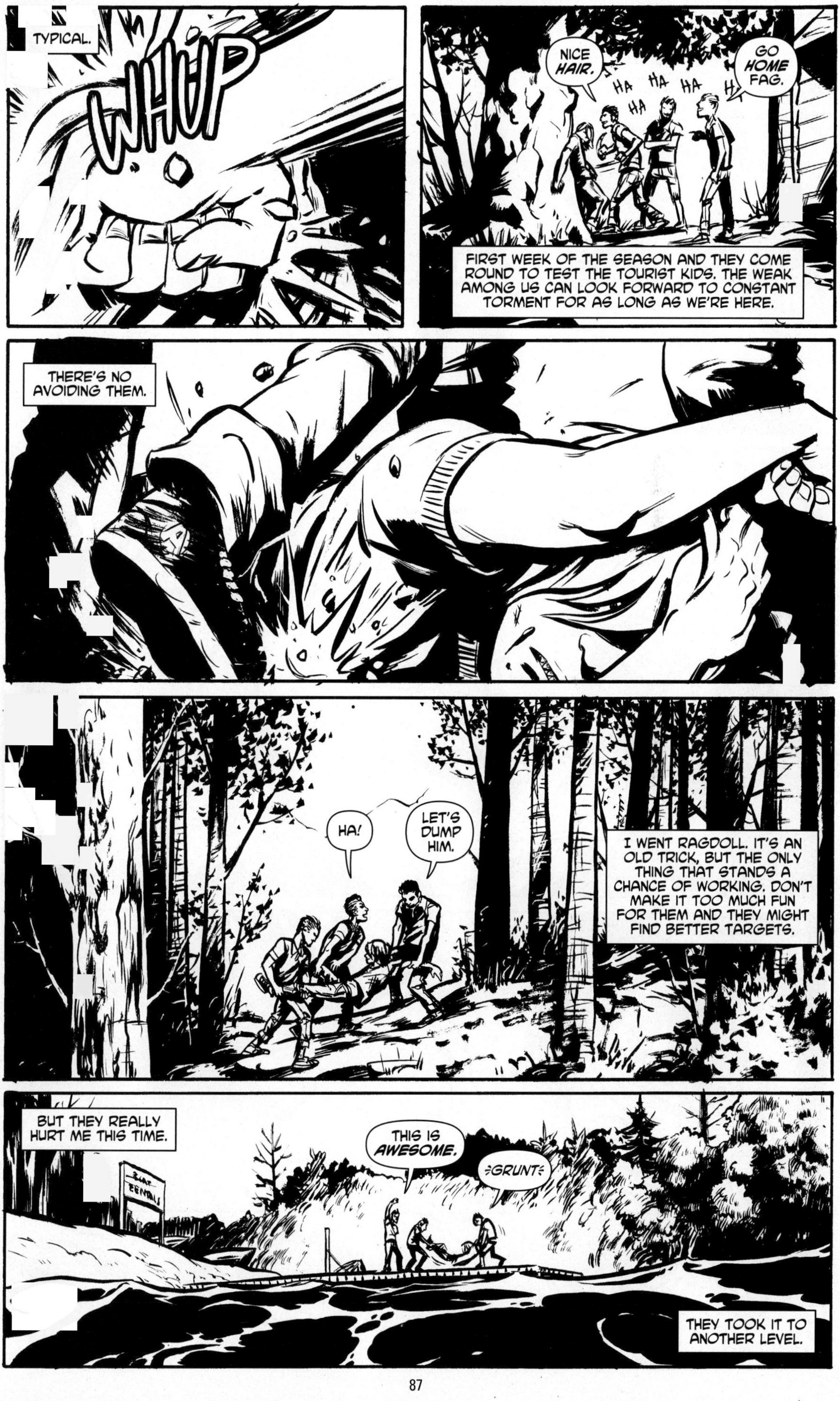
TYPICAL.
WHIP
NICE HAIR.
HA HA HA HA
GO HOME FAG.
FIRST WEEK OF THE SEASON AND THEY COME ROUND TO TEST THE TOURIST KIDS. THE WEAK AMONG US CAN LOOK FORWARD TO CONSTANT TORMENT FOR AS LONG AS WE'RE HERE.
THERE'S NO AVOIDING THEM.
HA!
LET'S DUMP HIM.
I WENT RAGDOLL. IT'S AN OLD TRICK, BUT THE ONLY THING THAT STANDS A CHANCE OF WORKING. DON'T MAKE IT TOO MUCH FUN FOR THEM AND THEY MIGHT FIND BETTER TARGETS.
BUT THEY REALLY HURT ME THIS TIME.
THIS IS AWESOME.
GRUNT
THEY TOOK IT TO ANOTHER LEVEL.

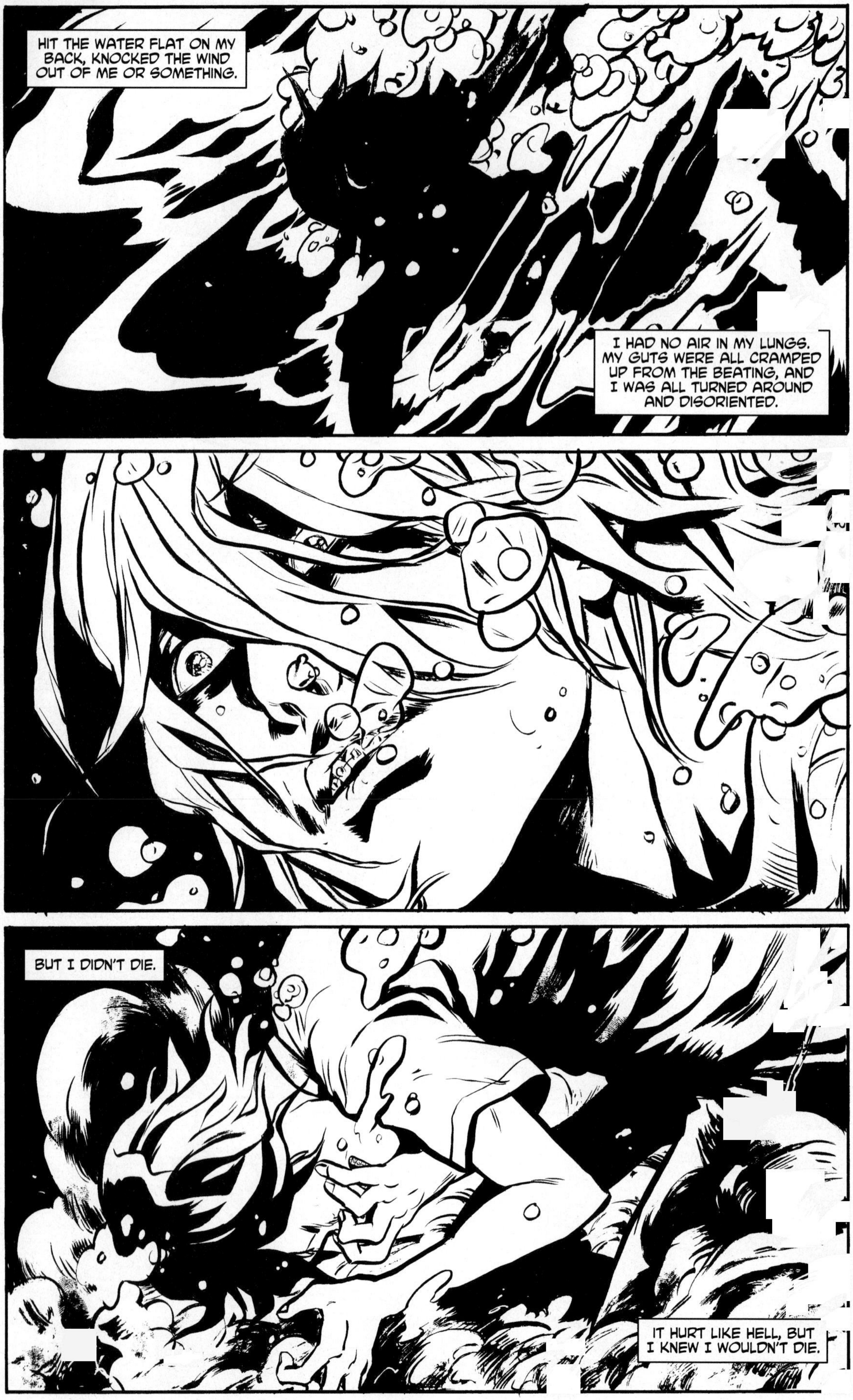
HIT THE WATER FLAT ON MY BACK, KNOCKED THE WIND OUT OF ME OR SOMETHING.
I HAD NO AIR IN MY LUNGS. MY GUTS WERE ALL CRAMPED UP FROM THE BEATING, AND I WAS ALL TURNED AROUND AND DISORIENTED.
BUT I DIDN'T DIE.
IT HURT LIKE HELL, BUT I KNEW I WOULDN'T DIE.

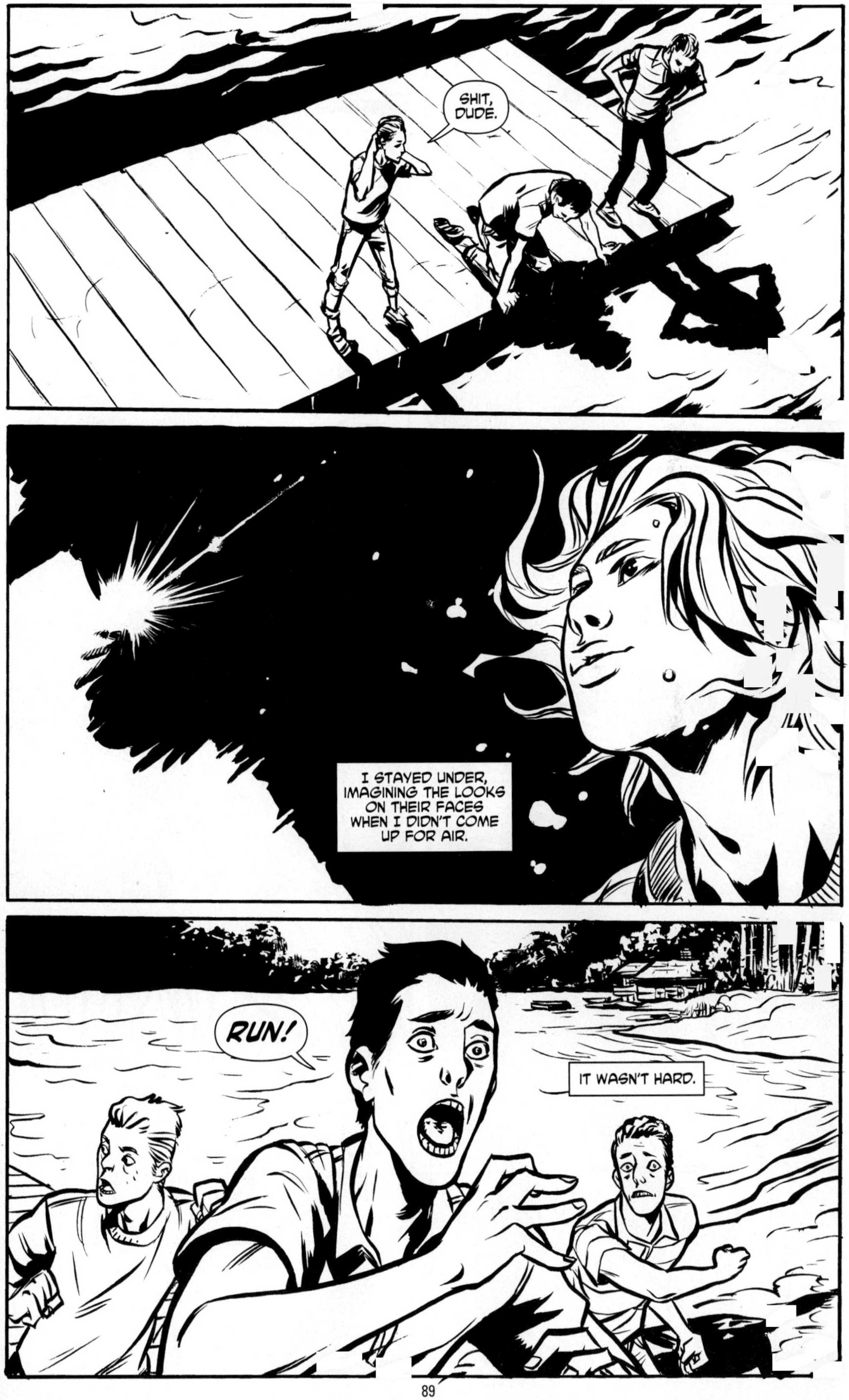
SHIT, DUDE.
I STAYED UNDER, IMAGINING THE LOOKS ON THEIR FACES WHEN I DIDN'T COME UP FOR AIR.
RUN!
IT WASN'T HARD.

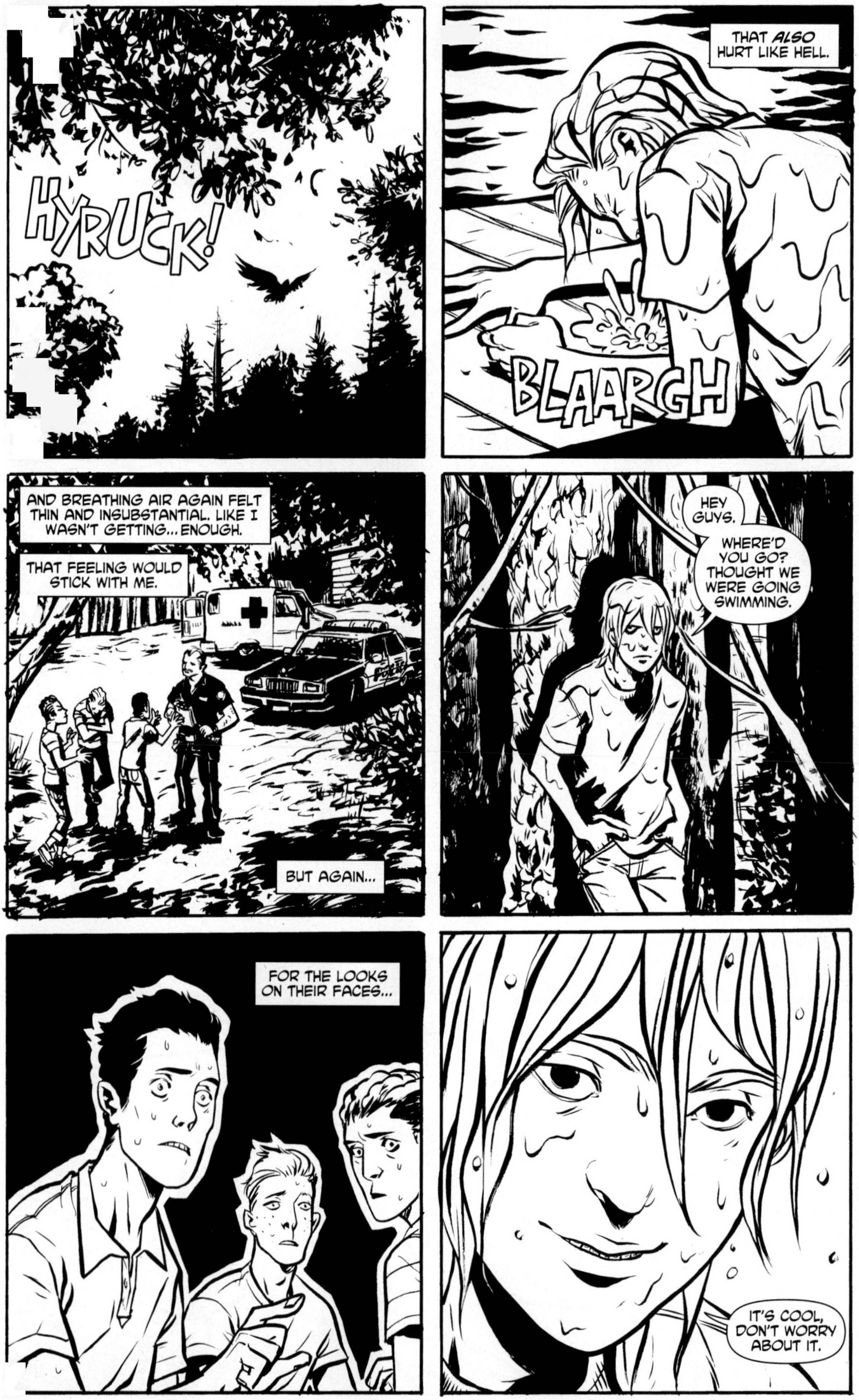
HYRUCK!
THAT ALSO HURT LIKE HELL.
BLAARGH
AND BREATHING AIR AGAIN FELT THIN AND INSUBSTANTIAL. LIKE I WASN'T GETTING... ENOUGH.
THAT FEELING WOULD STICK WITH ME.
BUT AGAIN...
HEY GUYS.
WHERE'D YOU GO? THOUGHT WE WERE GOING SWIMMING.
FOR THE LOOKS ON THEIR FACES...
IT'S COOL, DON'T WORRY ABOUT IT.

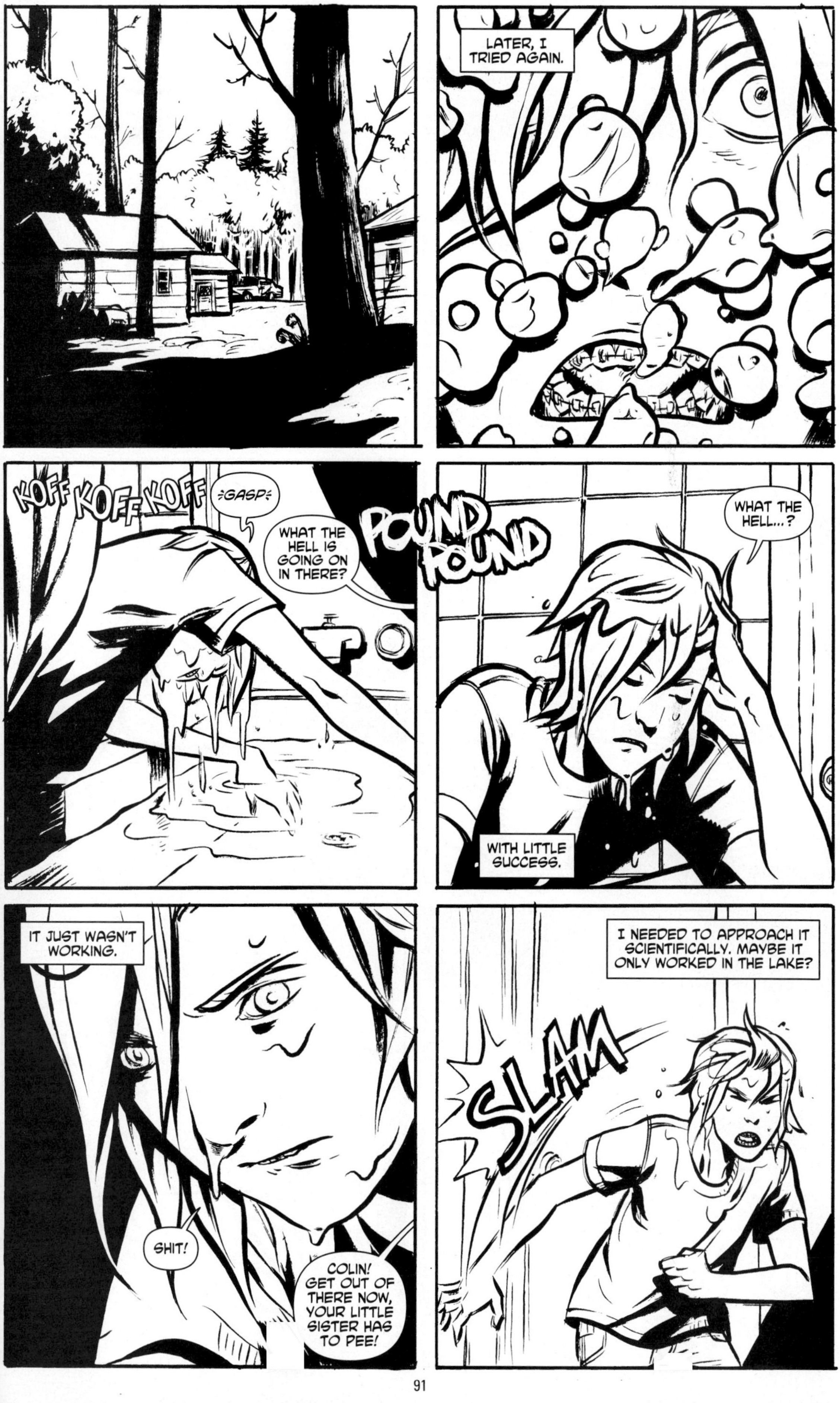
LATER, I TRIED AGAIN.
KOFF KOFF KOFF
GASP
WHAT THE HELL IS GOING ON IN THERE?
POUND POUND
WHAT THE HELL...?
WITH LITTLE SUCCESS.
IT JUST WASN'T WORKING.
SHIT!
COLIN! GET OUT OF THERE NOW, YOUR LITTLE SISTER HAS TO PEE!
I NEEDED TO APPROACH IT SCIENTIFICALLY. MAYBE IT ONLY WORKED IN THE LAKE?
SLAM

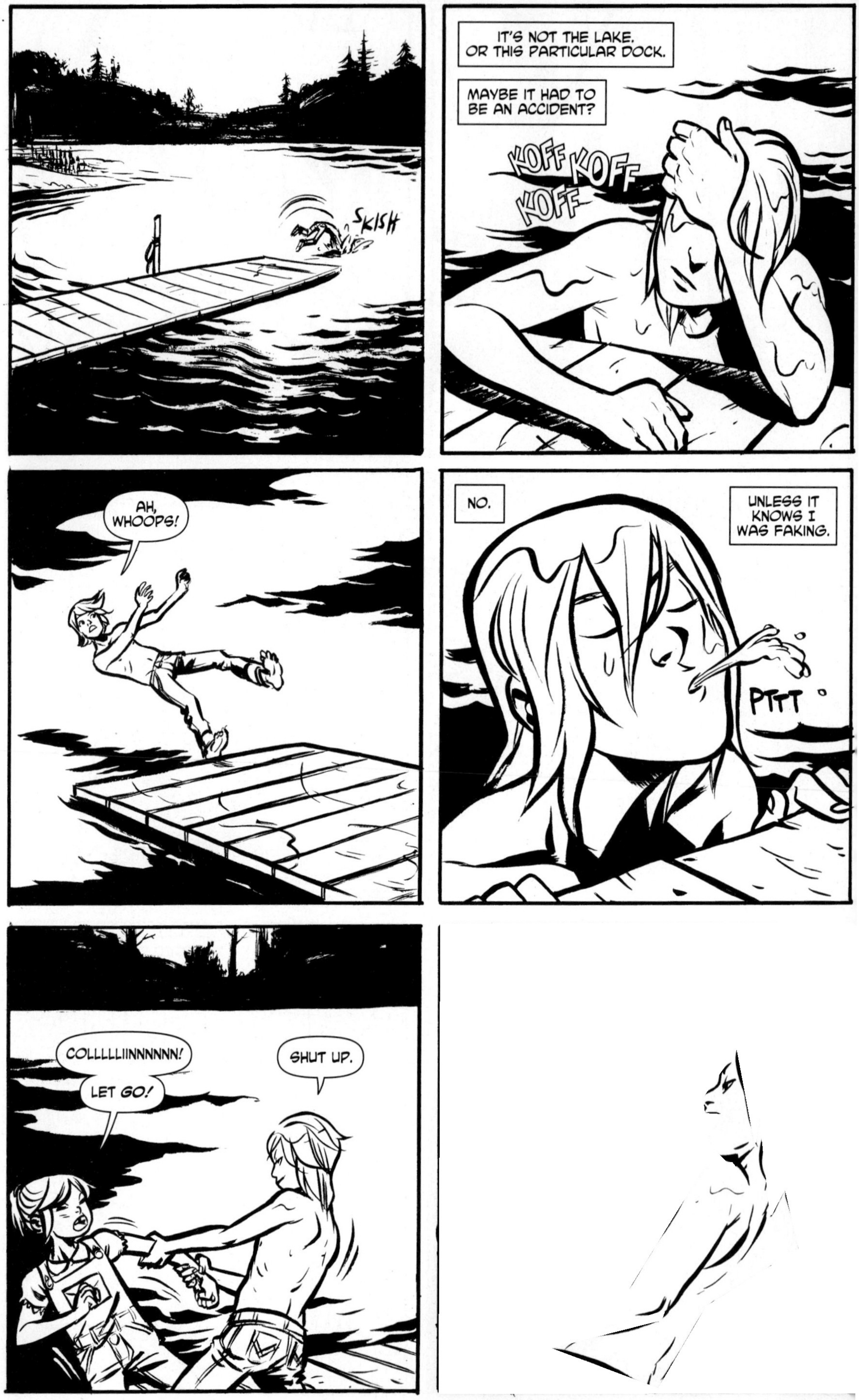
SKISH
IT'S NOT THE LAKE. OR THIS PARTICULAR DOCK.
MAYBE IT HAD TO BE AN ACCIDENT?
KOFF KOFF KOFF
AH, WHOOPS!
NO.
UNLESS IT KNOWS I WAS FAKING.
PTTT
COLLLLLIINNNNNN!
LET GO!
SHUT UP.

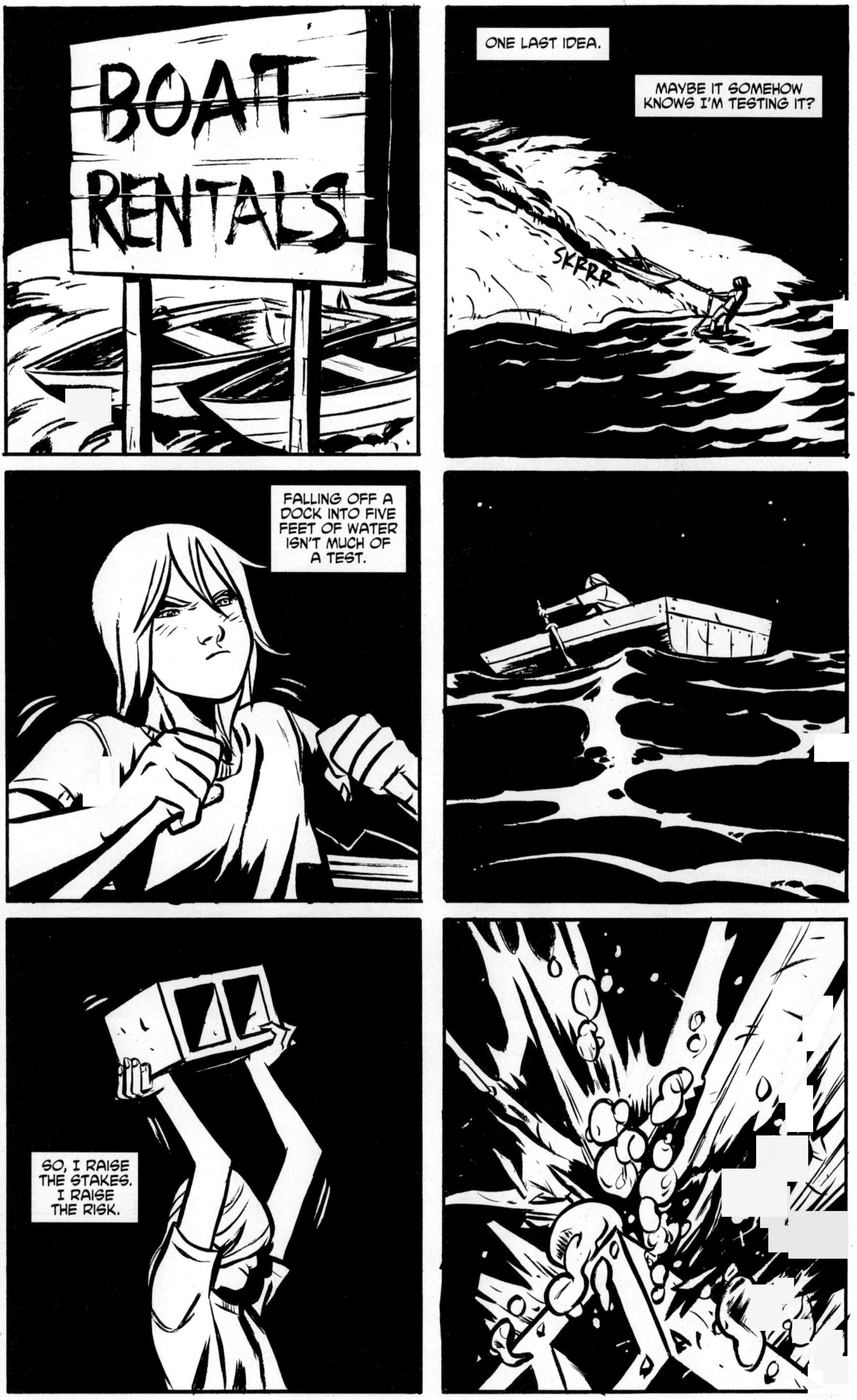
BOAT RENTALS
ONE LAST IDEA.
MAYBE IT SOMEHOW KNOWS I'M TESTING IT?
SKRRR
FALLING OFF A DOCK INTO FIVE FEET OF WATER ISN'T MUCH OF A TEST.
SO, I RAISE THE STAKES. I RAISE THE RISK.

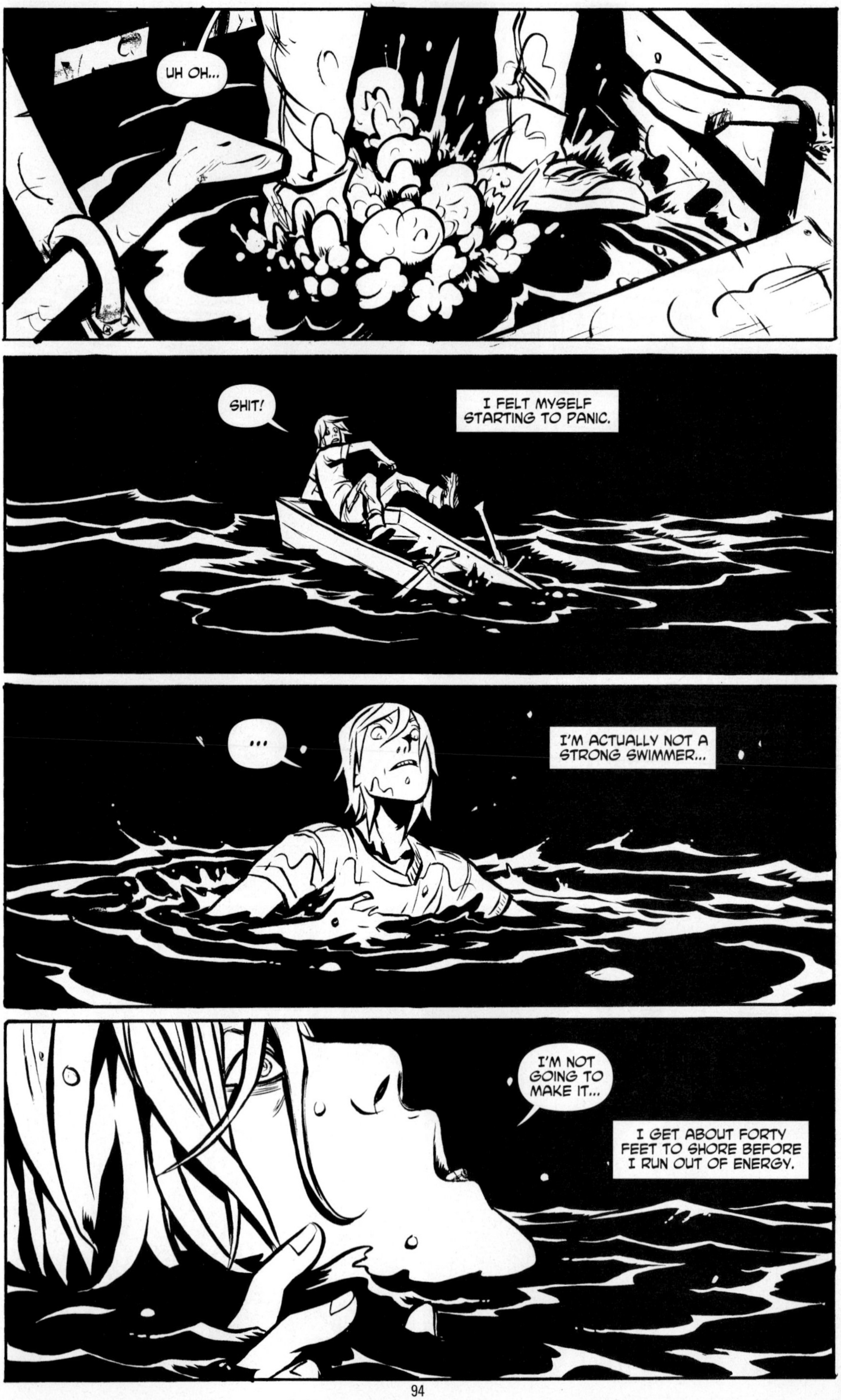
UH OH...
SHIT!
I FELT MYSELF STARTING TO PANIC.
...
I'M ACTUALLY NOT A STRONG SWIMMER...
I'M NOT GOING TO MAKE IT...
I GET ABOUT FORTY FEET TO SHORE BEFORE I RUN OUT OF ENERGY.

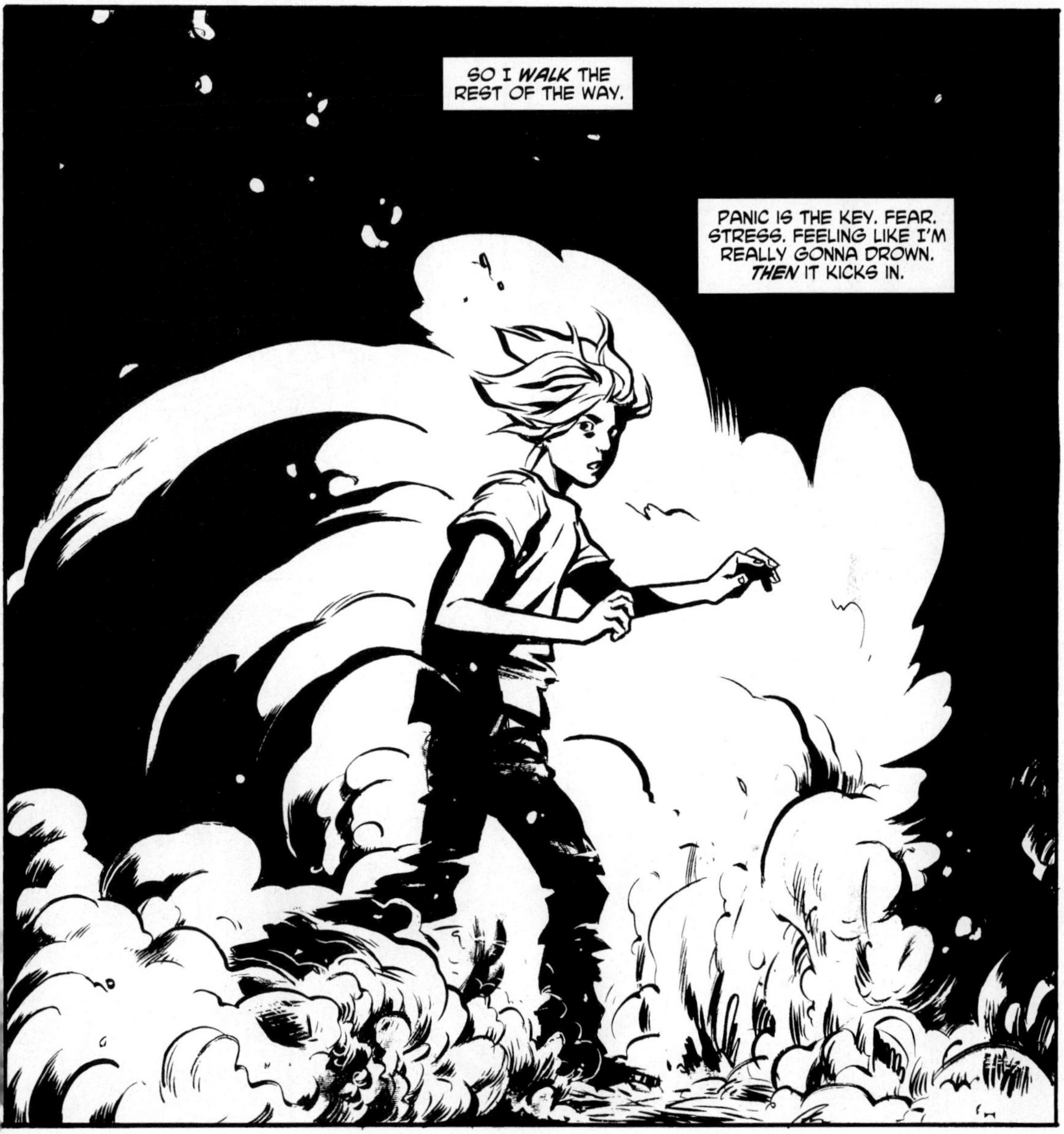
SO I WALK THE REST OF THE WAY.
PANIC IS THE KEY. FEAR. STRESS. FEELING LIKE I'M REALLY GONNA DROWN. THEN IT KICKS IN.

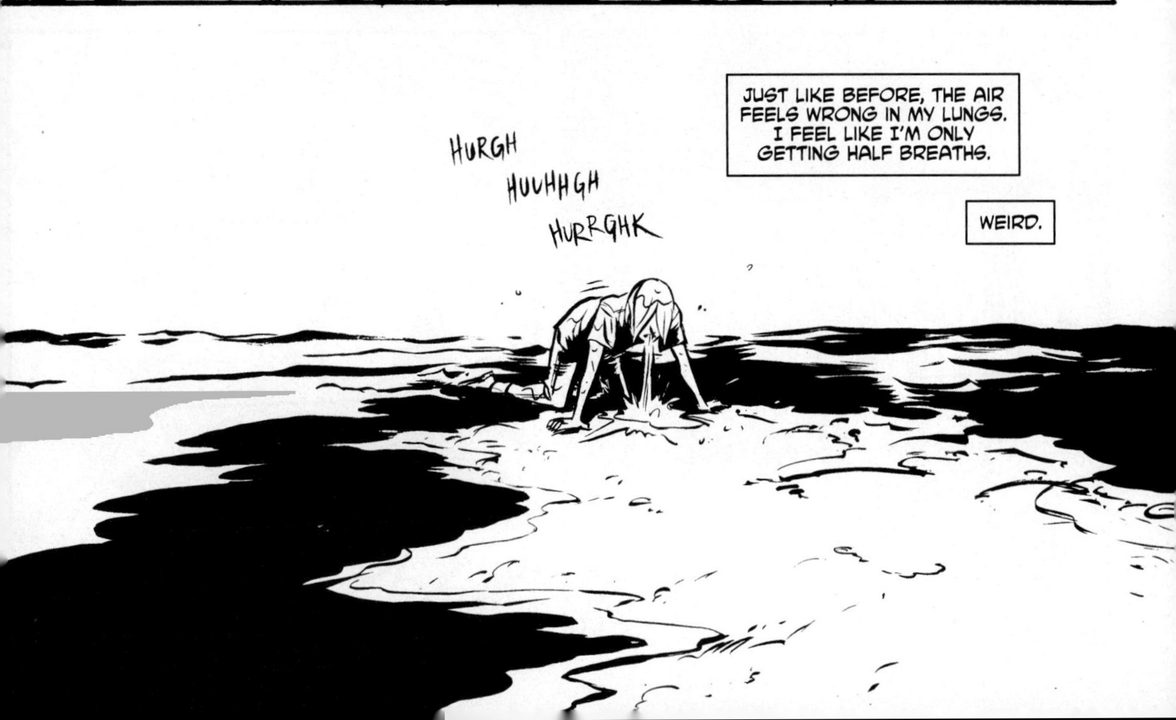
JUST LIKE BEFORE, THE AIR FEELS WRONG IN MY LUNGS. I FEEL LIKE I'M ONLY GETTING HALF BREATHS.
HURGH
HUUHHGH
HURRGHK
WEIRD.

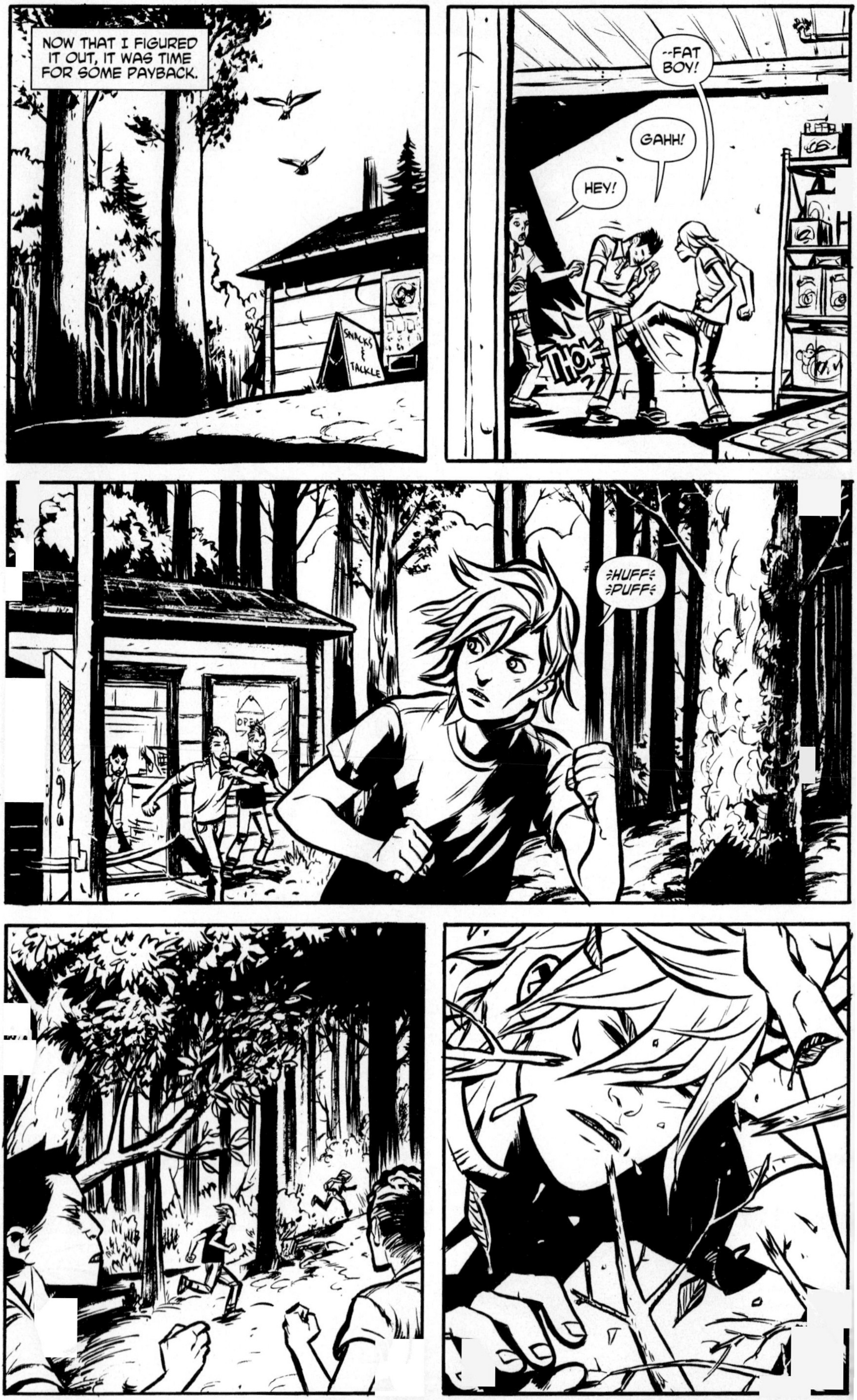
NOW THAT I FIGURED IT OUT, IT WAS TIME FOR SOME PAYBACK.
SNACKS & TACKLE
--FAT BOY!
GAHH!
HEY!
THOK
OPEN
HUFF PUFF

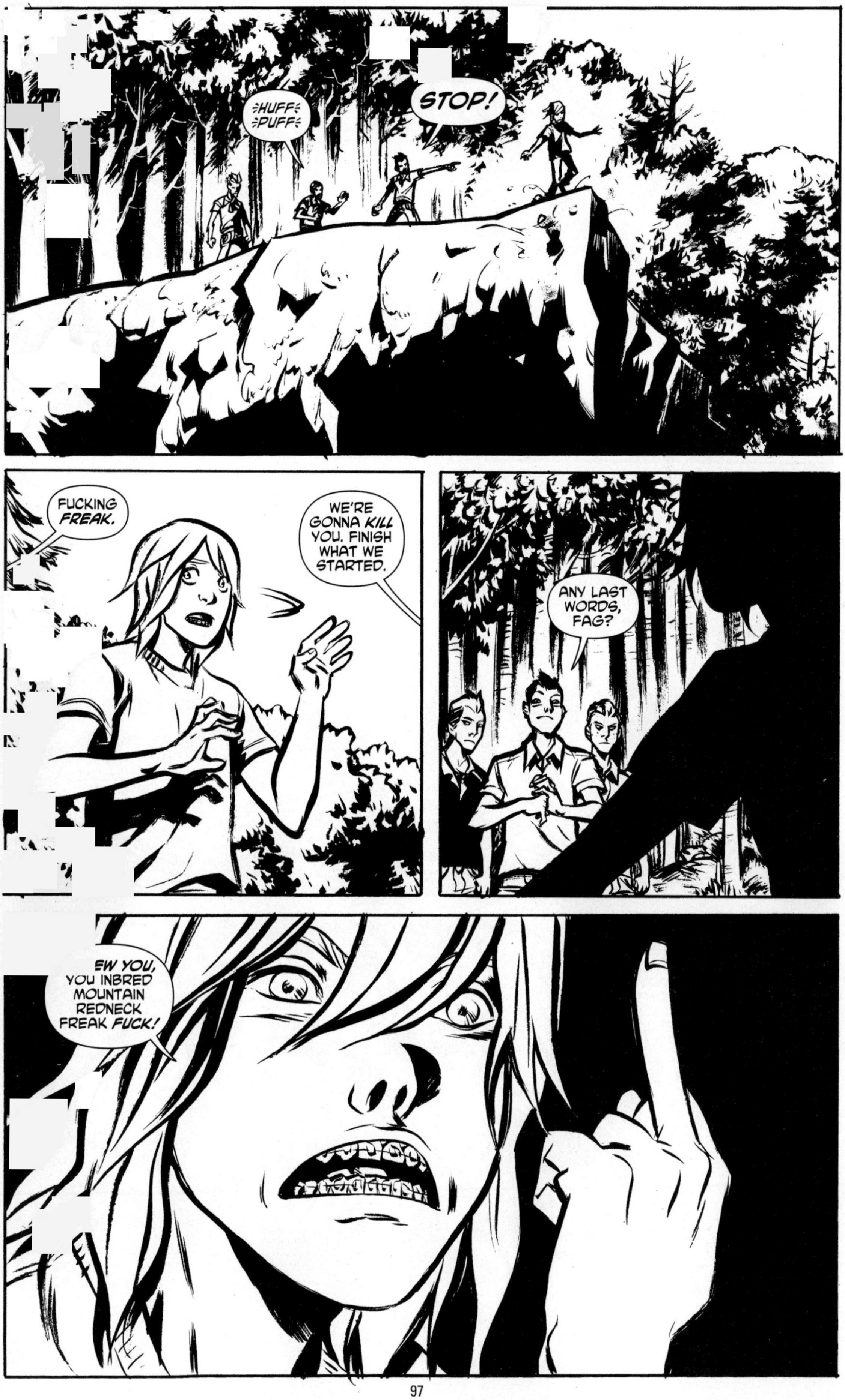
HUFF PUFF
STOP!
FUCKING FREAK.
WE'RE GONNA KILL YOU. FINISH WHAT WE STARTED.
ANY LAST WORDS, FAG?
EW YOU, YOU INBRED MOUNTAIN REDNECK FREAK FUCK!

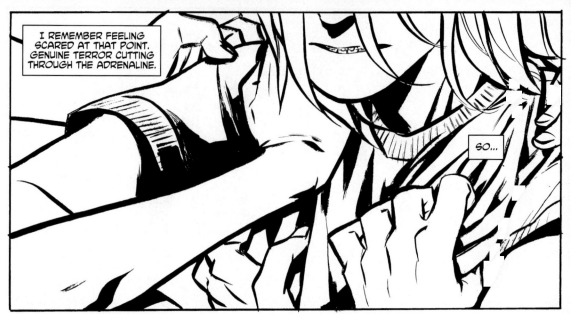

I REMEMBER FEELING SCARED AT THAT POINT. GENUINE TERROR CUTTING THROUGH THE ADRENALINE.

SO...

...I SIMPLY FELL BACKWARDS...

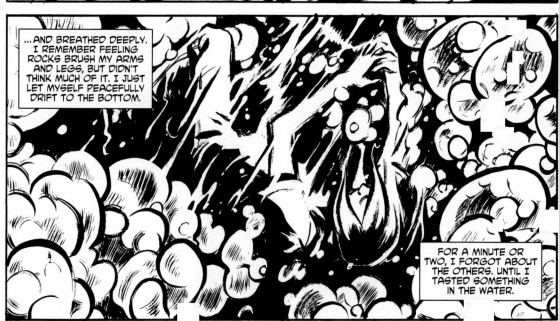

...AND BREATHED DEEPLY. I REMEMBER FEELING ROCKS BRUSH MY ARMS AND LEGS, BUT DIDN'T THINK MUCH OF IT. I JUST LET MYSELF PEACEFULLY DRIFT TO THE BOTTOM.

FOR A MINUTE OR TWO, I FORGOT ABOUT THE OTHERS. UNTIL I TASTED SOMETHING IN THE WATER.

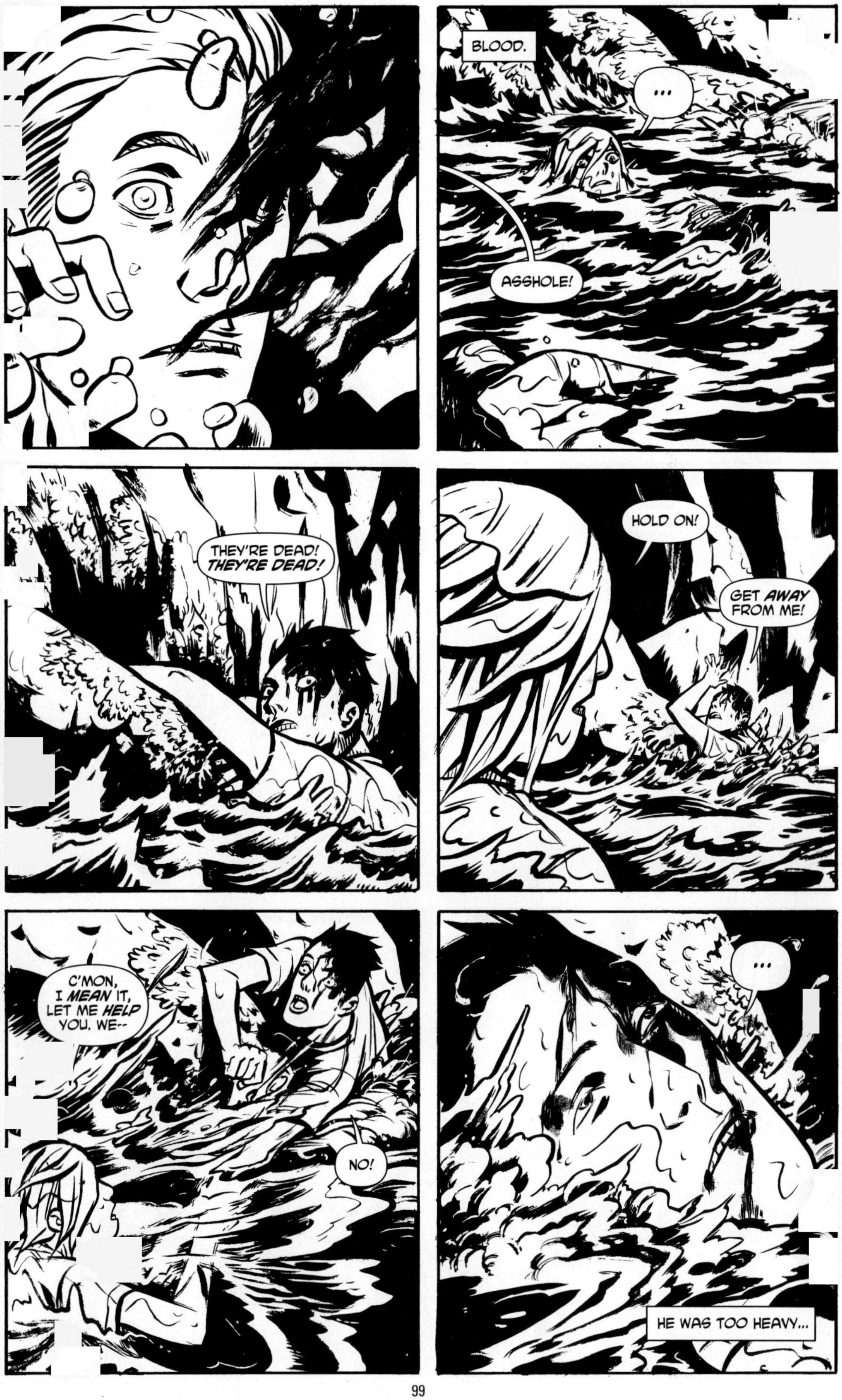
BLOOD.
...
ASSHOLE!
THEY'RE DEAD! THEY'RE DEAD!
HOLD ON!
GET AWAY FROM ME!
C'MON, I MEAN IT, LET ME HELP YOU. WE--
NO!
...
HE WAS TOO HEAVY...

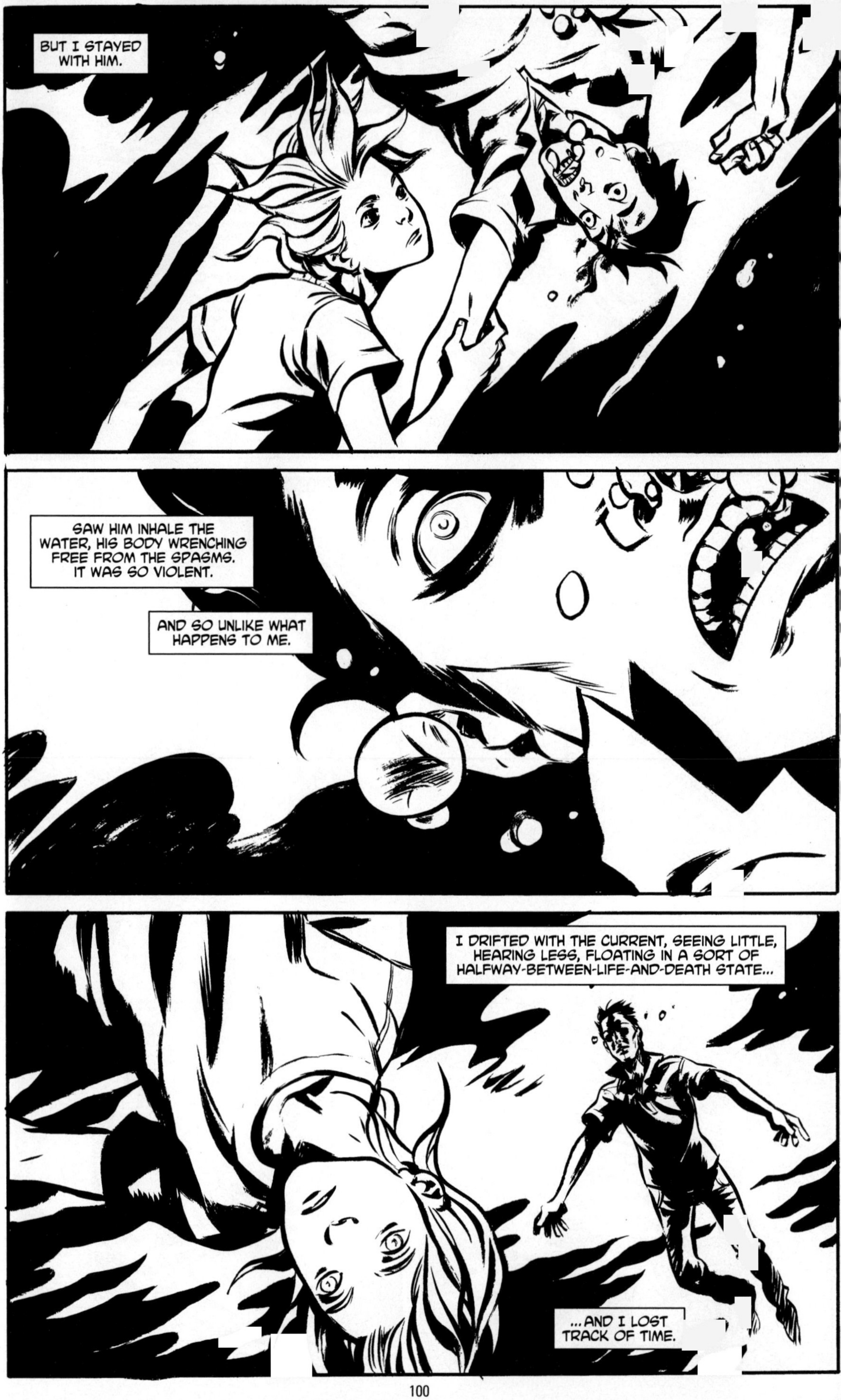
BUT I STAYED WITH HIM.
SAW HIM INHALE THE WATER, HIS BODY WRENCHING FREE FROM THE SPASMS. IT WAS SO VIOLENT.
AND SO UNLIKE WHAT HAPPENS TO ME.
I DRIFTED WITH THE CURRENT, SEEING LITTLE, HEARING LESS, FLOATING IN A SORT OF HALFWAY-BETWEEN-LIFE-AND-DEATH STATE...
...AND I LOST TRACK OF TIME.

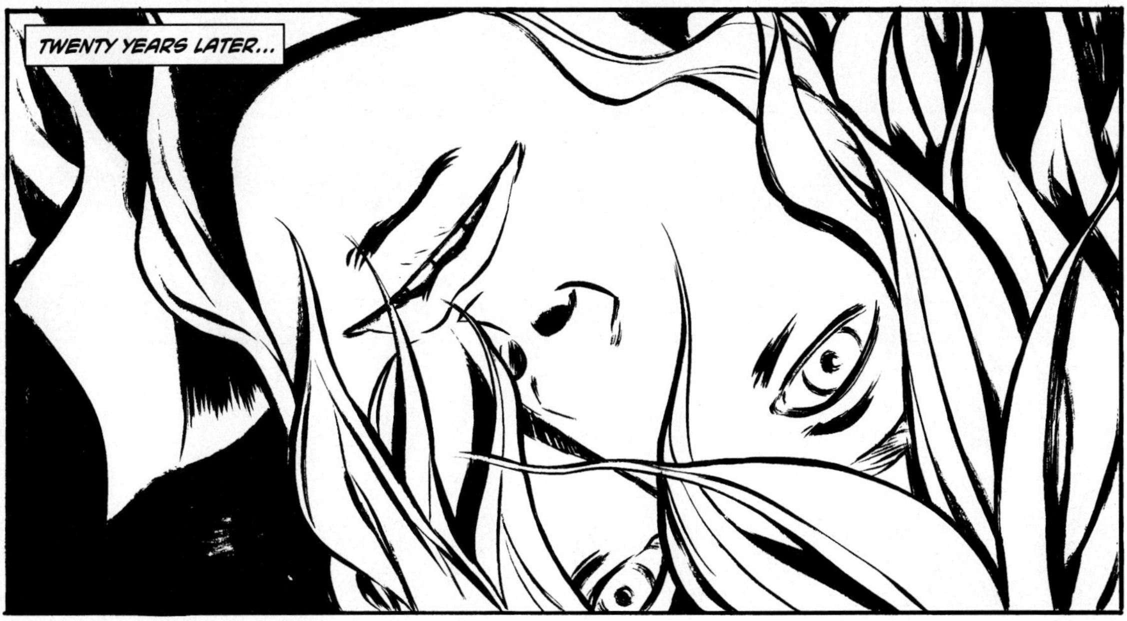
TWENTY YEARS LATER...

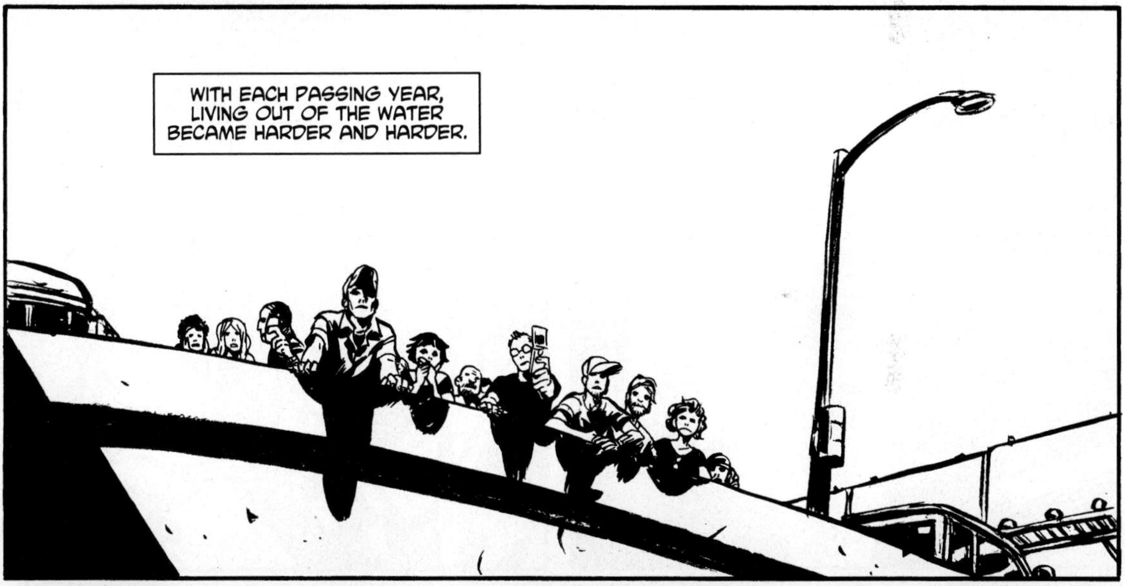
WITH EACH PASSING YEAR, LIVING OUT OF THE WATER BECAME HARDER AND HARDER.

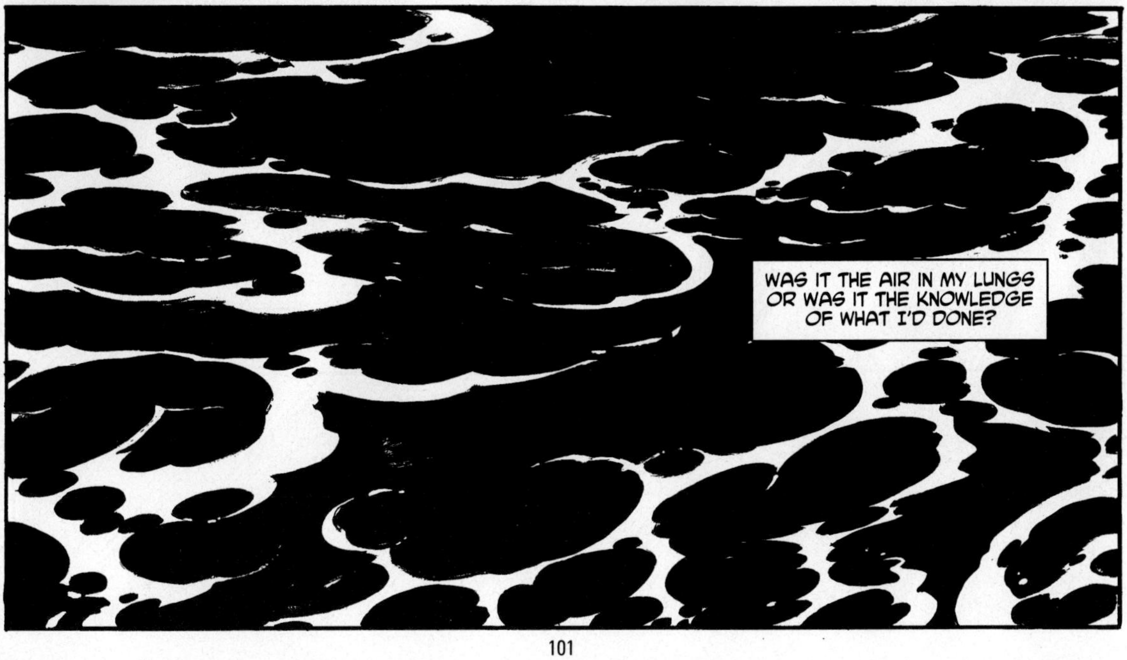
WAS IT THE AIR IN MY LUNGS OR WAS IT THE KNOWLEDGE OF WHAT I'D DONE?

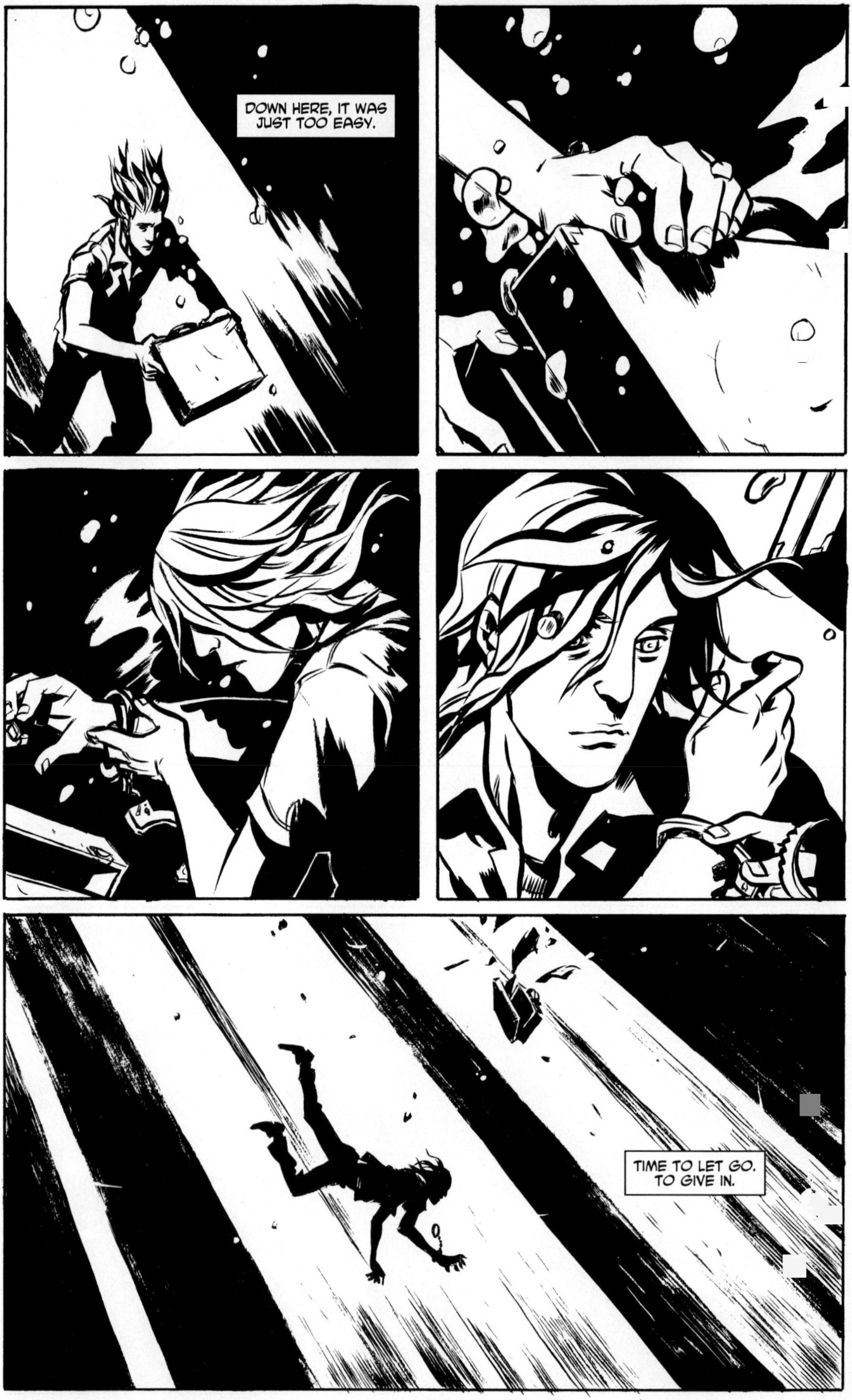
DOWN HERE, IT WAS JUST TOO EASY.
TIME TO LET GO. TO GIVE IN.

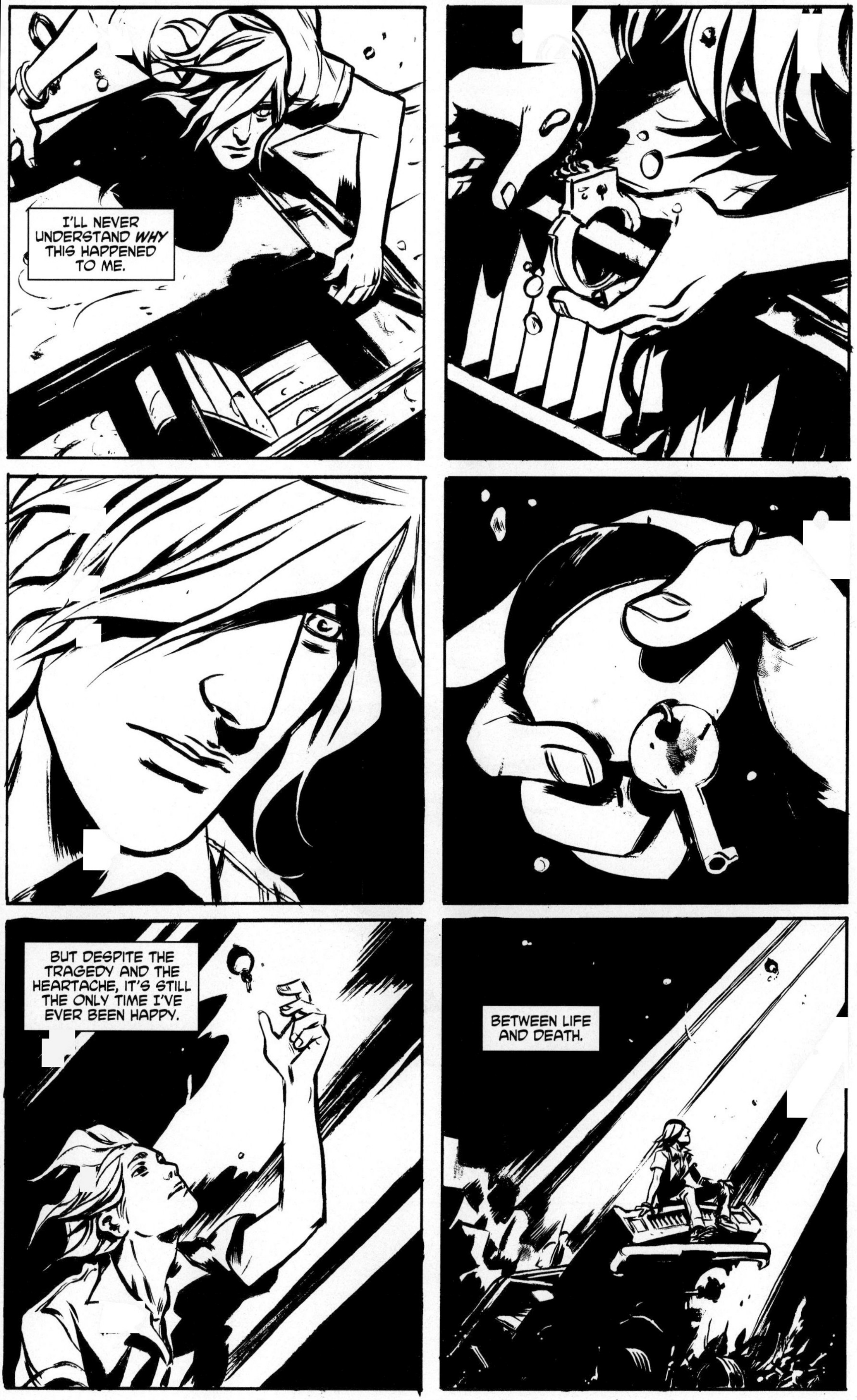
I'LL NEVER UNDERSTAND WHY THIS HAPPENED TO ME.
BUT DESPITE THE TRAGEDY AND THE HEARTACHE, IT'S STILL THE ONLY TIME I'VE EVER BEEN HAPPY.
BETWEEN LIFE AND DEATH.

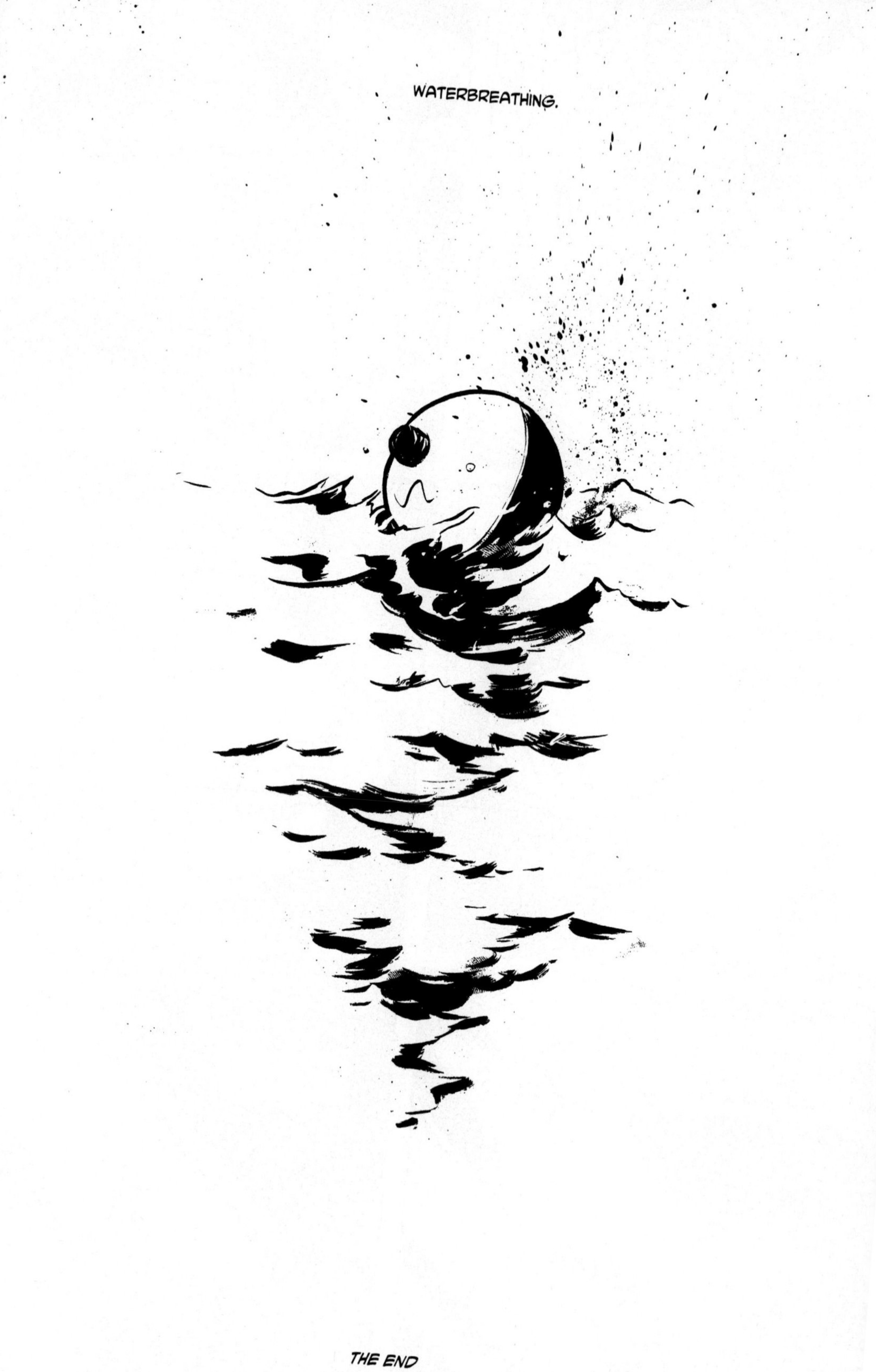
WATERBREATHING.
THE END

5

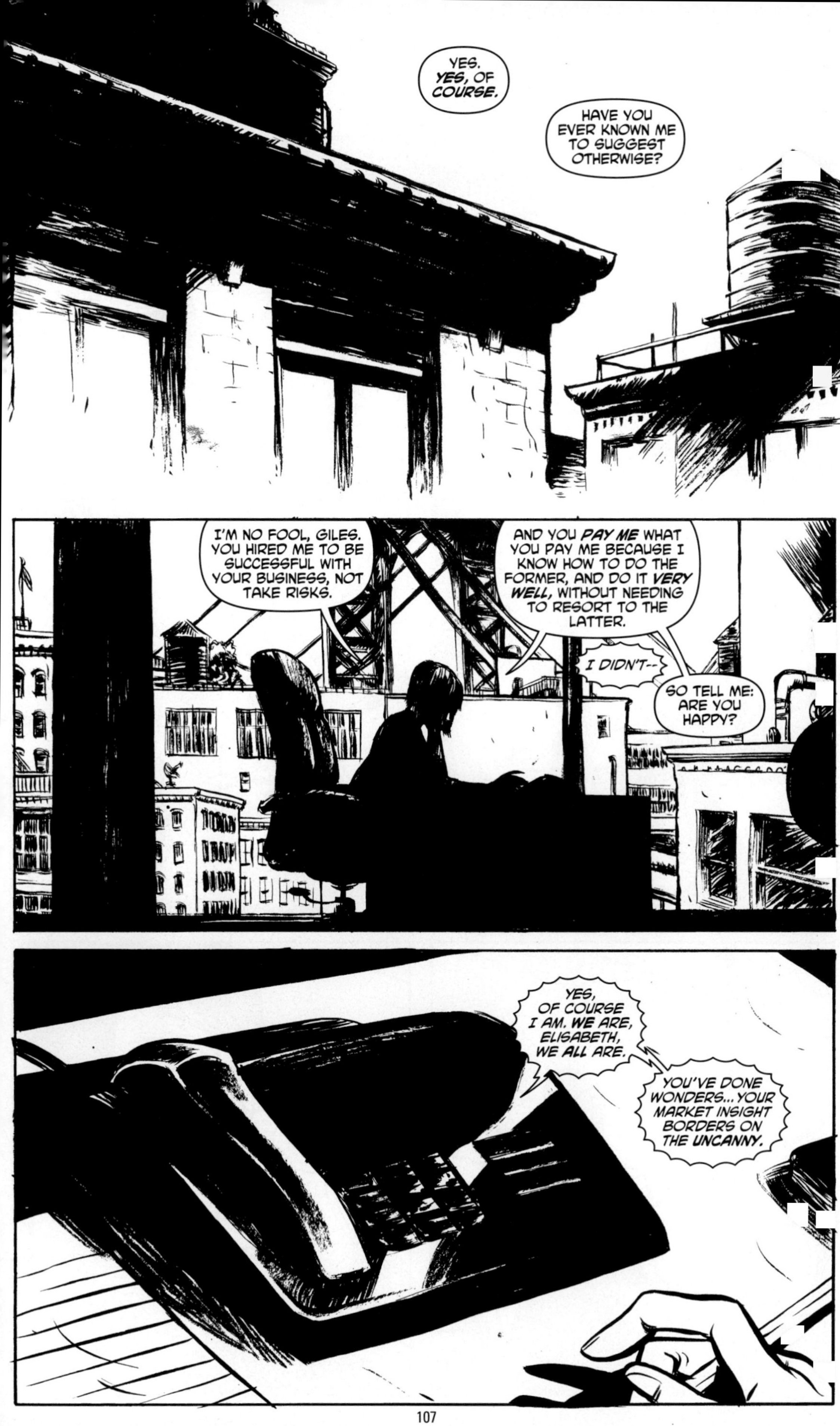
YES. YES, OF COURSE.
HAVE YOU EVER KNOWN ME TO SUGGEST OTHERWISE?
I'M NO FOOL, GILES. YOU HIRED ME TO BE SUCCESSFUL WITH YOUR BUSINESS, NOT TAKE RISKS.
AND YOU PAY ME WHAT YOU PAY ME BECAUSE I KNOW HOW TO DO THE FORMER, AND DO IT VERY WELL, WITHOUT NEEDING TO RESORT TO THE LATTER.
I DIDN'T--
SO TELL ME: ARE YOU HAPPY?
YES, OF COURSE I AM. WE ARE, ELISABETH, WE ALL ARE.
YOU'VE DONE WONDERS...YOUR MARKET INSIGHT BORDERS ON THE UNCANNY.

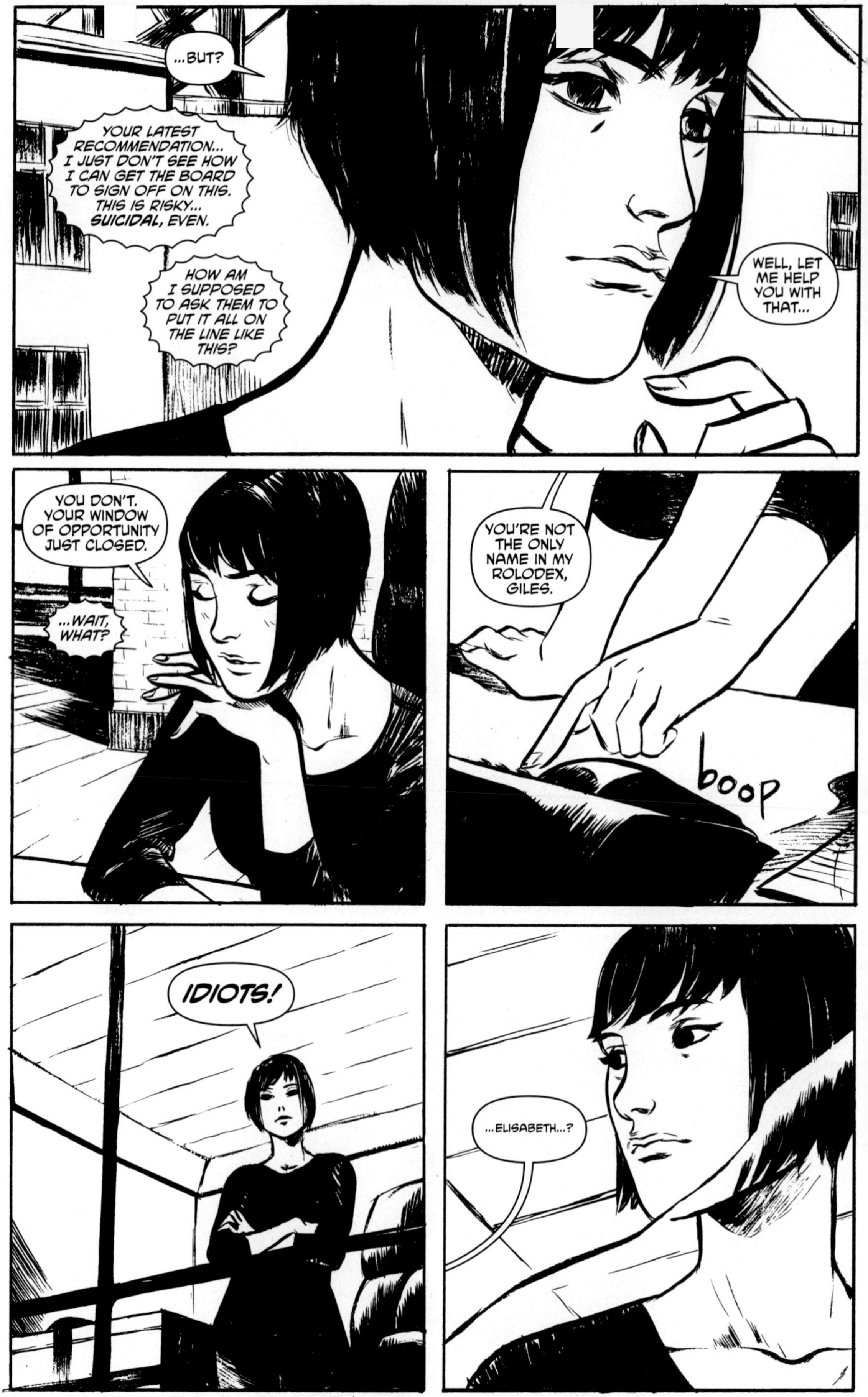

...BUT?
YOUR LATEST RECOMMENDATION... I JUST DON'T SEE HOW I CAN GET THE BOARD TO SIGN OFF ON THIS. THIS IS RISKY... SUICIDAL, EVEN.
HOW AM I SUPPOSED TO ASK THEM TO PUT IT ALL ON THE LINE LIKE THIS?
WELL, LET ME HELP YOU WITH THAT...
YOU DON'T. YOUR WINDOW OF OPPORTUNITY JUST CLOSED.
...WAIT, WHAT?
YOU'RE NOT THE ONLY NAME IN MY ROLODEX, GILES.
boop
IDIOTS!
...ELISABETH...?

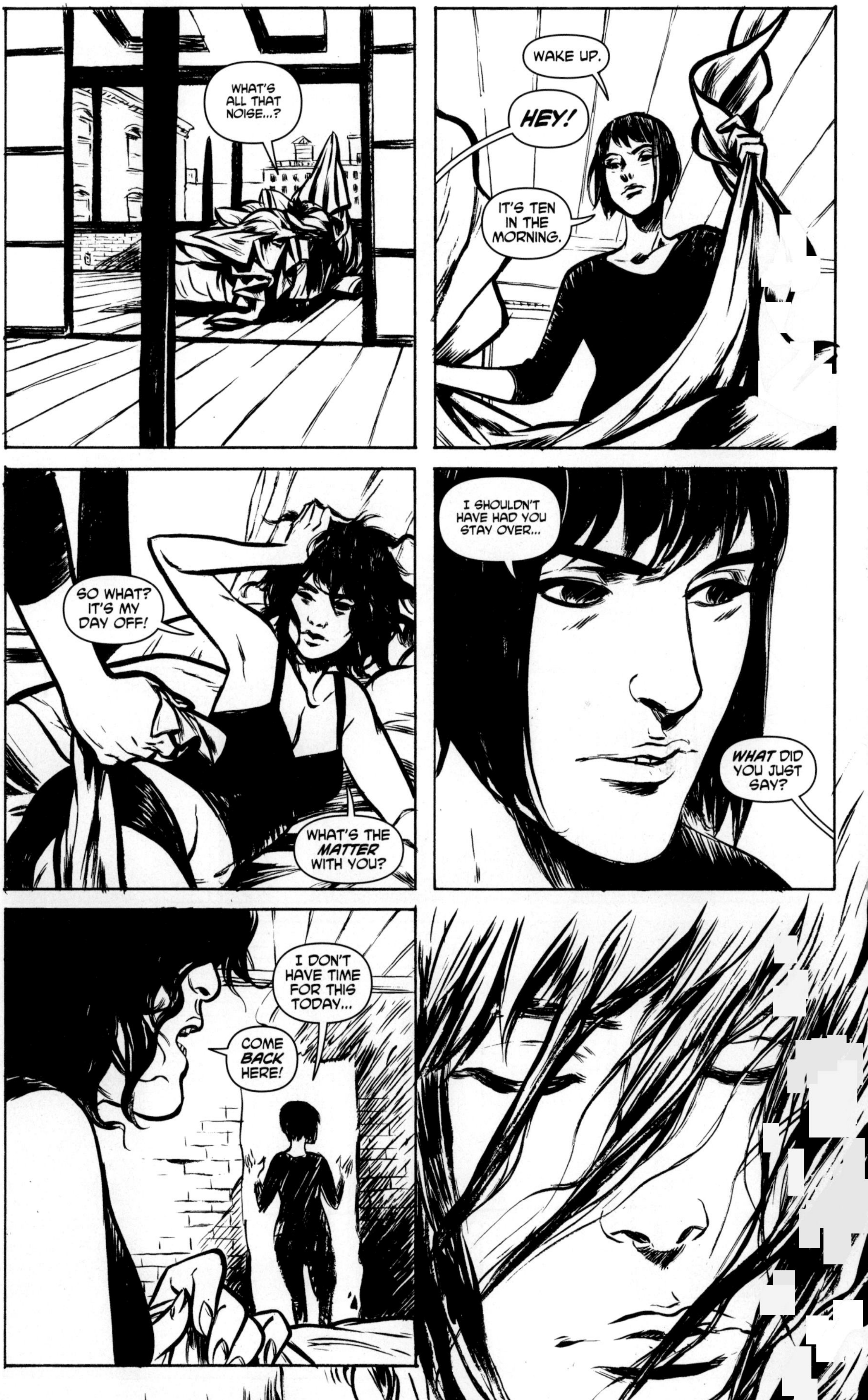
WHAT'S ALL THAT NOISE...?
WAKE UP.
HEY!
IT'S TEN IN THE MORNING.
SO WHAT? IT'S MY DAY OFF!
WHAT'S THE MATTER WITH YOU?
I SHOULDN'T HAVE HAD YOU STAY OVER...
WHAT DID YOU JUST SAY?
I DON'T HAVE TIME FOR THIS TODAY...
COME BACK HERE!

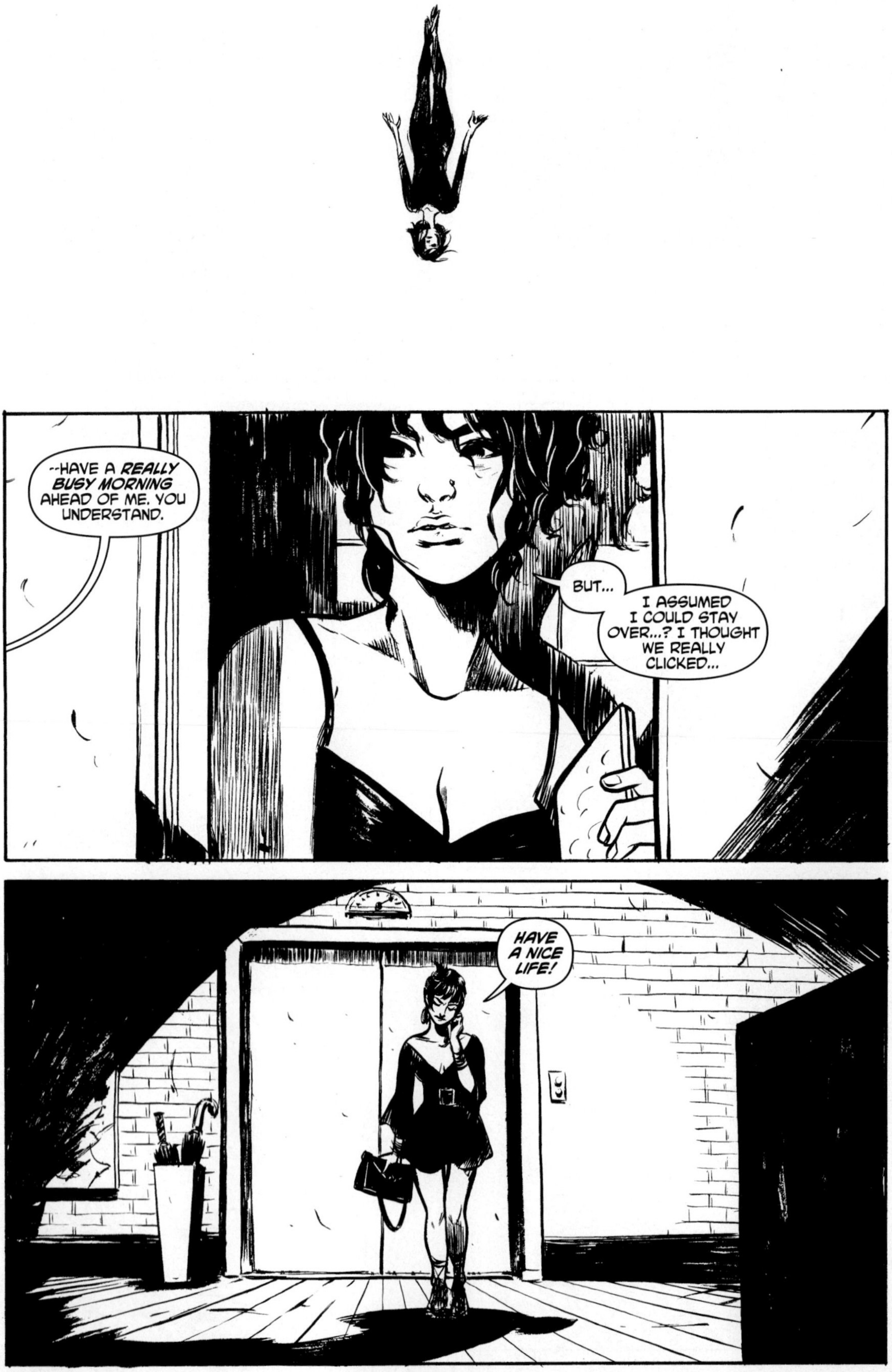
--HAVE A *REALLY BUSY MORNING* AHEAD OF ME. YOU UNDERSTAND.
BUT...
I ASSUMED I COULD STAY OVER...? I THOUGHT WE REALLY CLICKED...
HAVE A NICE LIFE!

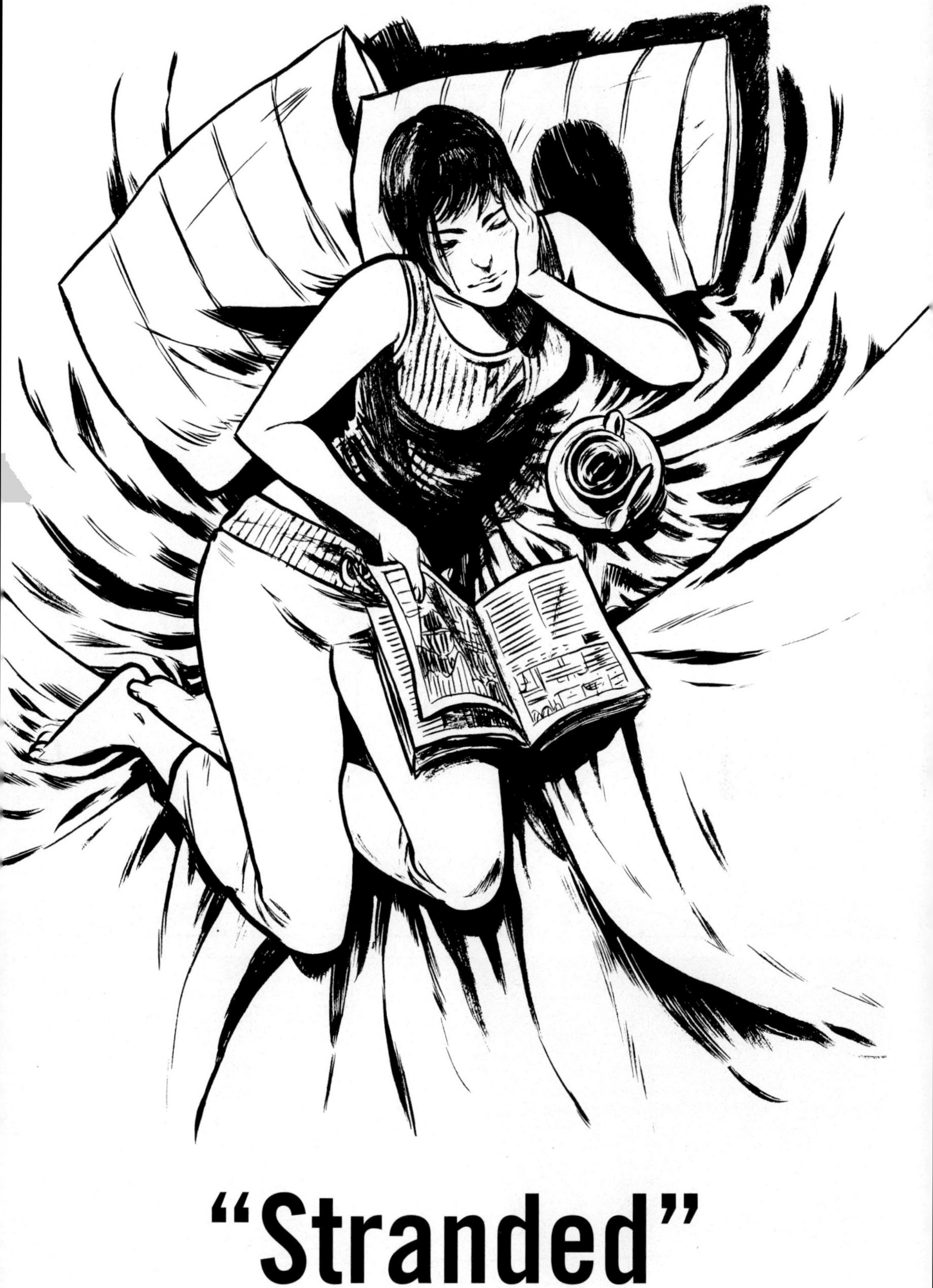

“Stranded”

"HI, MY NAME IS ELISABETH."

"I AM A CLICHÉ."

I ONCE DATED A GIRL WHO WOULD SAY THAT, IN THIS ANNOYING FALSETTO WHEN SHE'D TRY TO MAKE A POINT FOR THE TEN-THOUSANDTH TIME: YES, I AM THE VERY MODEL OF A MODERN YUPPIE BITCH.

SOMETIMES, IN A NORMAL VOICE, SHE'D TACK ON SOME PASSIVE-AGGRESSIVE COMMENT ABOUT HOW I'M ONLY A LESBIAN TO BUCK THE CLICHÉ.

THEN I SAY, IN A BORED MONOTONE, IF SHE THINKS SO, SHE NEEDS TO GET OUT MORE.

I KNOW I'M TOUGH. I CAN'T HELP MYSELF. AND THAT RELATIONSHIP BARELY LASTED TWO MONTHS. A RECORD FOR ME.

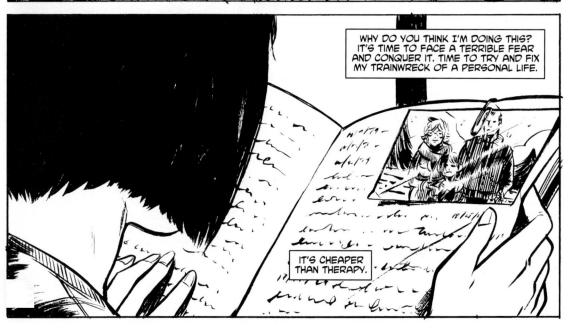

WHY DO YOU THINK I'M DOING THIS? IT'S TIME TO FACE A TERRIBLE FEAR AND CONQUER IT. TIME TO TRY AND FIX MY TRAINWRECK OF A PERSONAL LIFE.

IT'S CHEAPER THAN THERAPY.

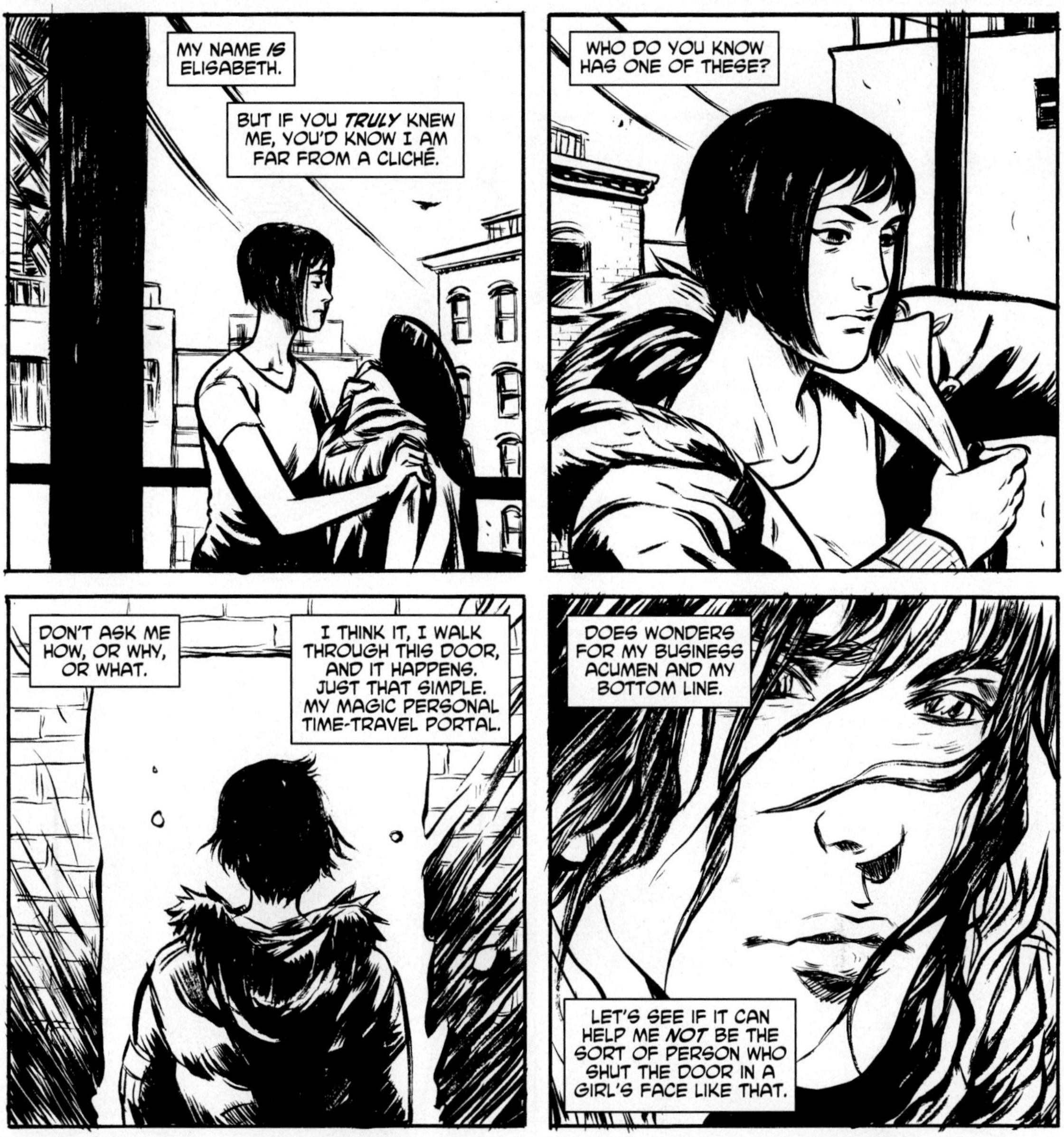
MY NAME *IS* ELISABETH.
BUT IF YOU *TRULY* KNEW ME, YOU'D KNOW I AM FAR FROM A CLICHÉ.
WHO DO YOU KNOW HAS ONE OF THESE?
DON'T ASK ME HOW, OR WHY, OR WHAT.
I THINK IT, I WALK THROUGH THIS DOOR, AND IT HAPPENS. JUST THAT SIMPLE. MY MAGIC PERSONAL TIME-TRAVEL PORTAL.
DOES WONDERS FOR MY BUSINESS ACUMEN AND MY BOTTOM LINE.
LET'S SEE IF IT CAN HELP ME *NOT* BE THE SORT OF PERSON WHO SHUT THE DOOR IN A GIRL'S FACE LIKE THAT.

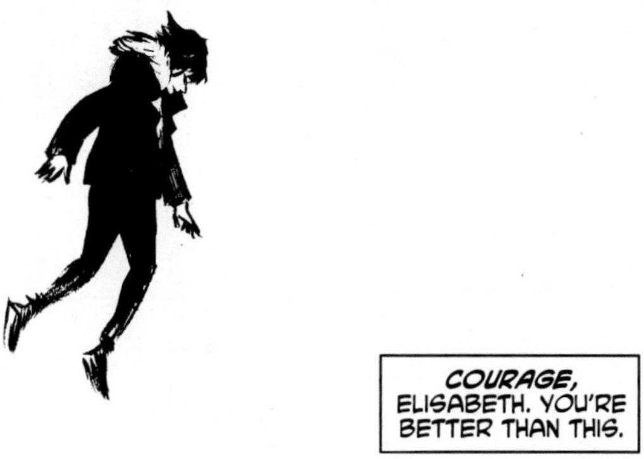
COURAGE, ELISABETH. YOU'RE BETTER THAN THIS.

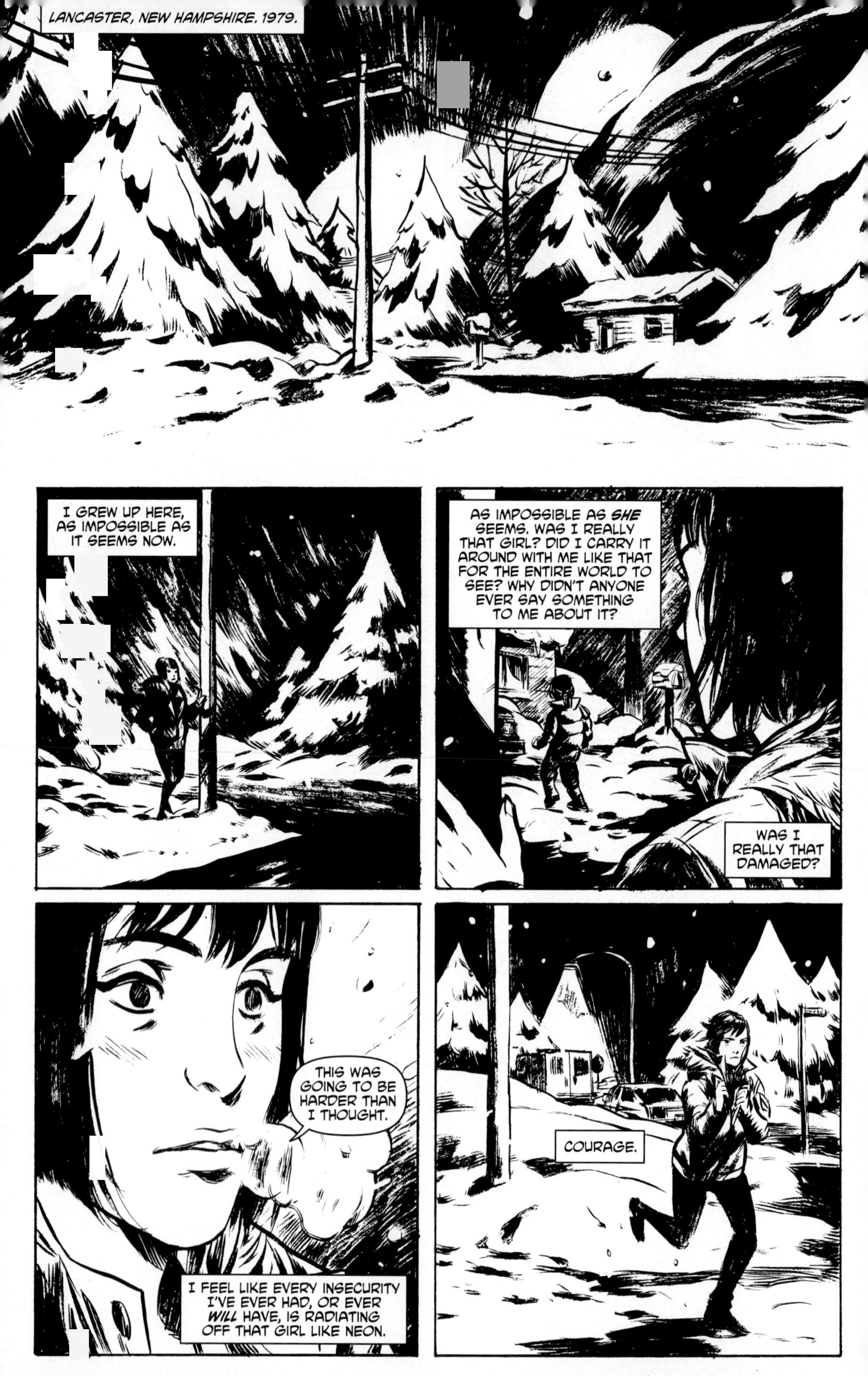
LANCASTER, NEW HAMPSHIRE. 1979.
I GREW UP HERE, AS IMPOSSIBLE AS IT SEEMS NOW.
AS IMPOSSIBLE AS SHE SEEMS. WAS I REALLY THAT GIRL? DID I CARRY IT AROUND WITH ME LIKE THAT FOR THE ENTIRE WORLD TO SEE? WHY DIDN'T ANYONE EVER SAY SOMETHING TO ME ABOUT IT?
WAS I REALLY THAT DAMAGED?
THIS WAS GOING TO BE HARDER THAN I THOUGHT.
I FEEL LIKE EVERY INSECURITY I'VE EVER HAD, OR EVER WILL HAVE, IS RADIATING OFF THAT GIRL LIKE NEON.
COURAGE.

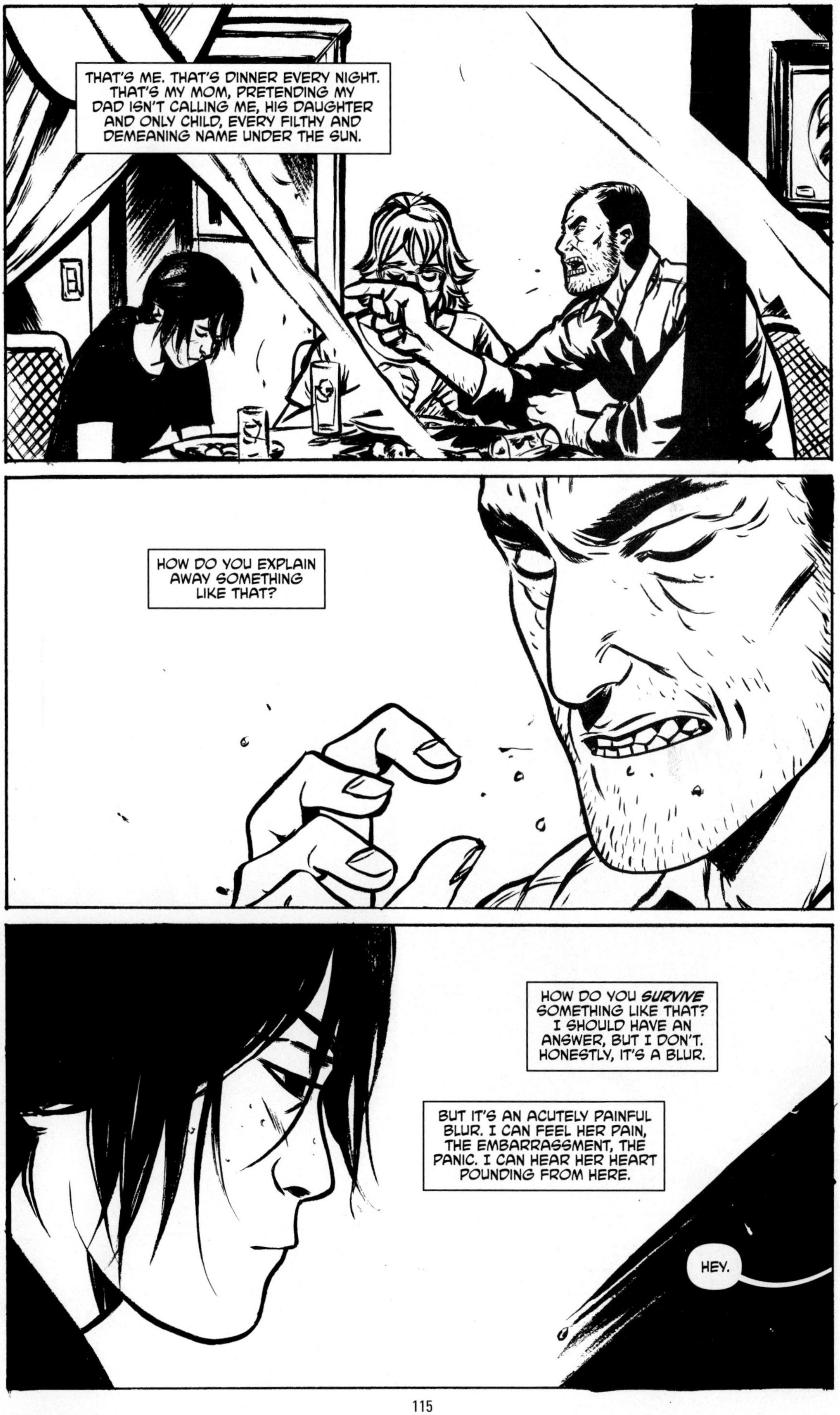
THAT'S ME. THAT'S DINNER EVERY NIGHT. THAT'S MY MOM, PRETENDING MY DAD ISN'T CALLING ME, HIS DAUGHTER AND ONLY CHILD, EVERY FILTHY AND DEMEANING NAME UNDER THE SUN.
HOW DO YOU EXPLAIN AWAY SOMETHING LIKE THAT?
HOW DO YOU *SURVIVE* SOMETHING LIKE THAT? I SHOULD HAVE AN ANSWER, BUT I DON'T. HONESTLY, IT'S A BLUR.
BUT IT'S AN ACUTELY PAINFUL BLUR. I CAN FEEL HER PAIN, THE EMBARRASSMENT, THE PANIC. I CAN HEAR HER HEART POUNDING FROM HERE.
HEY.

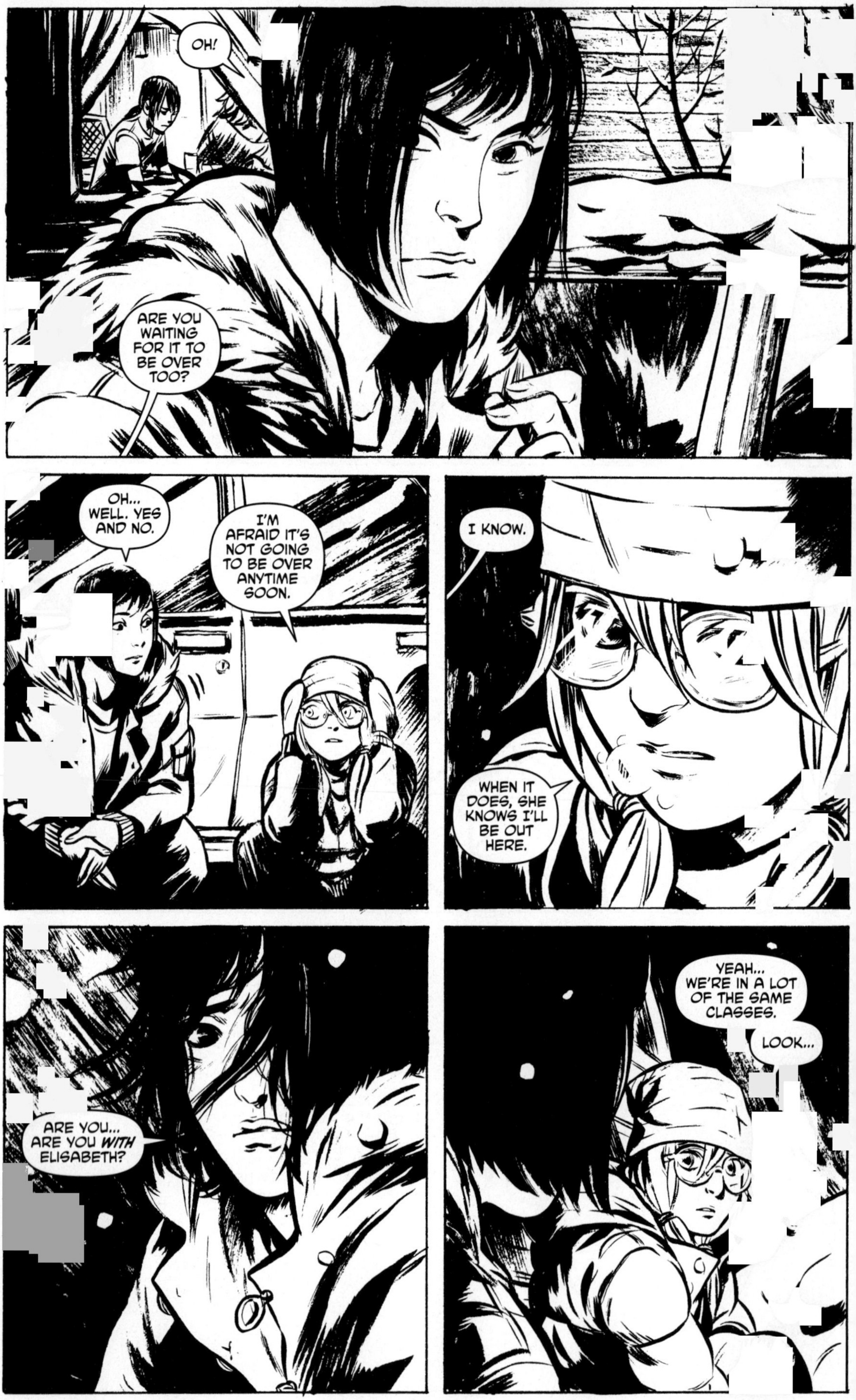

OH!
ARE YOU WAITING FOR IT TO BE OVER TOO?
OH... WELL. YES AND NO.
I'M AFRAID IT'S NOT GOING TO BE OVER ANYTIME SOON.
I KNOW.
WHEN IT DOES, SHE KNOWS I'LL BE OUT HERE.
ARE YOU... ARE YOU WITH ELISABETH?
YEAH... WE'RE IN A LOT OF THE SAME CLASSES.
LOOK...

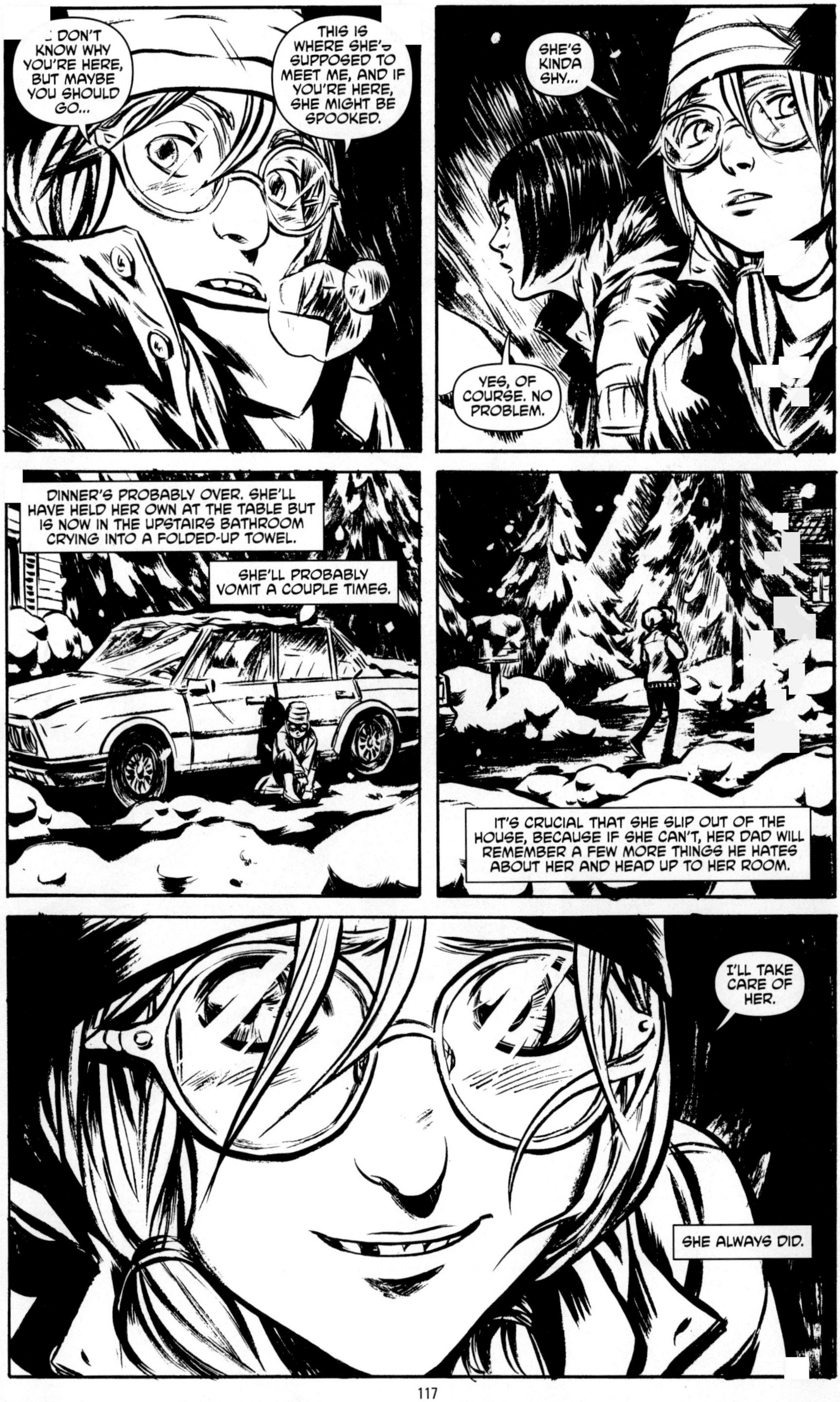

DON'T KNOW WHY YOU'RE HERE, BUT MAYBE YOU SHOULD GO...
THIS IS WHERE SHE'S SUPPOSED TO MEET ME, AND IF YOU'RE HERE, SHE MIGHT BE SPOOKED.
SHE'S KINDA SHY...
YES, OF COURSE. NO PROBLEM.
DINNER'S PROBABLY OVER. SHE'LL HAVE HELD HER OWN AT THE TABLE BUT IS NOW IN THE UPSTAIRS BATHROOM CRYING INTO A FOLDED-UP TOWEL.
SHE'LL PROBABLY VOMIT A COUPLE TIMES.
IT'S CRUCIAL THAT SHE SLIP OUT OF THE HOUSE, BECAUSE IF SHE CAN'T, HER DAD WILL REMEMBER A FEW MORE THINGS HE HATES ABOUT HER AND HEAD UP TO HER ROOM.
I'LL TAKE CARE OF HER.
SHE ALWAYS DID.

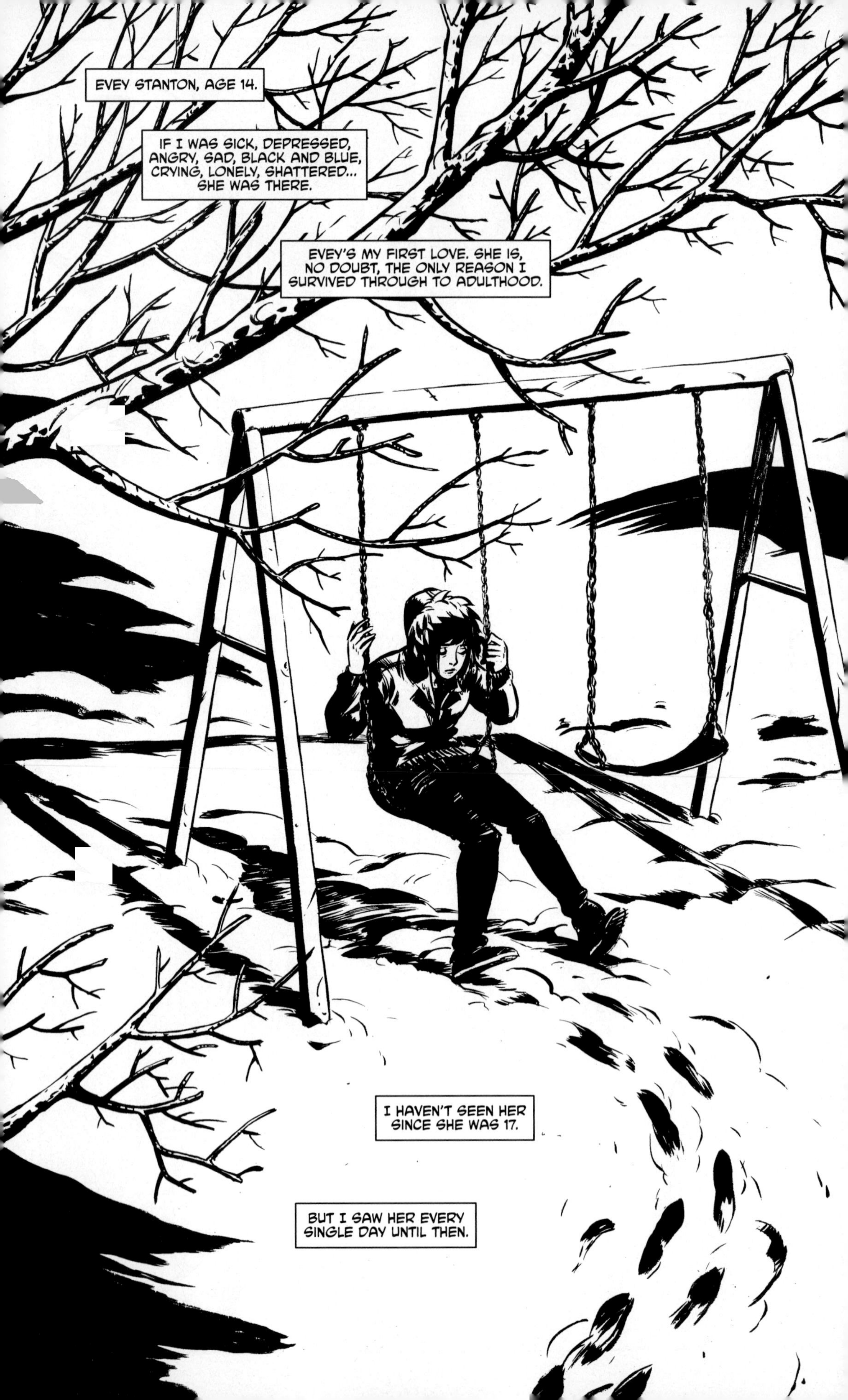
EVEY STANTON, AGE 14.
IF I WAS SICK, DEPRESSED, ANGRY, SAD, BLACK AND BLUE, CRYING, LONELY, SHATTERED... SHE WAS THERE.
EVEY'S MY FIRST LOVE. SHE IS, NO DOUBT, THE ONLY REASON I SURVIVED THROUGH TO ADULTHOOD.
I HAVEN'T SEEN HER SINCE SHE WAS 17.
BUT I SAW HER EVERY SINGLE DAY UNTIL THEN.

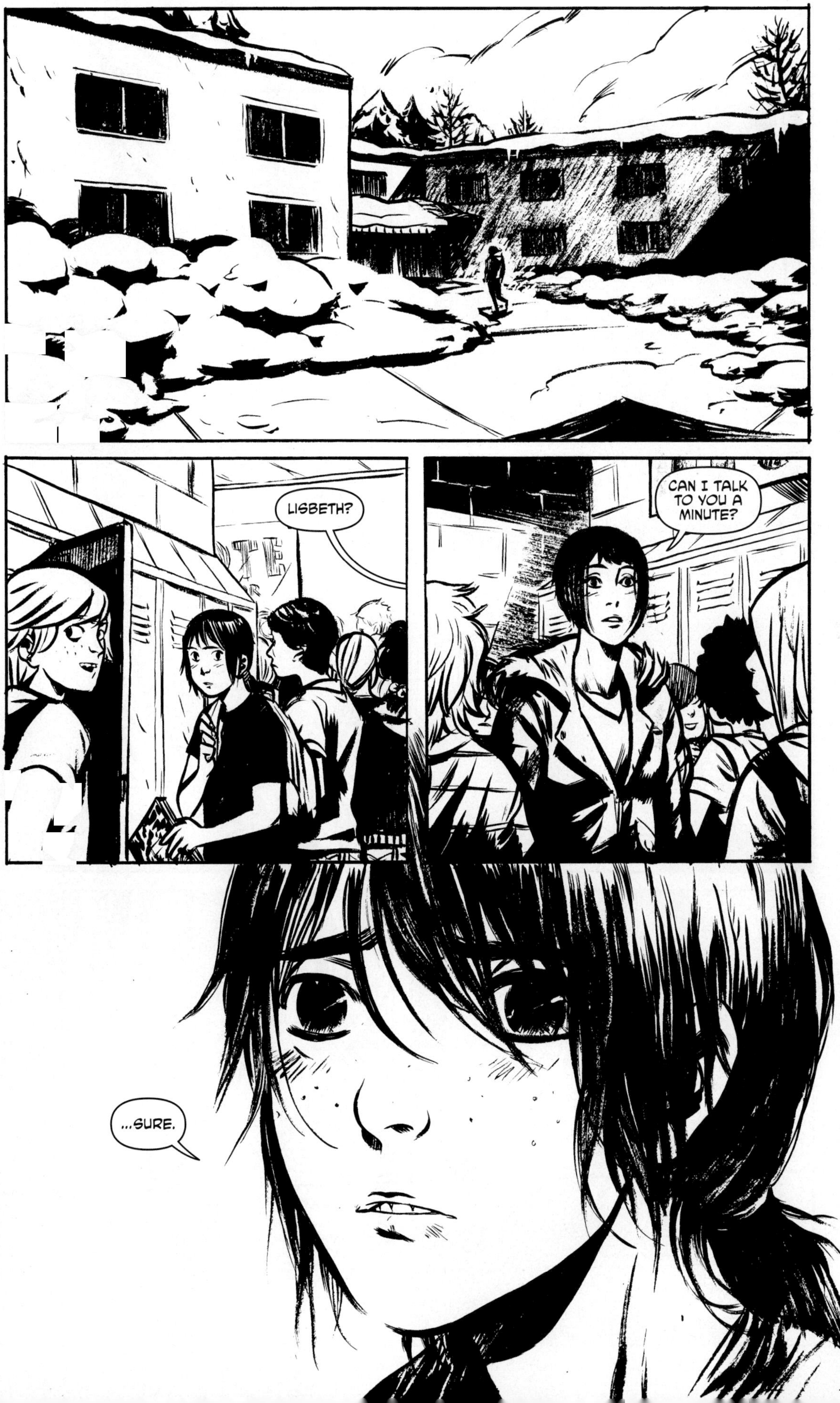
LISBETH?
CAN I TALK TO YOU A MINUTE?
...SURE.

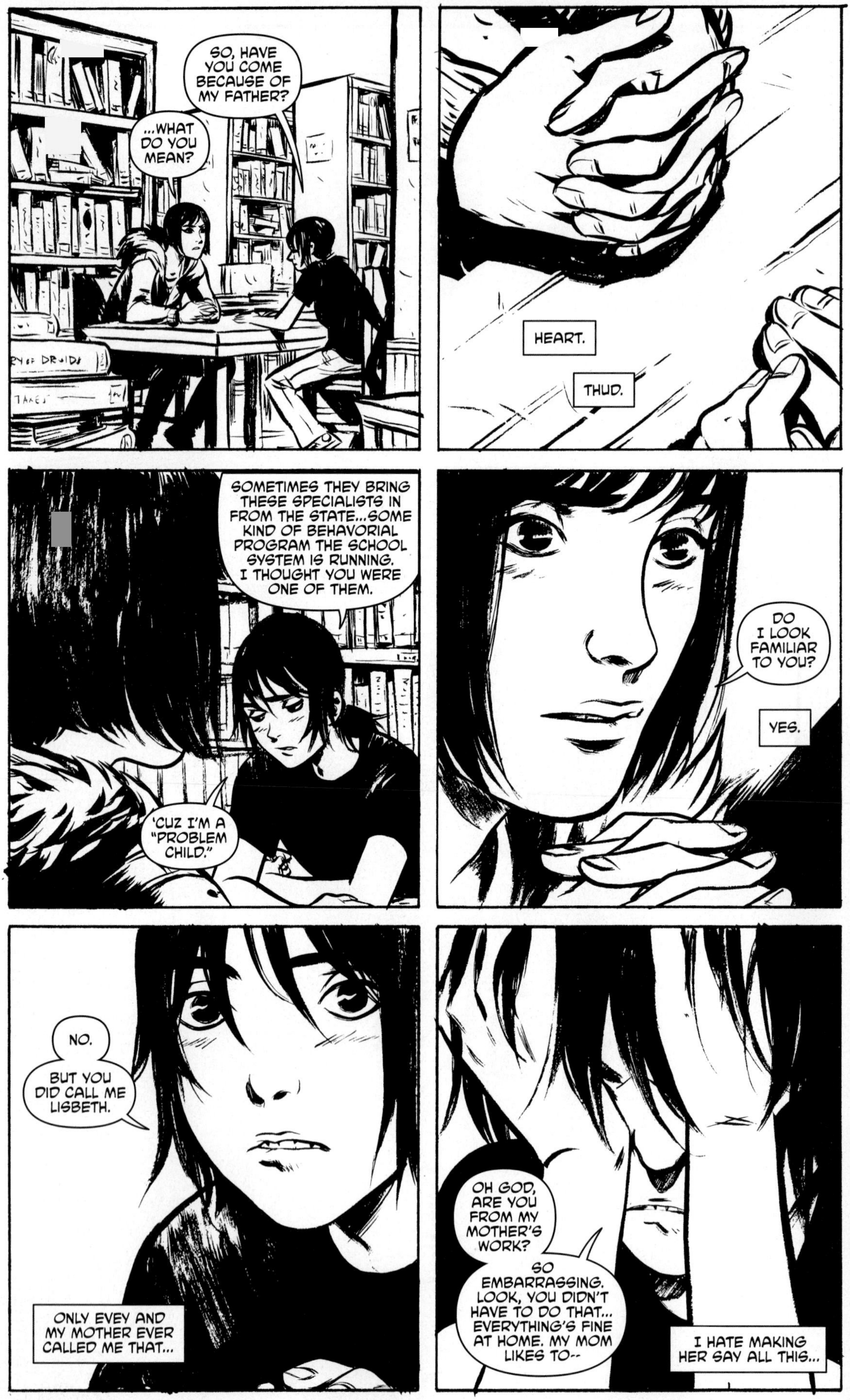
SO, HAVE YOU COME BECAUSE OF MY FATHER?
...WHAT DO YOU MEAN?
HEART.
THUD.
SOMETIMES THEY BRING THESE SPECIALISTS IN FROM THE STATE...SOME KIND OF BEHAVORIAL PROGRAM THE SCHOOL SYSTEM IS RUNNING. I THOUGHT YOU WERE ONE OF THEM.
'CUZ I'M A "PROBLEM CHILD."
DO I LOOK FAMILIAR TO YOU?
YES.
NO.
BUT YOU DID CALL ME LISBETH.
ONLY EVEY AND MY MOTHER EVER CALLED ME THAT...
OH GOD, ARE YOU FROM MY MOTHER'S WORK?
SO EMBARRASSING. LOOK, YOU DIDN'T HAVE TO DO THAT... EVERYTHING'S FINE AT HOME. MY MOM LIKES TO--
I HATE MAKING HER SAY ALL THIS...

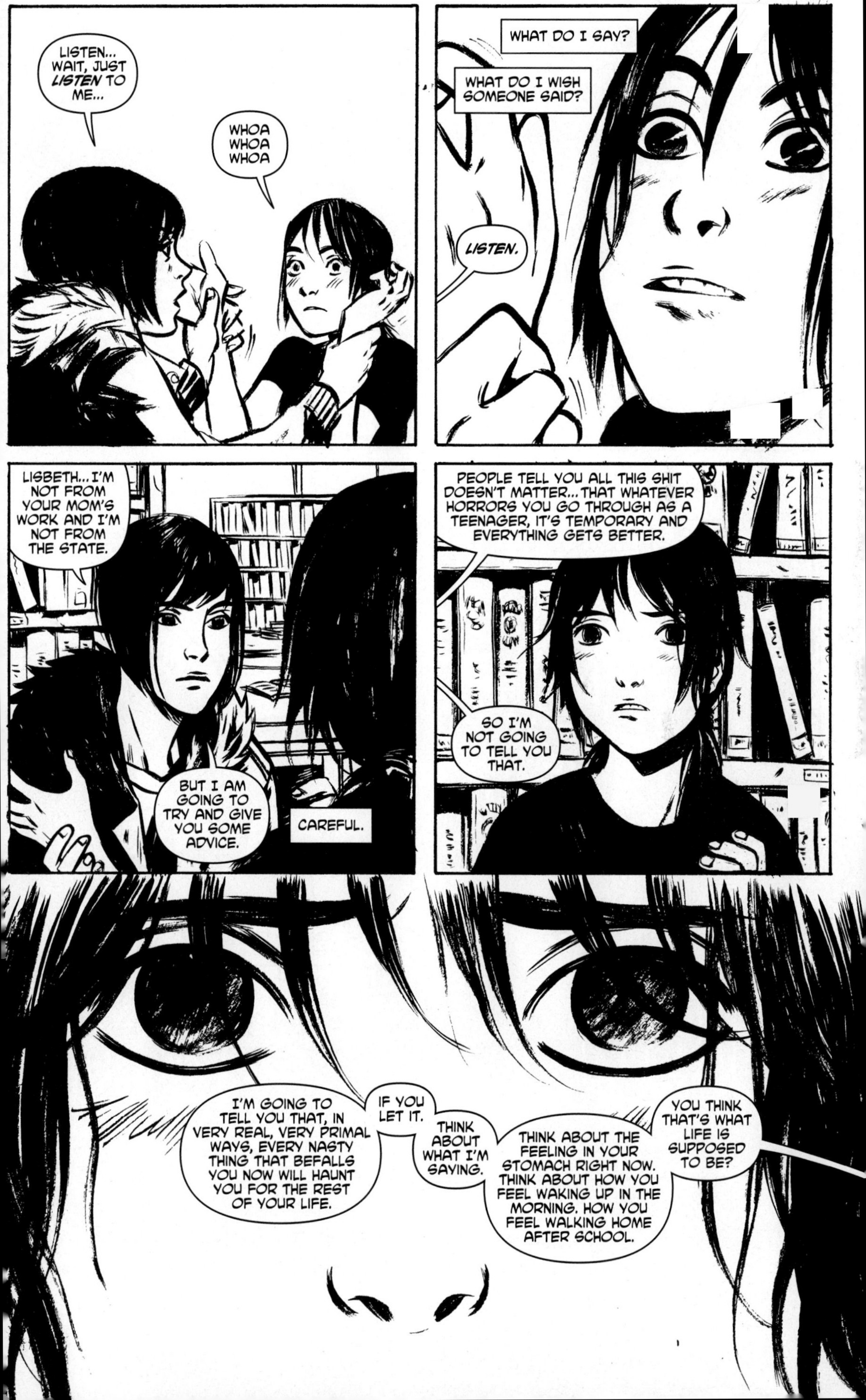
LISTEN... WAIT, JUST *LISTEN* TO ME...
WHOA WHOA WHOA
WHAT DO I SAY?
WHAT DO I WISH SOMEONE SAID?
LISTEN.
LISBETH... I'M NOT FROM YOUR MOM'S WORK AND I'M NOT FROM THE STATE.
BUT I AM GOING TO TRY AND GIVE YOU SOME ADVICE.
CAREFUL.
PEOPLE TELL YOU ALL THIS SHIT DOESN'T MATTER... THAT WHATEVER HORRORS YOU GO THROUGH AS A TEENAGER, IT'S TEMPORARY AND EVERYTHING GETS BETTER.
SO I'M NOT GOING TO TELL YOU THAT.
I'M GOING TO TELL YOU THAT, IN VERY REAL, VERY PRIMAL WAYS, EVERY NASTY THING THAT BEFALLS YOU NOW WILL HAUNT YOU FOR THE REST OF YOUR LIFE.
IF YOU LET IT.
THINK ABOUT WHAT I'M SAYING.
THINK ABOUT THE FEELING IN YOUR STOMACH RIGHT NOW. THINK ABOUT HOW YOU FEEL WAKING UP IN THE MORNING. HOW YOU FEEL WALKING HOME AFTER SCHOOL.
YOU THINK THAT'S WHAT LIFE IS SUPPOSED TO BE?

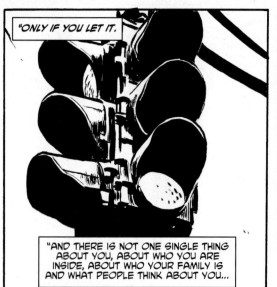

"ONLY IF YOU LET IT.

"AND THERE IS NOT ONE SINGLE THING ABOUT YOU, ABOUT WHO YOU ARE INSIDE, ABOUT WHO YOUR FAMILY IS AND WHAT PEOPLE THINK ABOUT YOU...

"...THAT MEANS YOU HAVE TO TAKE A SHRED OF SHIT FROM ANYONE. OR LET ANYONE OR ANYTHING DEFINE YOUR LIFE FOR YOU.

"YOU GIVE AN INCH ON THAT, AND YOU'LL BE PAYING FOR IT FOR YEARS TO COME.

"EVEY? HOLD ON TO HER. WITH EVERY MOLECULE YOU'VE GOT, HOLD ON TO HER. SHE IS BY FAR THE ONLY THING IN THIS TOWN WORTH THAT KIND OF EFFORT.

"AND ONCE YOU TWO LEAVE HERE, IT'LL MAKE MUCH MORE SENSE.

"PROMISE ME, LISBETH.

"DON'T WRITE ME OFF AS ANOTHER ONE OF THESE CLUELESS ADULTS.

"I'M THE ONLY ONE WHO'S EVER GOING TO BE THIS HONEST WITH YOU."

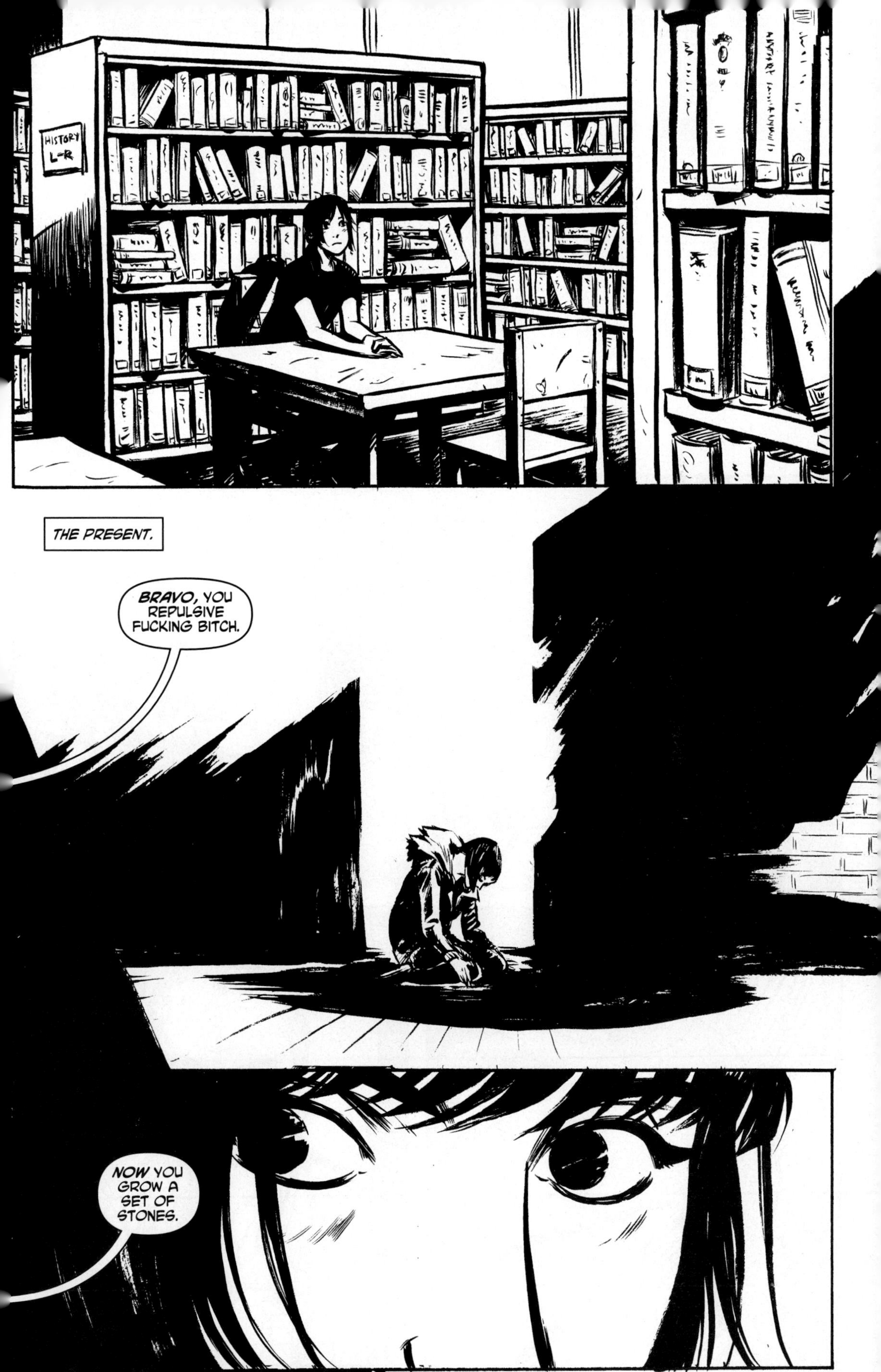
HISTORY L-R
THE PRESENT.
BRAVO, YOU REPULSIVE FUCKING BITCH.
NOW YOU GROW A SET OF STONES.

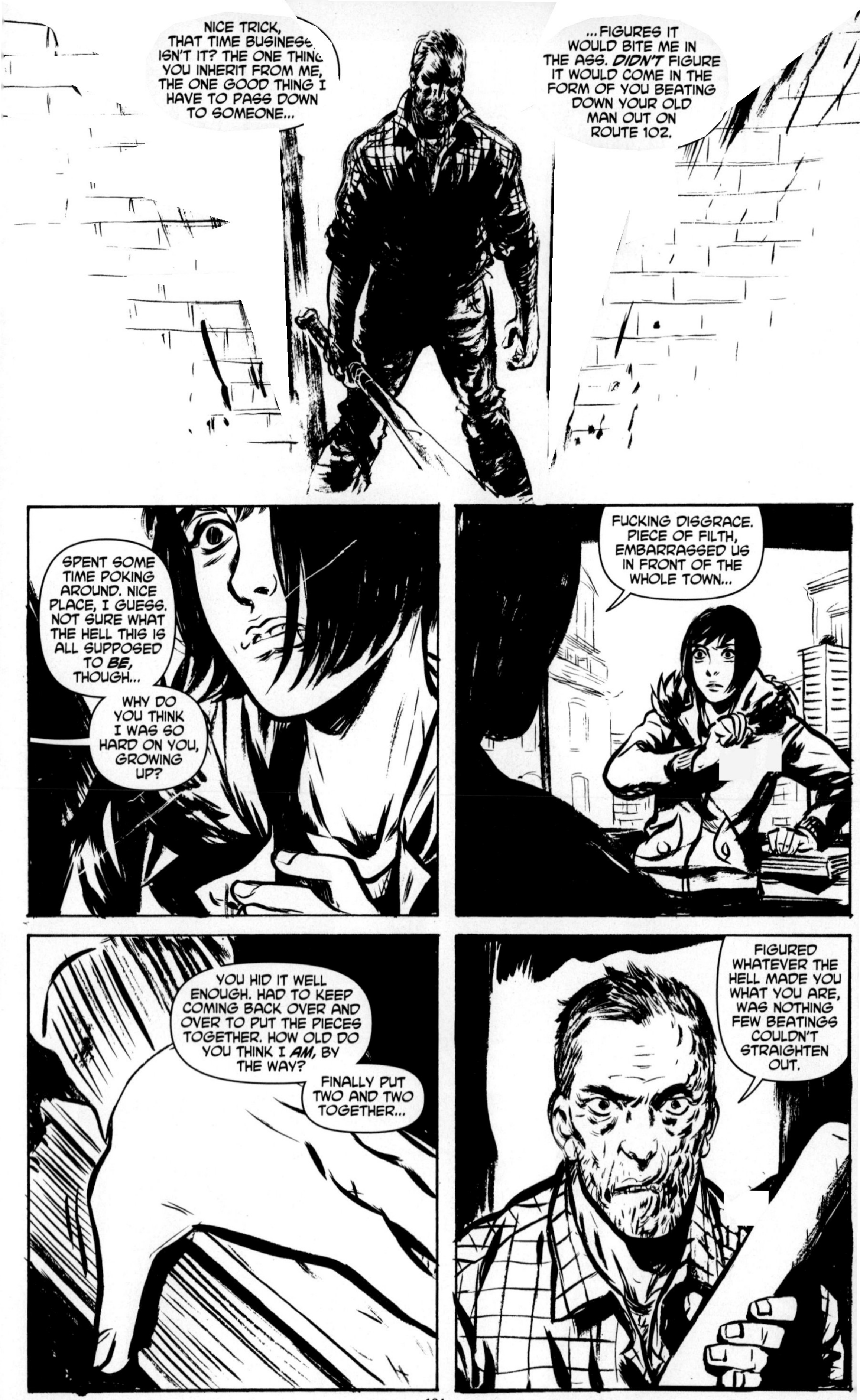
NICE TRICK, THAT TIME BUSINESS, ISN'T IT? THE ONE THING YOU INHERIT FROM ME, THE ONE GOOD THING I HAVE TO PASS DOWN TO SOMEONE...
...FIGURES IT WOULD BITE ME IN THE ASS. DIDN'T FIGURE IT WOULD COME IN THE FORM OF YOU BEATING DOWN YOUR OLD MAN OUT ON ROUTE 102.
SPENT SOME TIME POKING AROUND. NICE PLACE, I GUESS. NOT SURE WHAT THE HELL THIS IS ALL SUPPOSED TO BE, THOUGH...
WHY DO YOU THINK I WAS SO HARD ON YOU, GROWING UP?
FUCKING DISGRACE. PIECE OF FILTH, EMBARRASSED US IN FRONT OF THE WHOLE TOWN...
YOU HID IT WELL ENOUGH. HAD TO KEEP COMING BACK OVER AND OVER TO PUT THE PIECES TOGETHER. HOW OLD DO YOU THINK I AM, BY THE WAY?
FINALLY PUT TWO AND TWO TOGETHER...
FIGURED WHATEVER THE HELL MADE YOU WHAT YOU ARE, WAS NOTHING FEW BEATINGS COULDN'T STRAIGHTEN OUT.

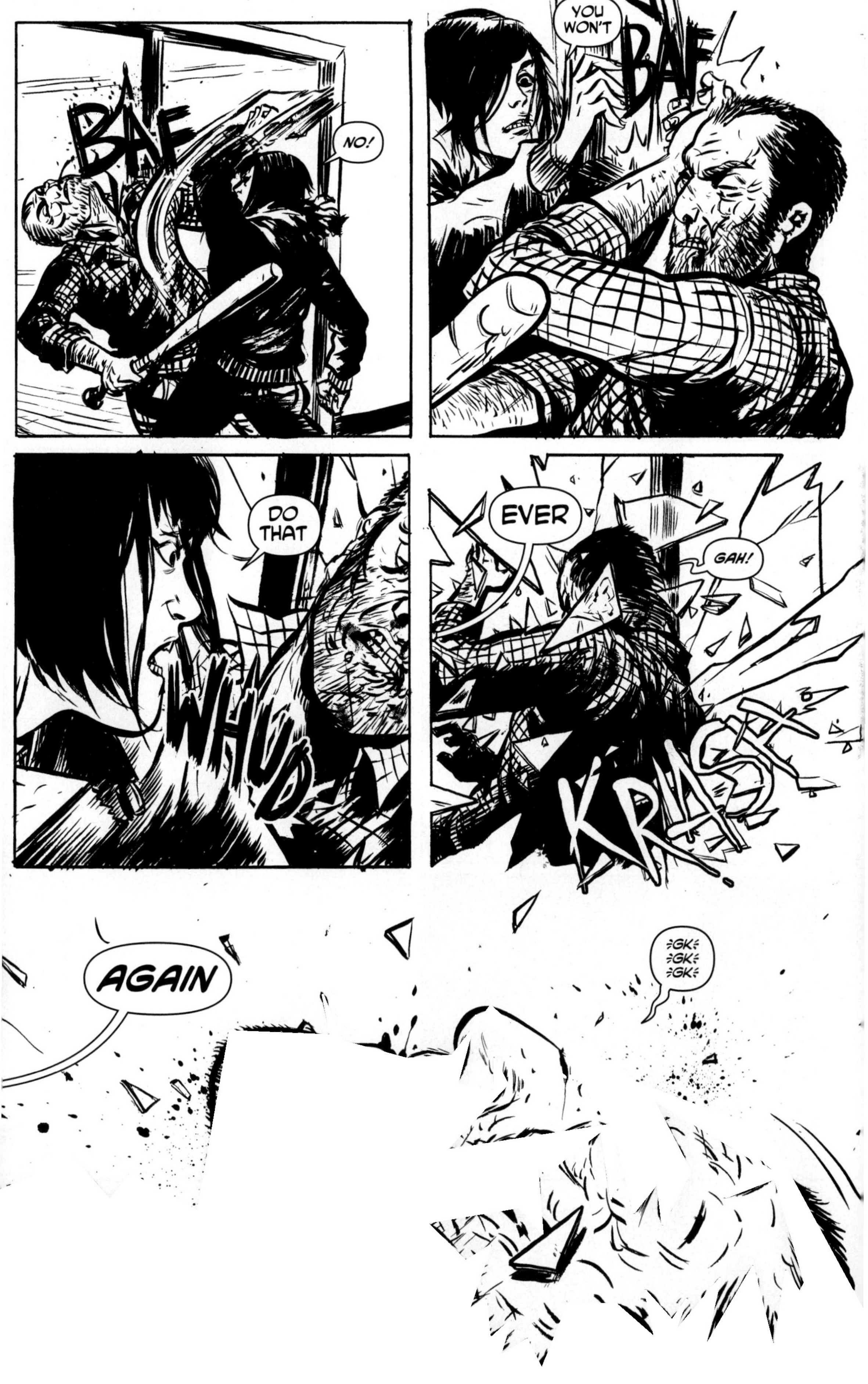
BAF
NO!
YOU WON'T
BAF
DO THAT
WHUD
EVER
GAH!
KRASSH
AGAIN
GK GK GK

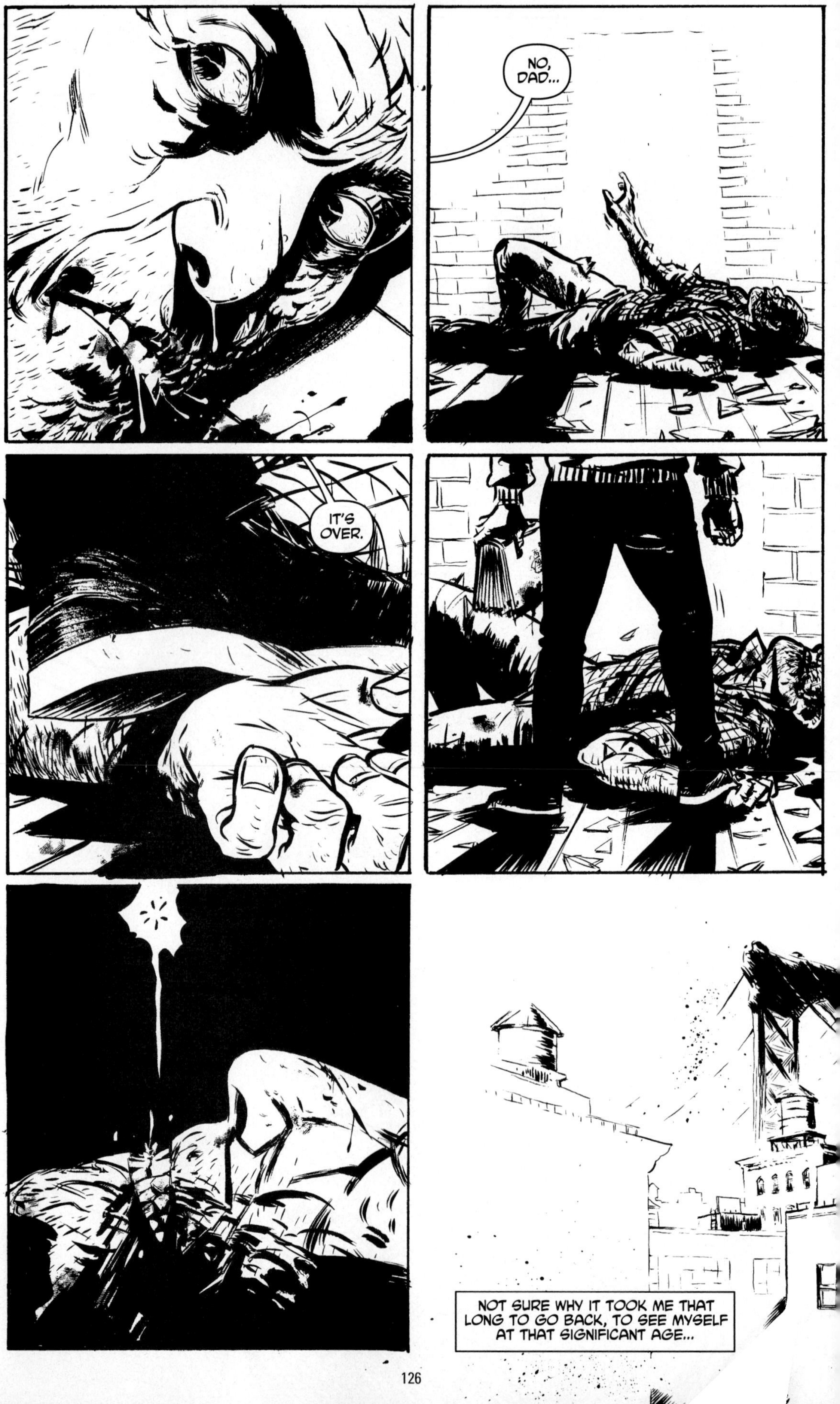
NO, DAD...
IT'S OVER.
NOT SURE WHY IT TOOK ME THAT LONG TO GO BACK, TO SEE MYSELF AT THAT SIGNIFICANT AGE...

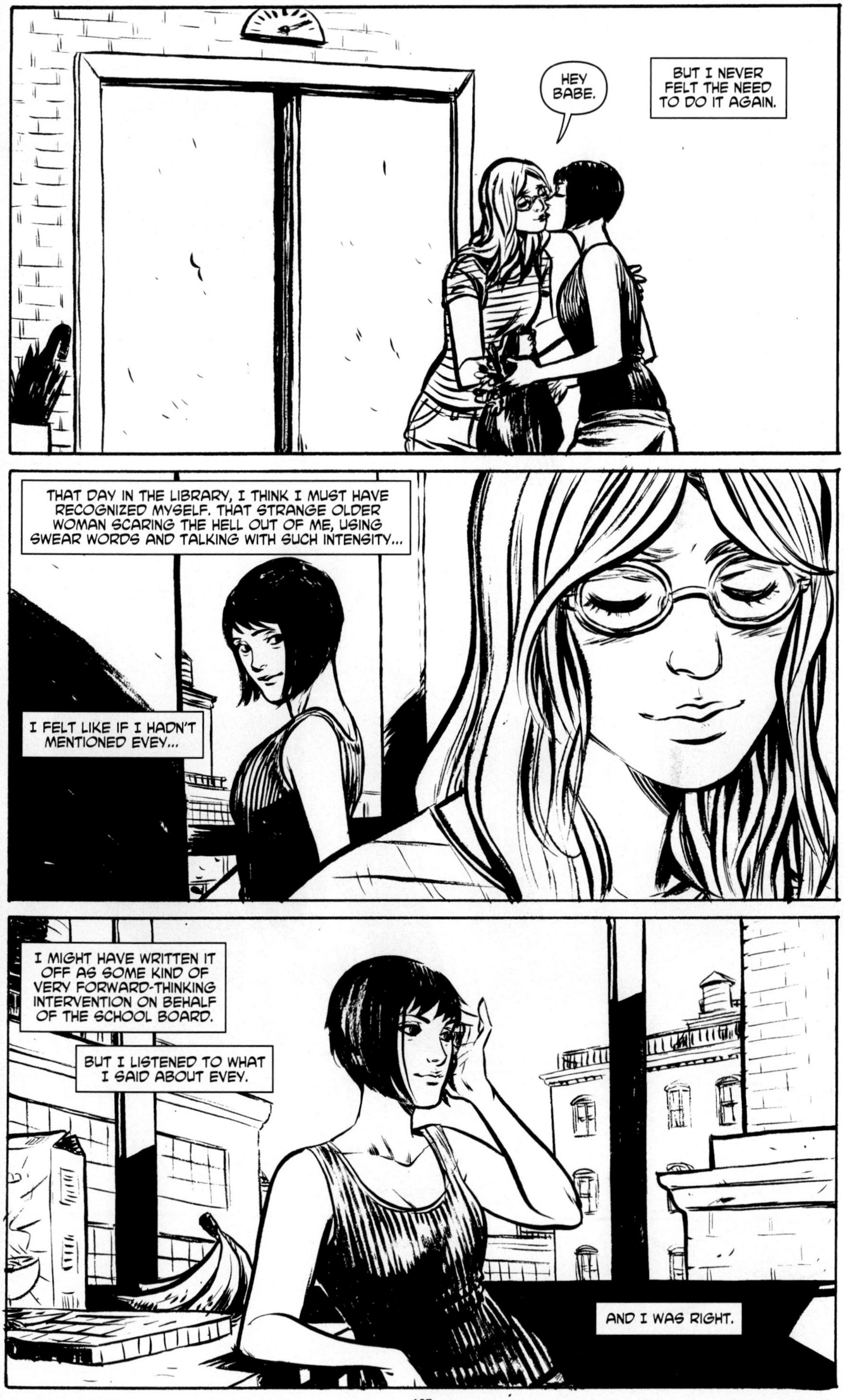
HEY BABE.
BUT I NEVER FELT THE NEED TO DO IT AGAIN.
THAT DAY IN THE LIBRARY, I THINK I MUST HAVE RECOGNIZED MYSELF. THAT STRANGE OLDER WOMAN SCARING THE HELL OUT OF ME, USING SWEAR WORDS AND TALKING WITH SUCH INTENSITY...
I FELT LIKE IF I HADN'T MENTIONED EVEY...
I MIGHT HAVE WRITTEN IT OFF AS SOME KIND OF VERY FORWARD-THINKING INTERVENTION ON BEHALF OF THE SCHOOL BOARD.
BUT I LISTENED TO WHAT I SAID ABOUT EVEY.
AND I WAS RIGHT.

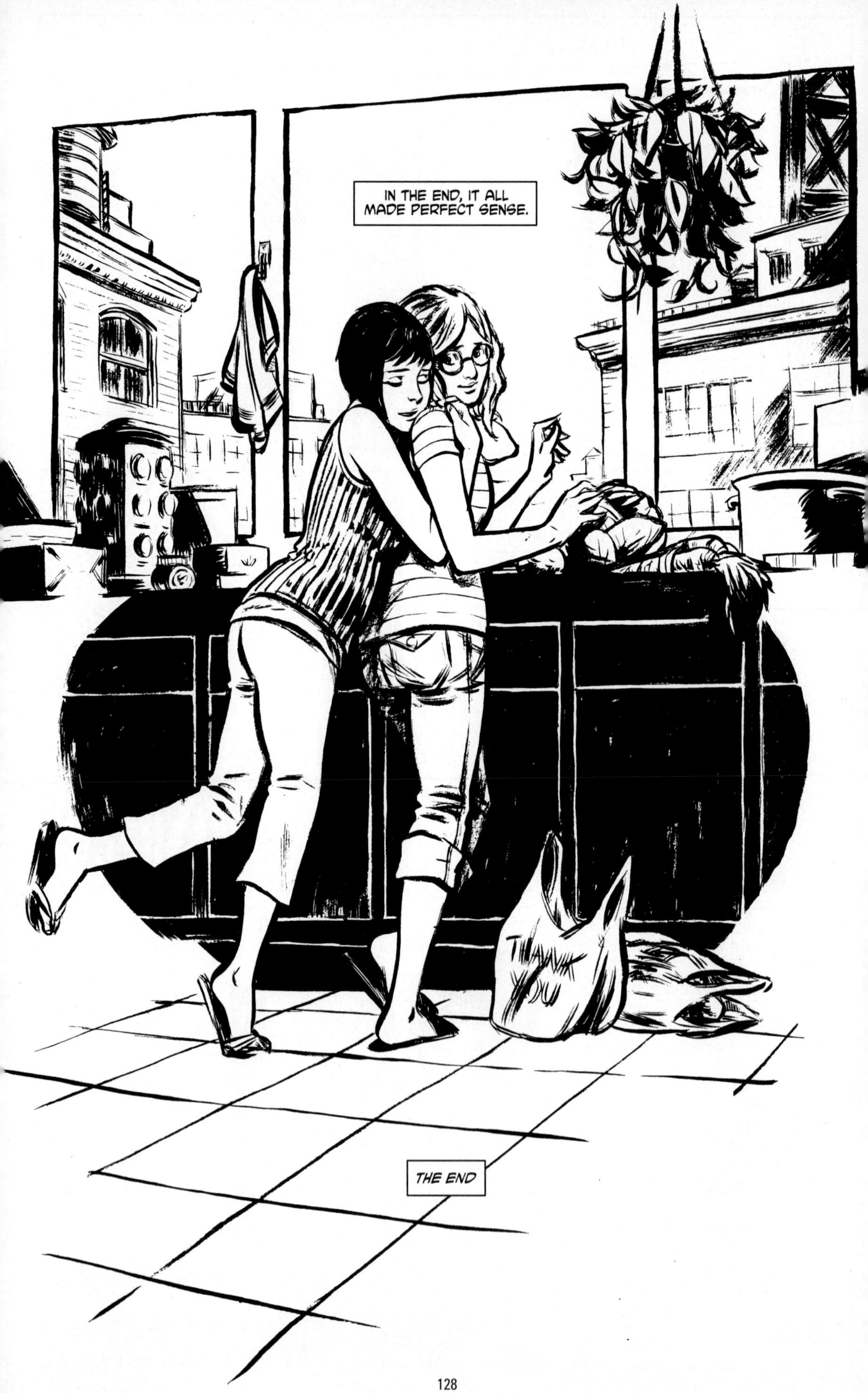
IN THE END, IT ALL MADE PERFECT SENSE.
THANK YOU
THE END

6

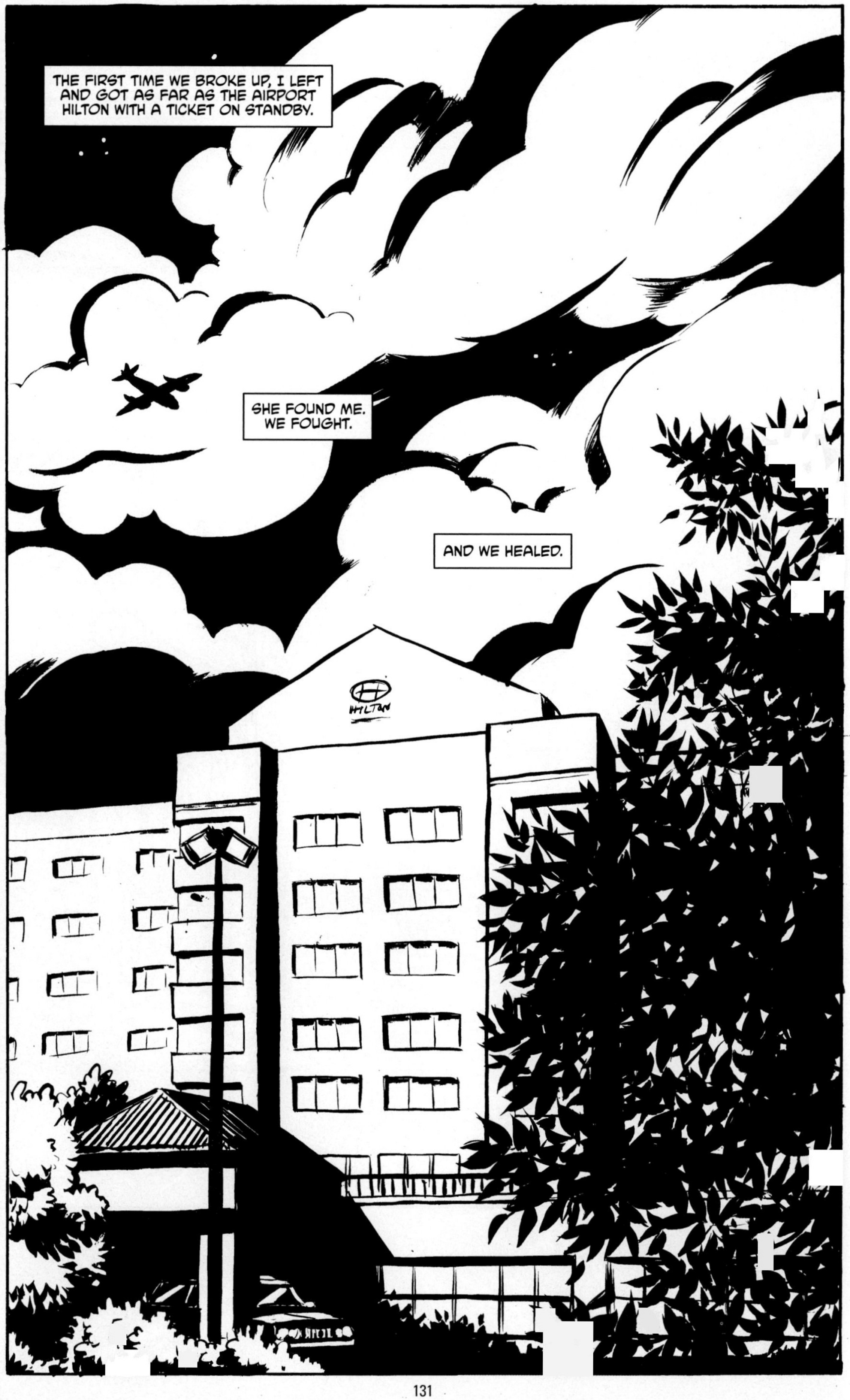
THE FIRST TIME WE BROKE UP, I LEFT AND GOT AS FAR AS THE AIRPORT HILTON WITH A TICKET ON STANDBY.
SHE FOUND ME. WE FOUGHT.
AND WE HEALED.
HILTON

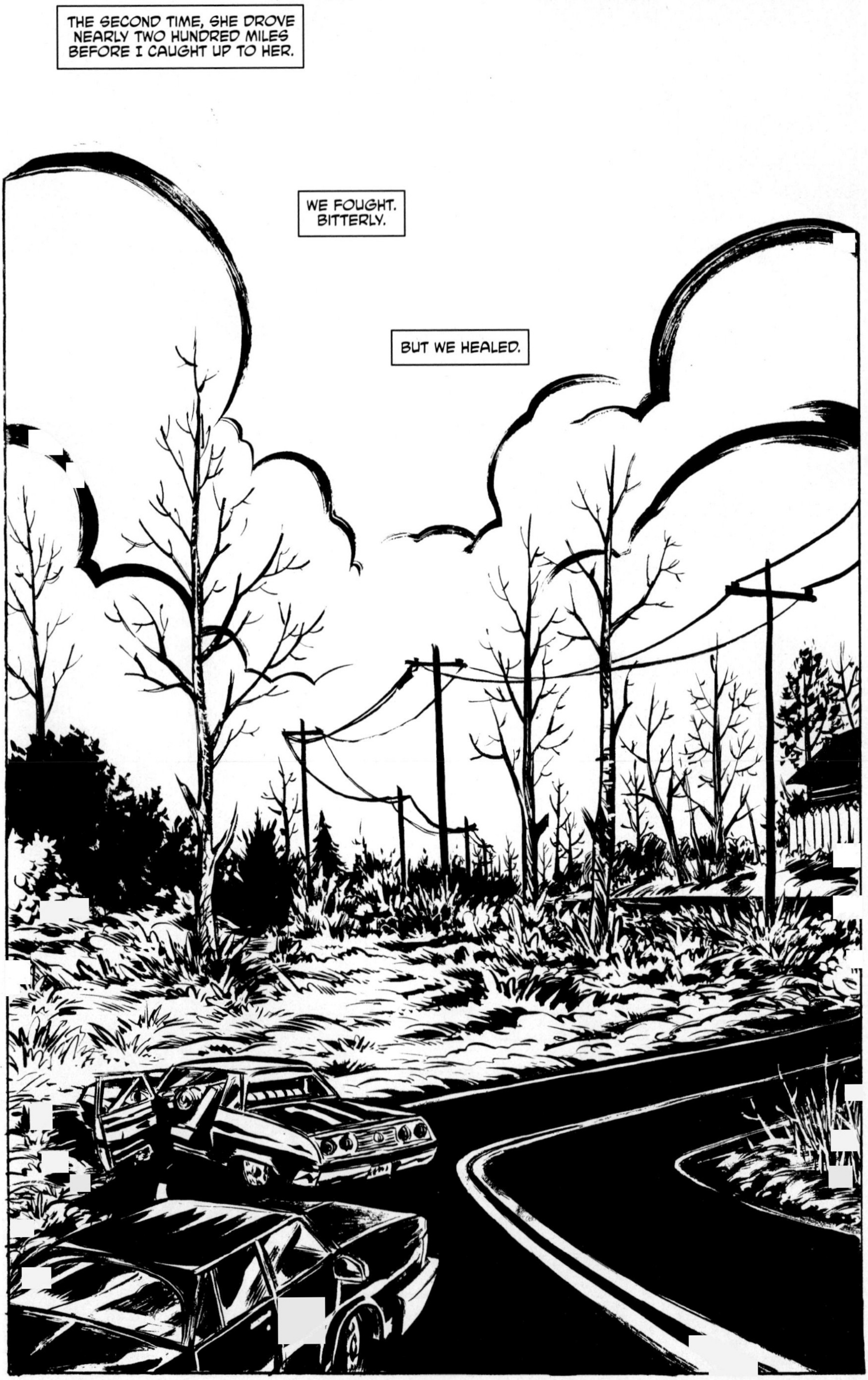
THE SECOND TIME, SHE DROVE NEARLY TWO HUNDRED MILES BEFORE I CAUGHT UP TO HER.
WE FOUGHT. BITTERLY.
BUT WE HEALED.

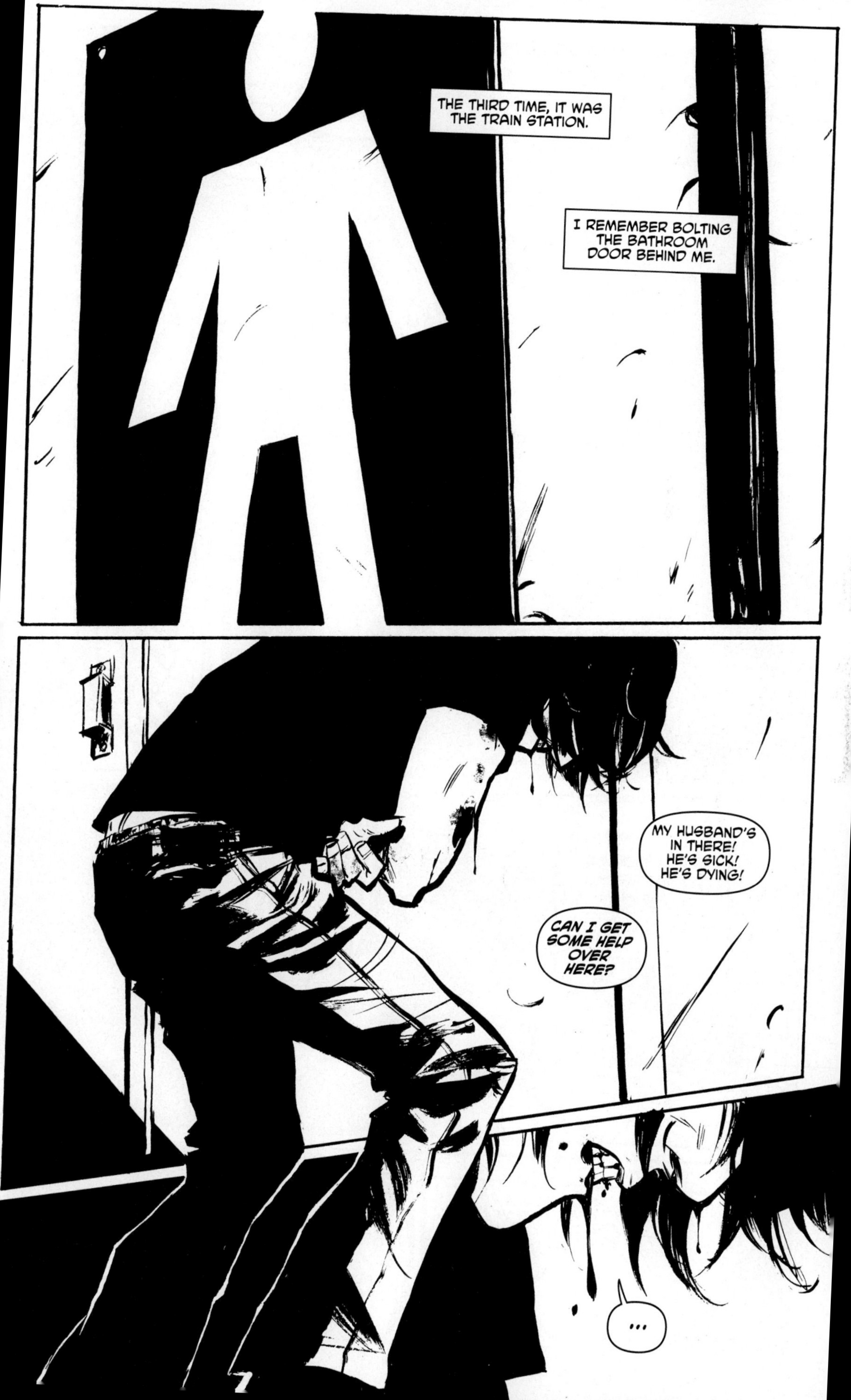
THE THIRD TIME, IT WAS THE TRAIN STATION.
I REMEMBER BOLTING THE BATHROOM DOOR BEHIND ME.
MY HUSBAND'S IN THERE! HE'S SICK! HE'S DYING!
CAN I GET SOME HELP OVER HERE?
...

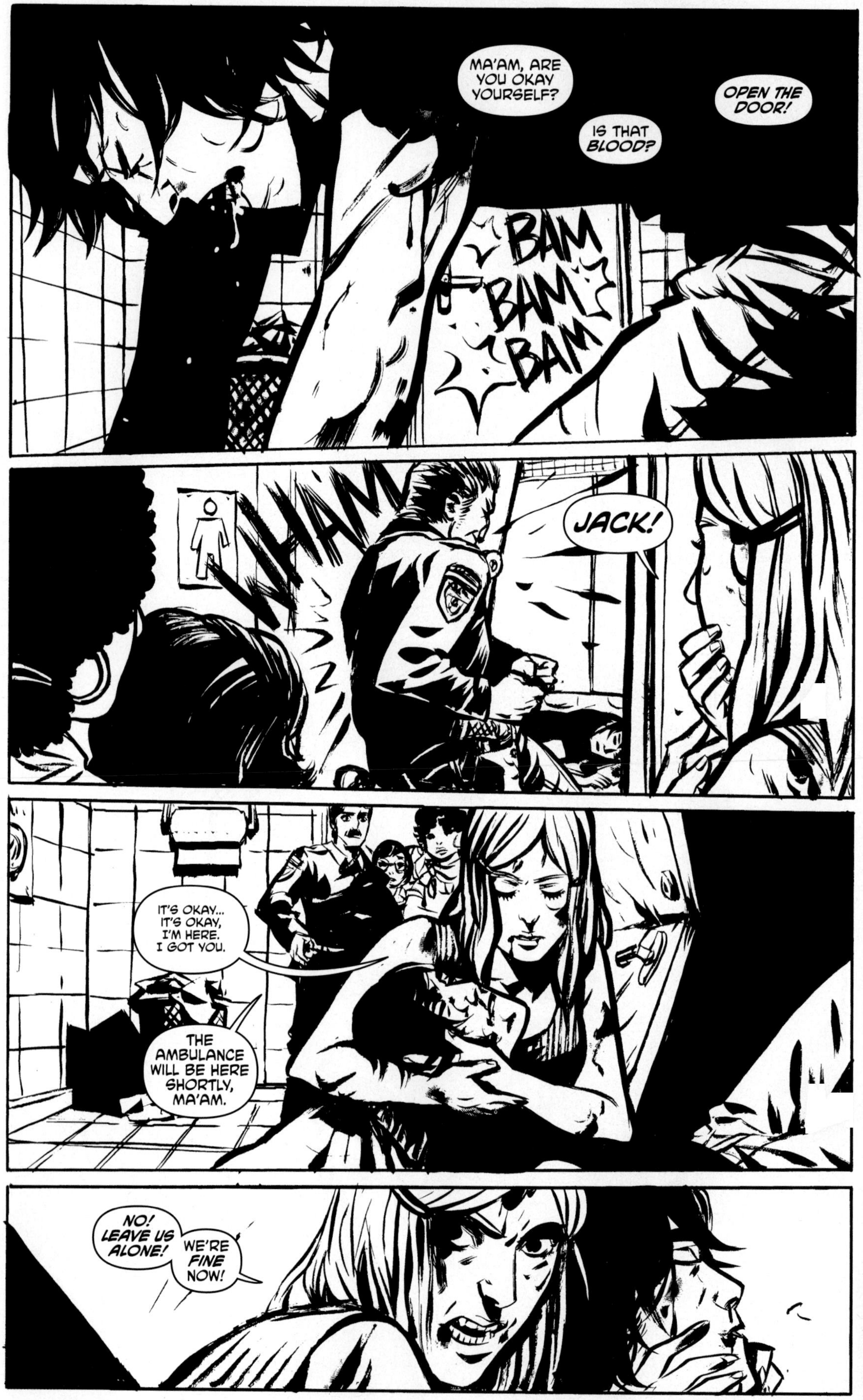
MA'AM, ARE YOU OKAY YOURSELF?
IS THAT BLOOD?
OPEN THE DOOR!
BAM BAM BAM
WHAM
JACK!
IT'S OKAY... IT'S OKAY, I'M HERE. I GOT YOU.
THE AMBULANCE WILL BE HERE SHORTLY, MA'AM.
NO! LEAVE US ALONE!
WE'RE FINE NOW!

AND WE HEALED.

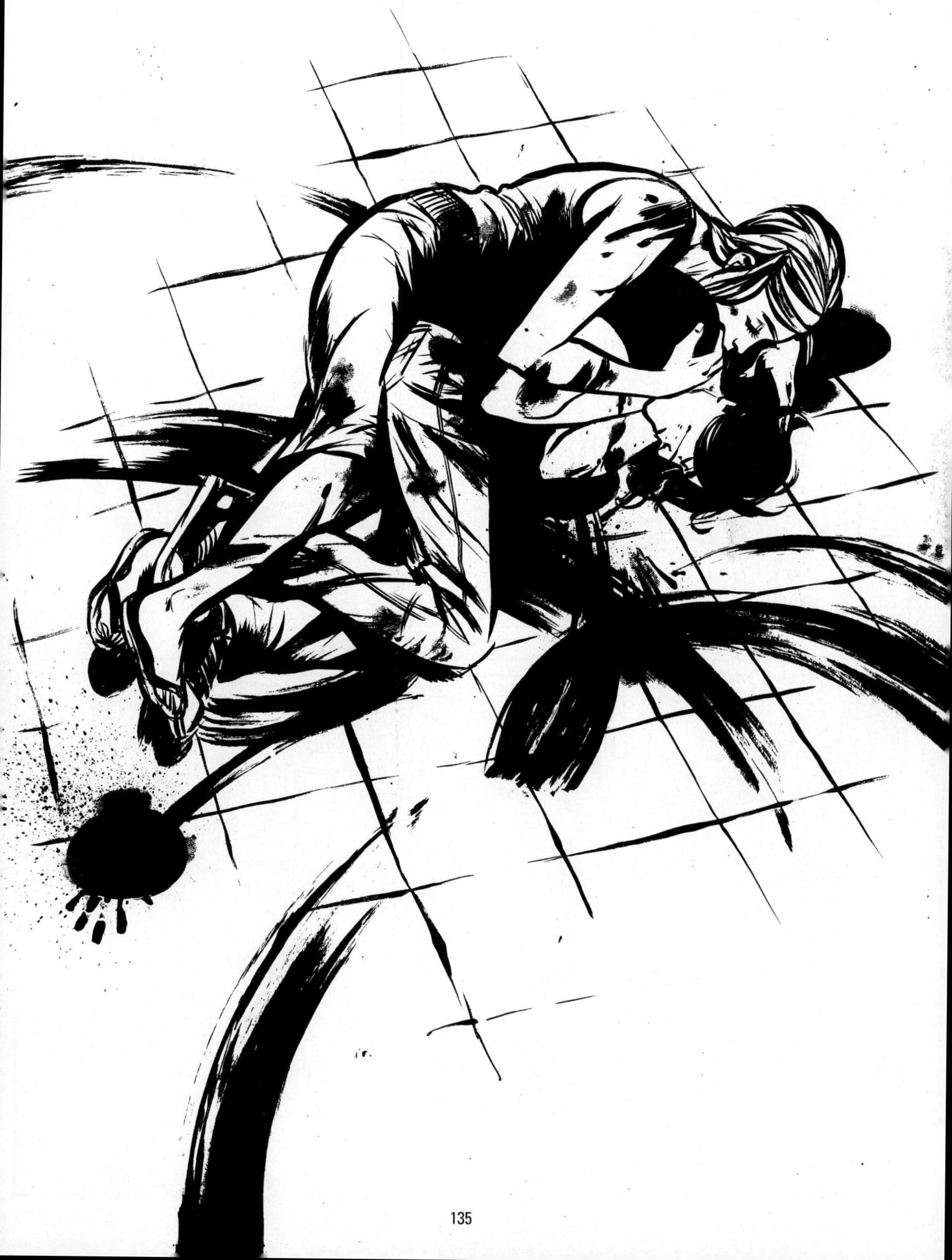

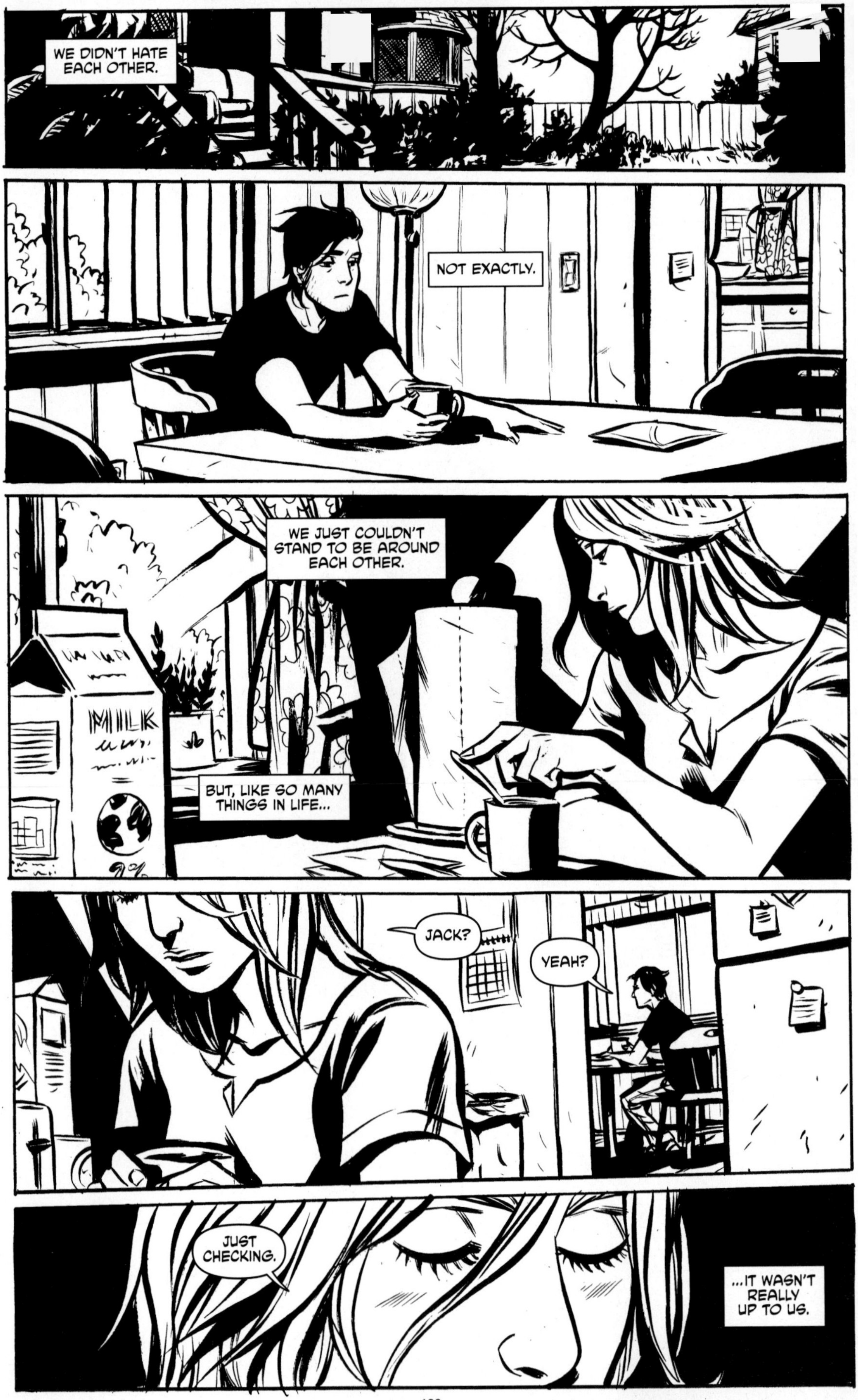
WE DIDN'T HATE EACH OTHER.
NOT EXACTLY.
WE JUST COULDN'T STAND TO BE AROUND EACH OTHER.
BUT, LIKE SO MANY THINGS IN LIFE...
JACK?
YEAH?
JUST CHECKING.
...IT WASN'T REALLY UP TO US.

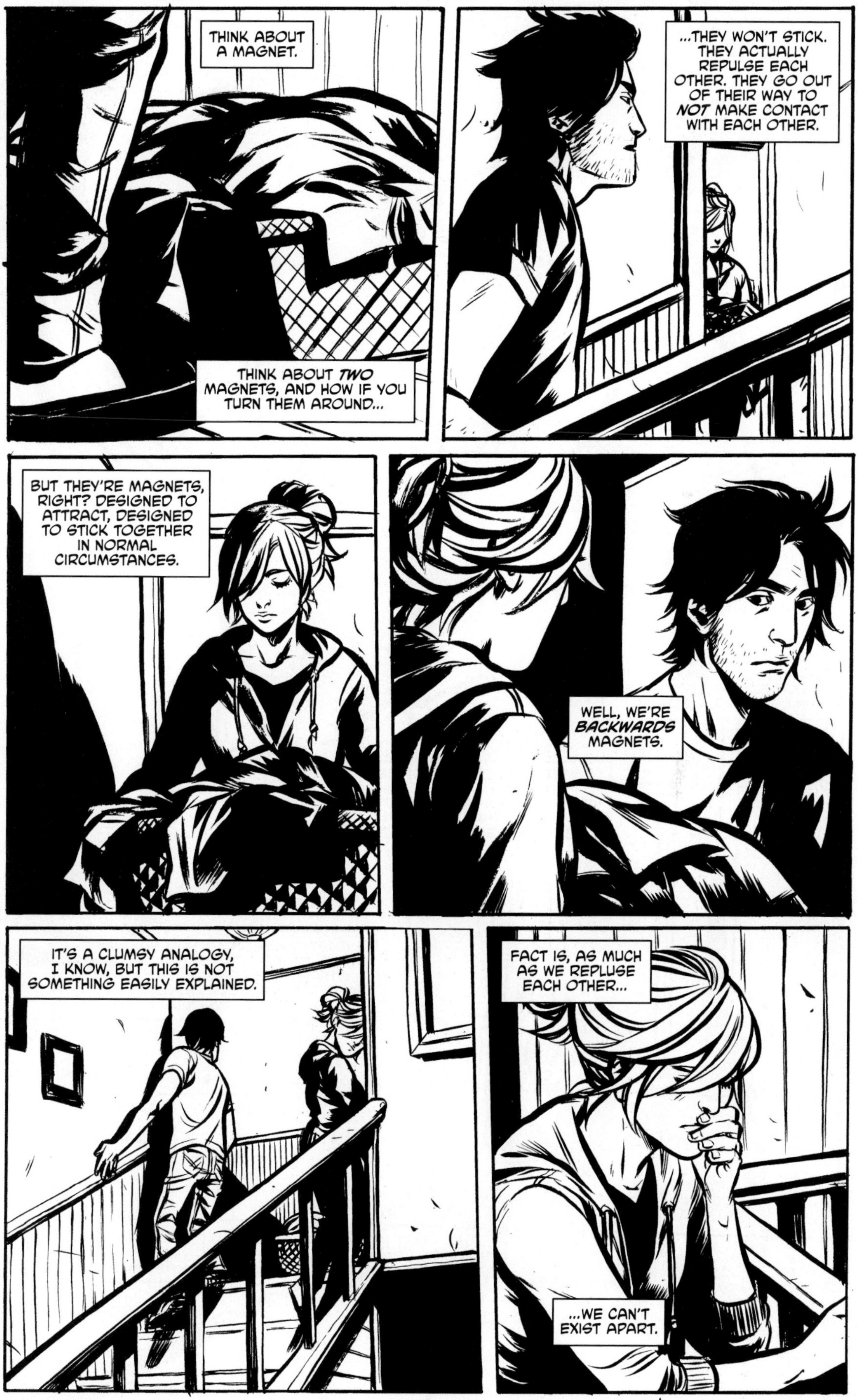
THINK ABOUT A MAGNET.
THINK ABOUT *TWO* MAGNETS, AND HOW IF YOU TURN THEM AROUND...
...THEY WON'T STICK. THEY ACTUALLY REPULSE EACH OTHER. THEY GO OUT OF THEIR WAY TO *NOT* MAKE CONTACT WITH EACH OTHER.
BUT THEY'RE MAGNETS, RIGHT? DESIGNED TO ATTRACT, DESIGNED TO STICK TOGETHER IN NORMAL CIRCUMSTANCES.
WELL, WE'RE *BACKWARDS* MAGNETS.
IT'S A CLUMSY ANALOGY, I KNOW, BUT THIS IS NOT SOMETHING EASILY EXPLAINED.
FACT IS, AS MUCH AS WE REPLUSE EACH OTHER...
...WE CAN'T EXIST APART.

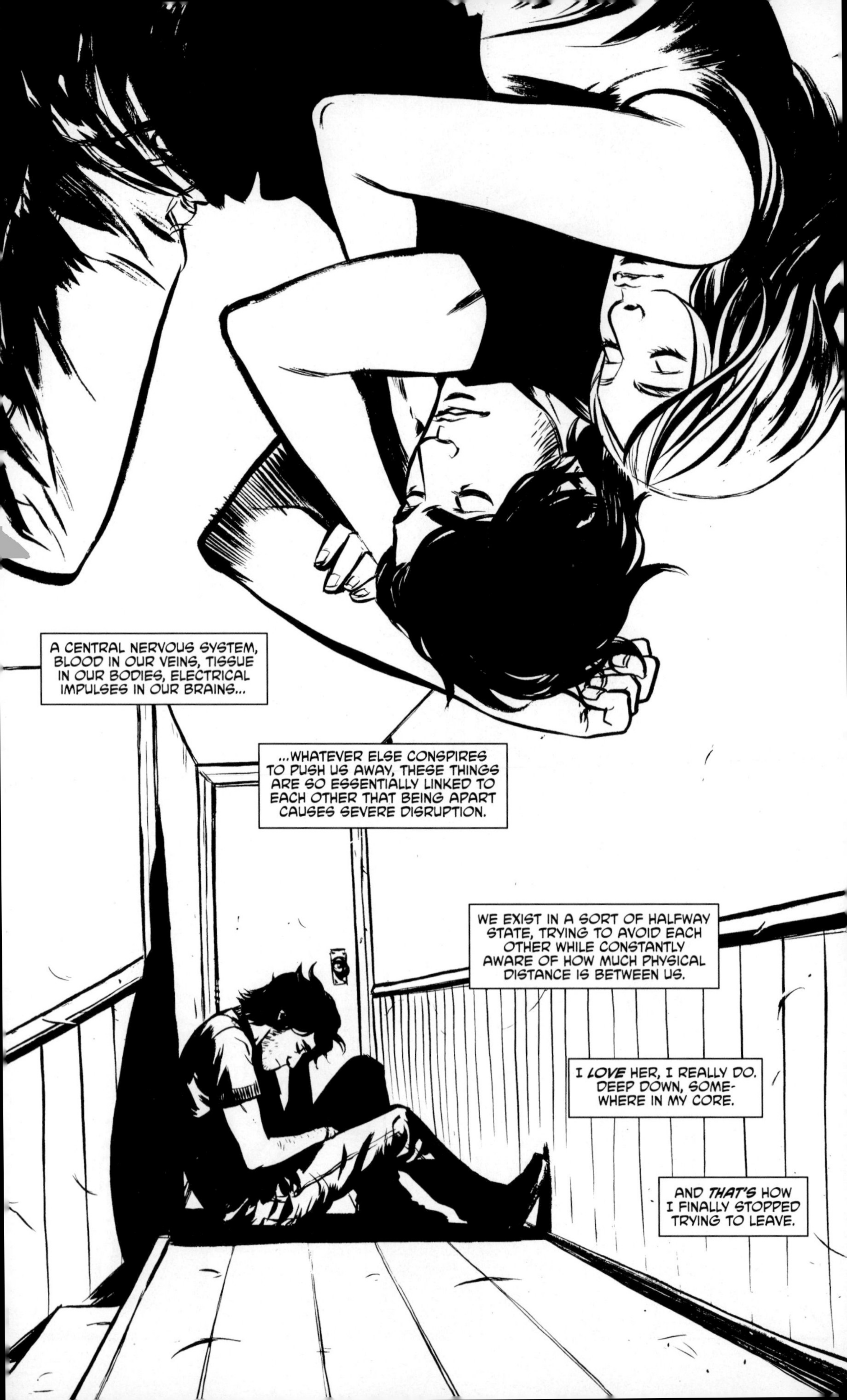
A CENTRAL NERVOUS SYSTEM, BLOOD IN OUR VEINS, TISSUE IN OUR BODIES, ELECTRICAL IMPULSES IN OUR BRAINS...
...WHATEVER ELSE CONSPIRES TO PUSH US AWAY, THESE THINGS ARE SO ESSENTIALLY LINKED TO EACH OTHER THAT BEING APART CAUSES SEVERE DISRUPTION.
WE EXIST IN A SORT OF HALFWAY STATE, TRYING TO AVOID EACH OTHER WHILE CONSTANTLY AWARE OF HOW MUCH PHYSICAL DISTANCE IS BETWEEN US.
I *LOVE* HER, I REALLY DO. DEEP DOWN, SOME-WHERE IN MY CORE.
AND *THAT'S* HOW I FINALLY STOPPED TRYING TO LEAVE.

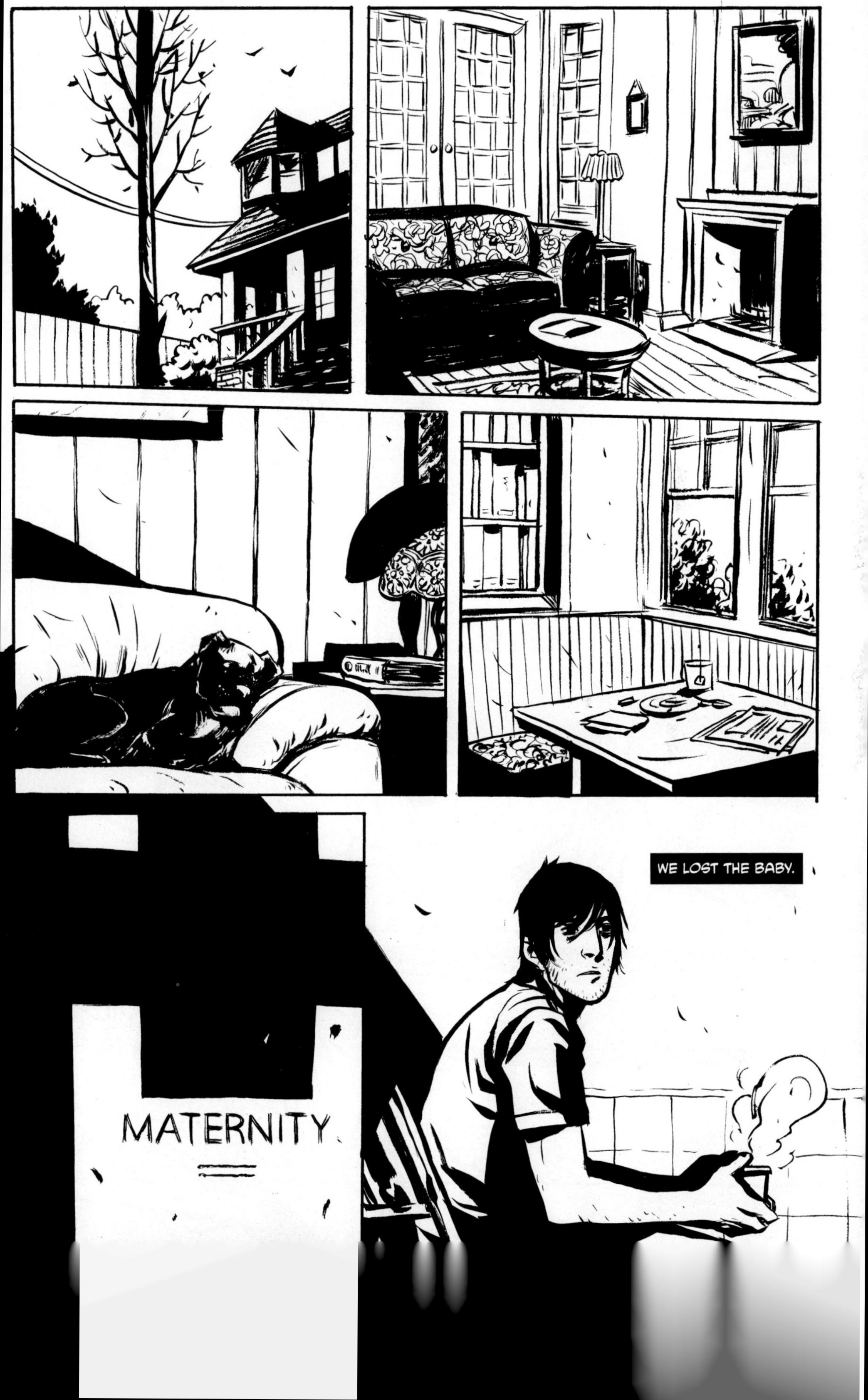
WE LOST THE BABY.
MATERNITY

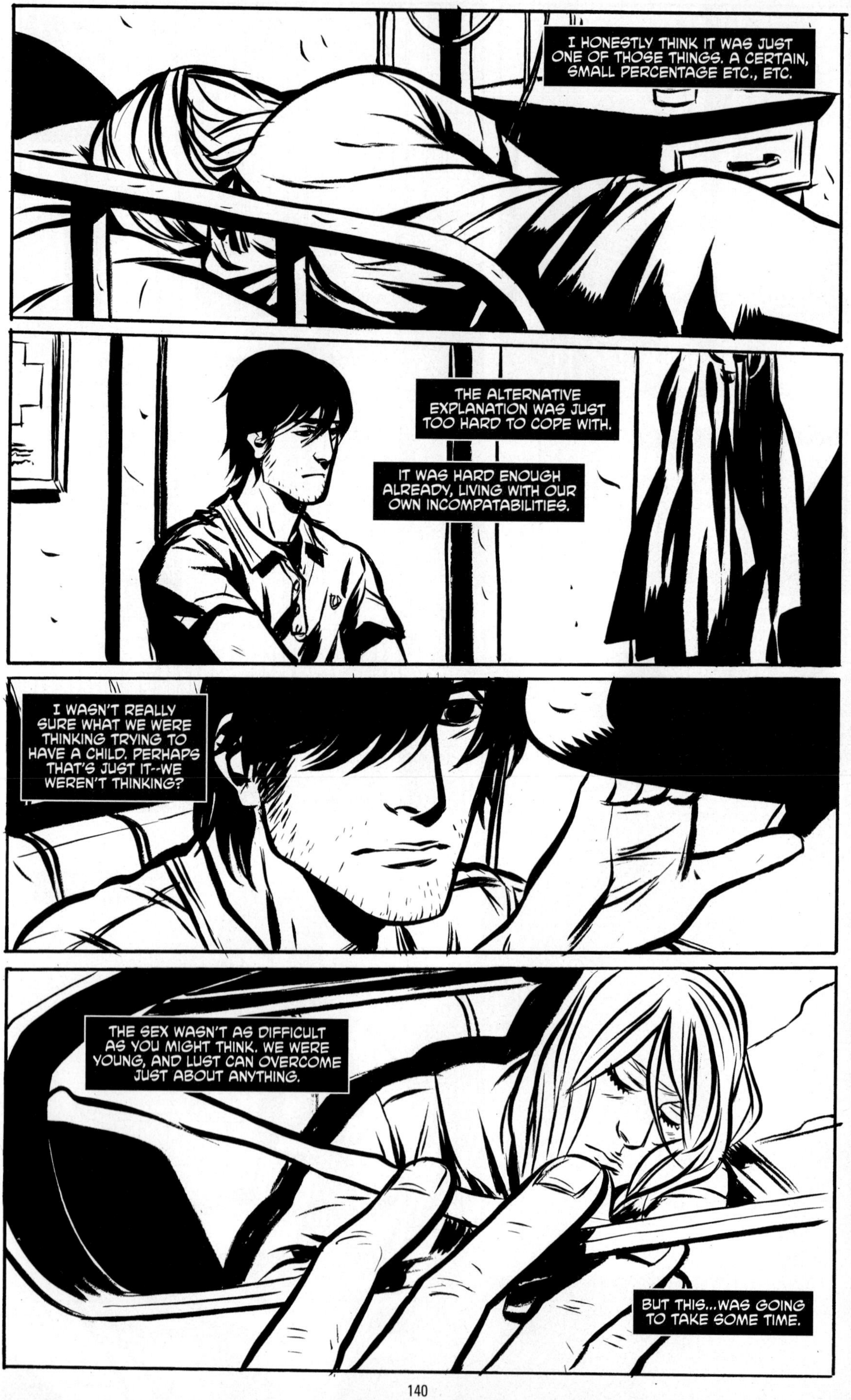
I HONESTLY THINK IT WAS JUST ONE OF THOSE THINGS. A CERTAIN, SMALL PERCENTAGE ETC., ETC.
THE ALTERNATIVE EXPLANATION WAS JUST TOO HARD TO COPE WITH.
IT WAS HARD ENOUGH ALREADY, LIVING WITH OUR OWN INCOMPATABILITIES.
I WASN'T REALLY SURE WHAT WE WERE THINKING TRYING TO HAVE A CHILD. PERHAPS THAT'S JUST IT--WE WEREN'T THINKING?
THE SEX WASN'T AS DIFFICULT AS YOU MIGHT THINK. WE WERE YOUNG, AND LUST CAN OVERCOME JUST ABOUT ANYTHING.
BUT THIS...WAS GOING TO TAKE SOME TIME.

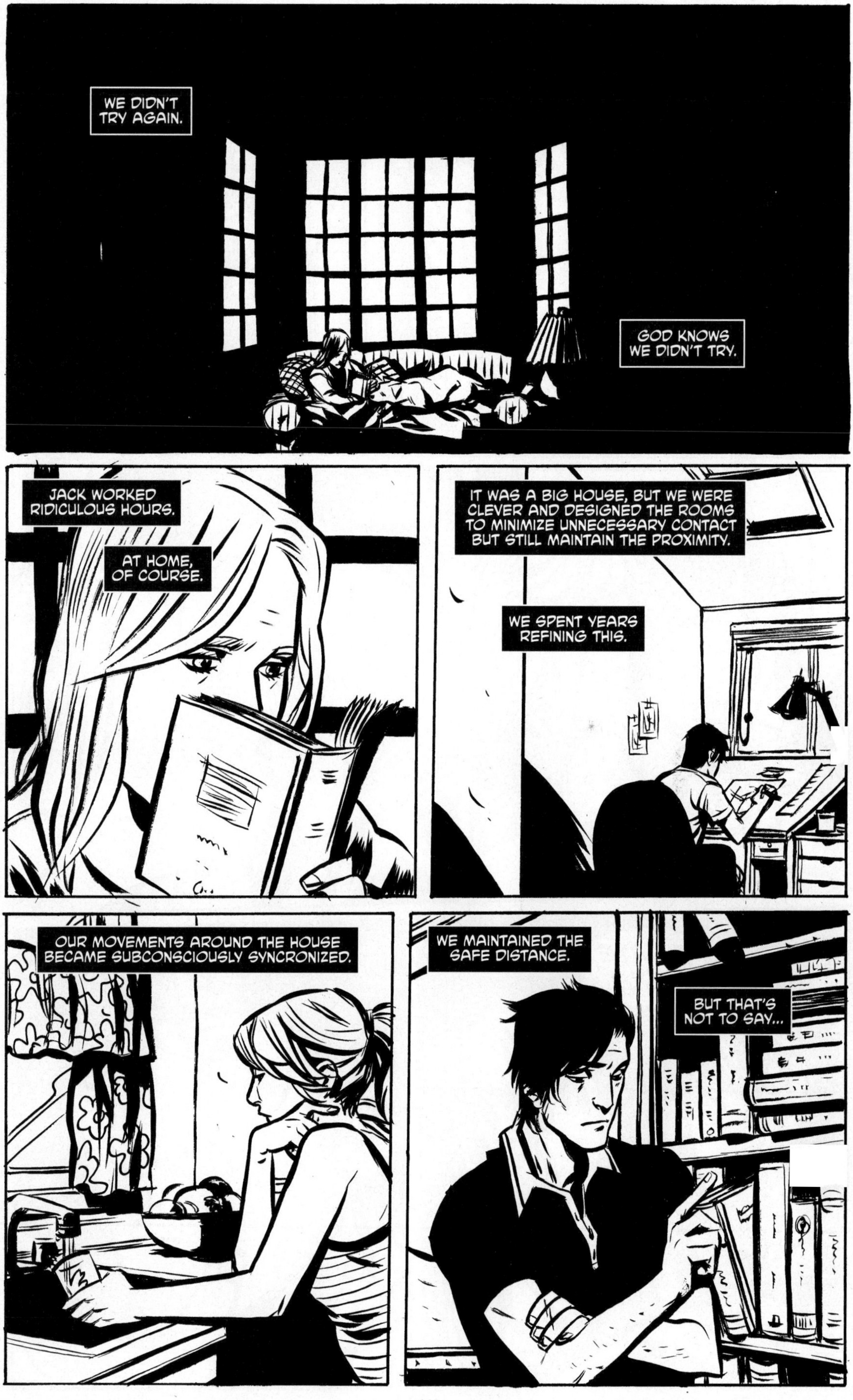
WE DIDN'T TRY AGAIN.
GOD KNOWS WE DIDN'T TRY.
JACK WORKED RIDICULOUS HOURS.
AT HOME, OF COURSE.
IT WAS A BIG HOUSE, BUT WE WERE CLEVER AND DESIGNED THE ROOMS TO MINIMIZE UNNECESSARY CONTACT BUT STILL MAINTAIN THE PROXIMITY.
WE SPENT YEARS REFINING THIS.
OUR MOVEMENTS AROUND THE HOUSE BECAME SUBCONSCIOUSLY SYNCRONIZED.
WE MAINTAINED THE SAFE DISTANCE.
BUT THAT'S NOT TO SAY...

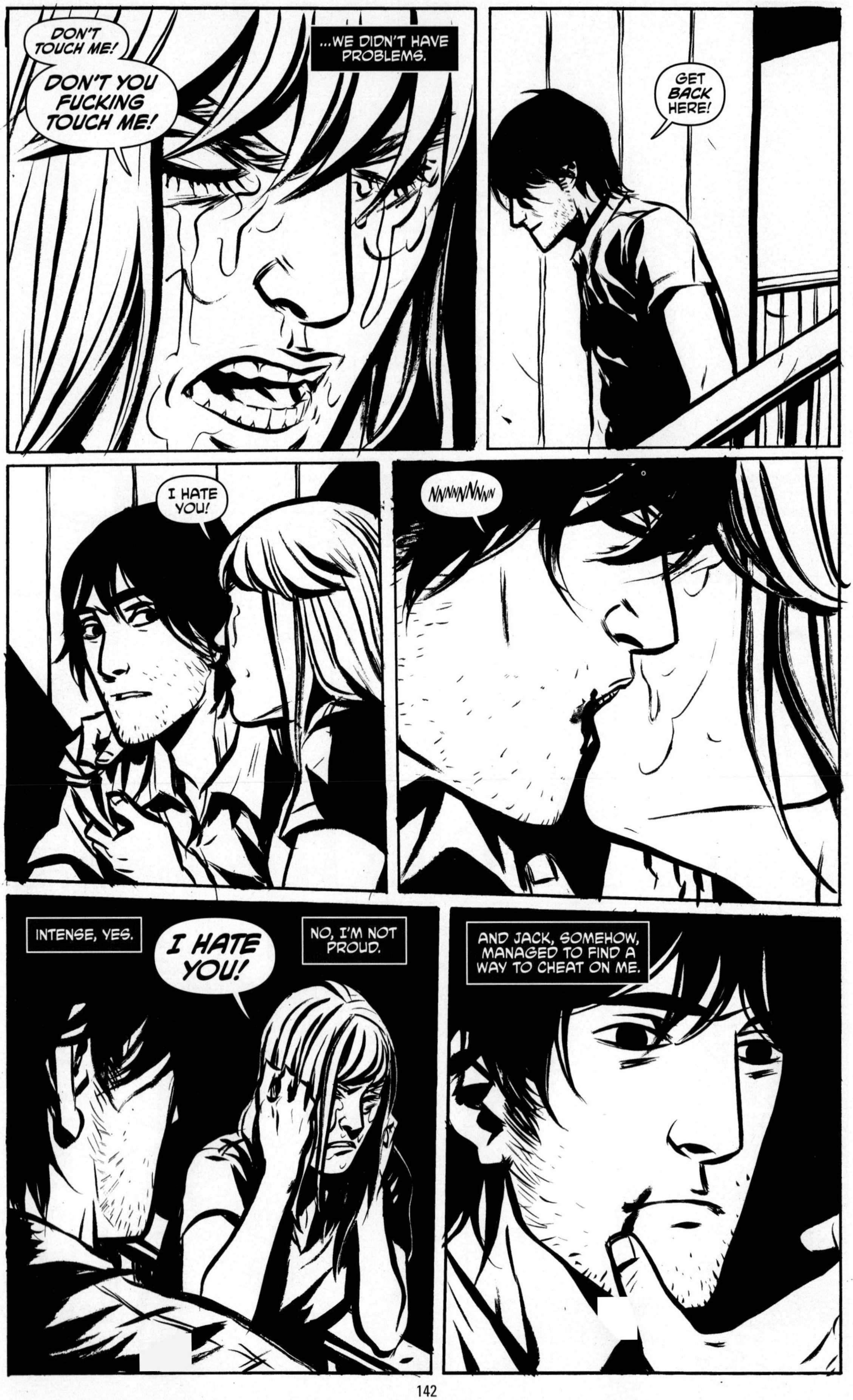
DON'T TOUCH ME!
DON'T YOU FUCKING TOUCH ME!
...WE DIDN'T HAVE PROBLEMS.
GET BACK HERE!
I HATE YOU!
NNNNNNNN
INTENSE, YES.
I HATE YOU!
NO, I'M NOT PROUD.
AND JACK, SOMEHOW, MANAGED TO FIND A WAY TO CHEAT ON ME.

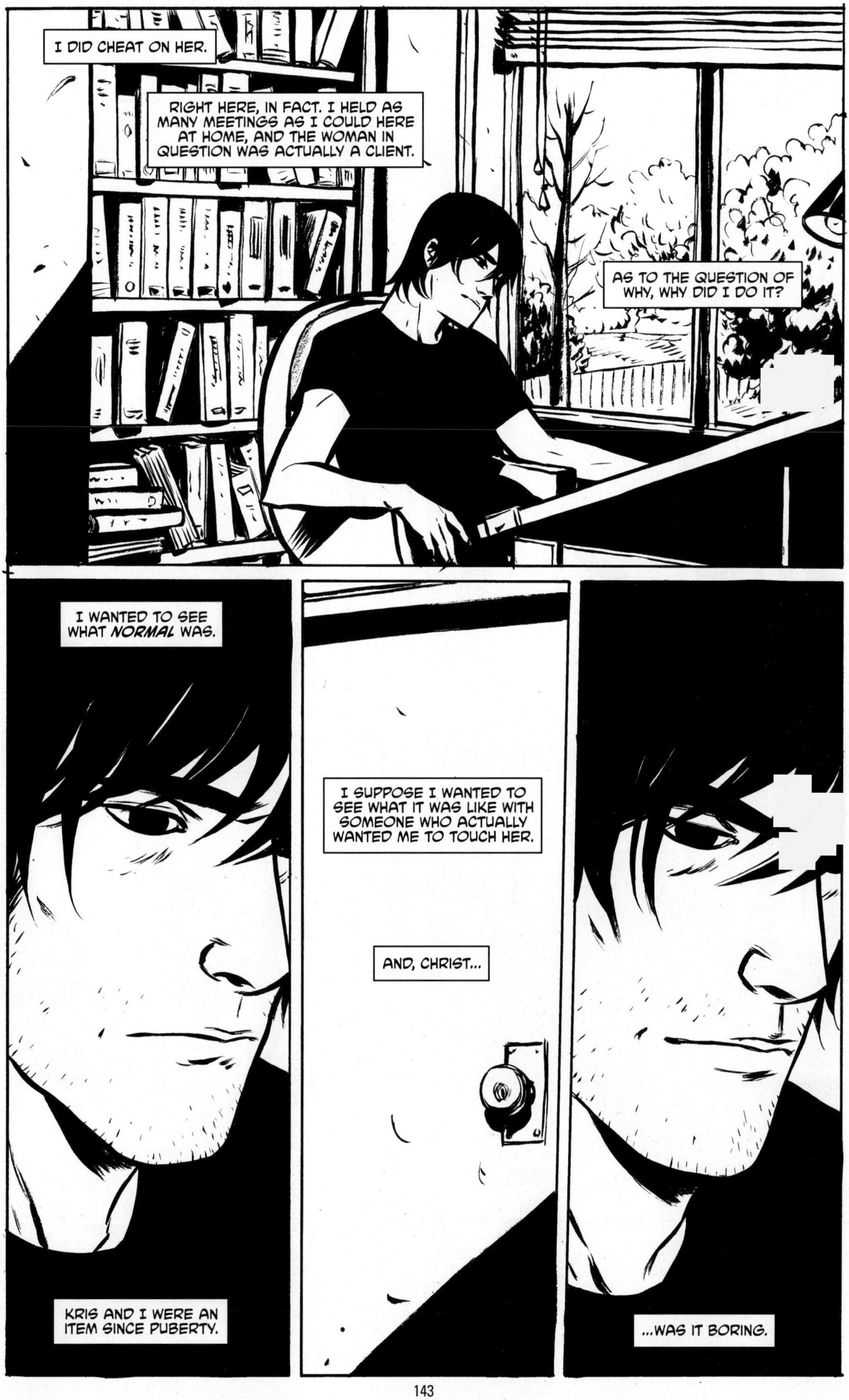
I DID CHEAT ON HER.
RIGHT HERE, IN FACT. I HELD AS MANY MEETINGS AS I COULD HERE AT HOME, AND THE WOMAN IN QUESTION WAS ACTUALLY A CLIENT.
AS TO THE QUESTION OF WHY, WHY DID I DO IT?
I WANTED TO SEE WHAT *NORMAL* WAS.
KRIS AND I WERE AN ITEM SINCE PUBERTY.
I SUPPOSE I WANTED TO SEE WHAT IT WAS LIKE WITH SOMEONE WHO ACTUALLY WANTED ME TO TOUCH HER.
AND, CHRIST...
...WAS IT BORING.

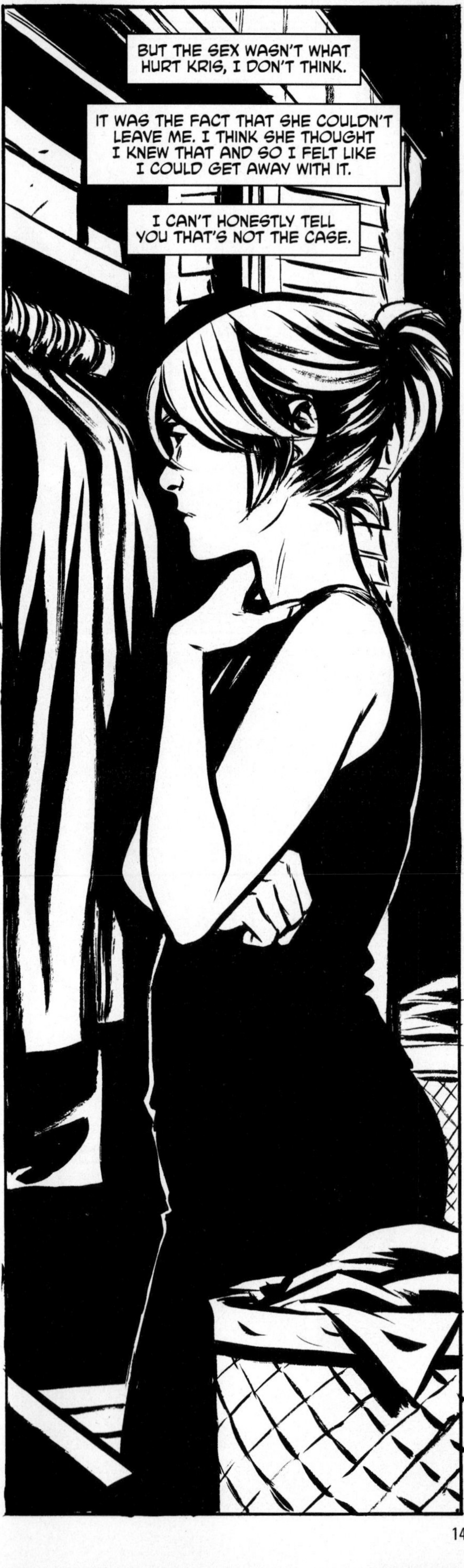

BUT THE SEX WASN'T WHAT HURT KRIS, I DON'T THINK.
IT WAS THE FACT THAT SHE COULDN'T LEAVE ME. I THINK SHE THOUGHT I KNEW THAT AND SO I FELT LIKE I COULD GET AWAY WITH IT.
I CAN'T HONESTLY TELL YOU THAT'S NOT THE CASE.

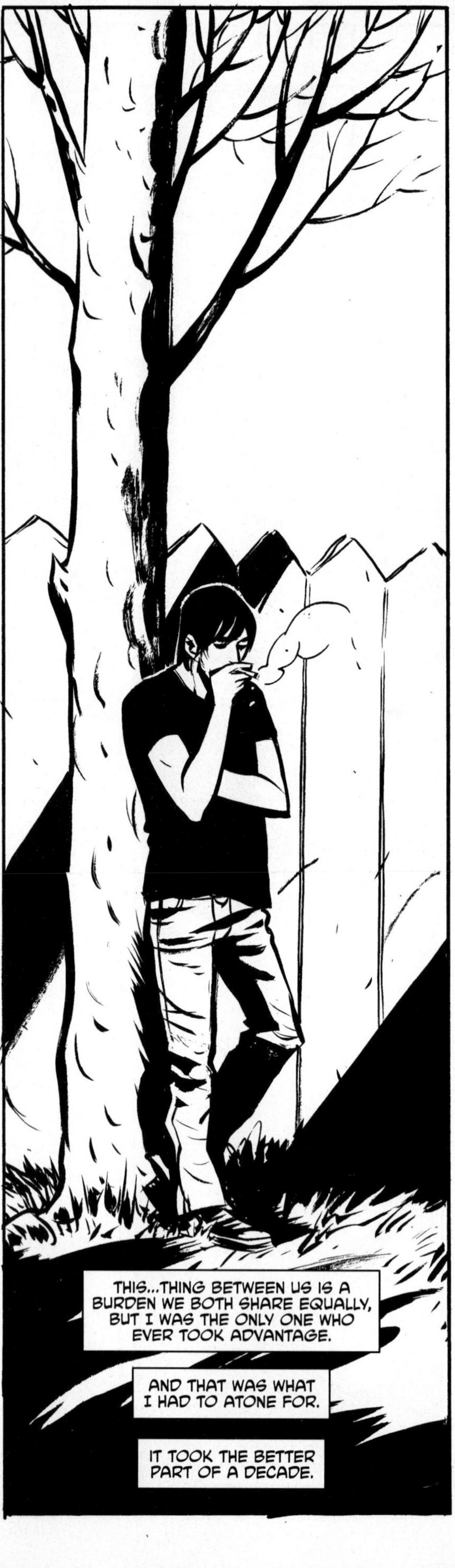

THIS...THING BETWEEN US IS A BURDEN WE BOTH SHARE EQUALLY, BUT I WAS THE ONLY ONE WHO EVER TOOK ADVANTAGE.
AND THAT WAS WHAT I HAD TO ATONE FOR.
IT TOOK THE BETTER PART OF A DECADE.

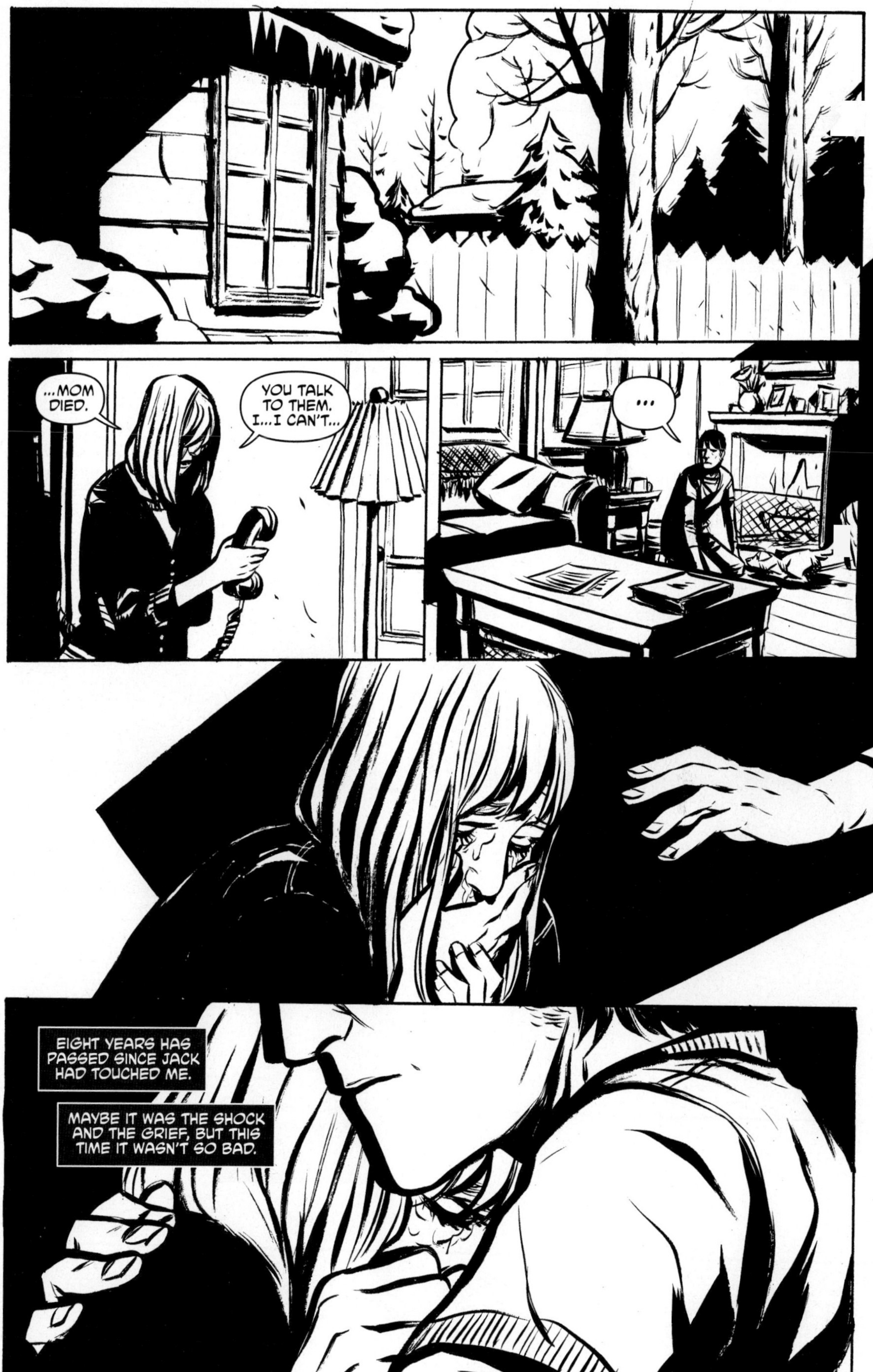
...MOM DIED.
YOU TALK TO THEM. I...I CAN'T...
...
EIGHT YEARS HAS PASSED SINCE JACK HAD TOUCHED ME.
MAYBE IT WAS THE SHOCK AND THE GRIEF, BUT THIS TIME IT WASN'T SO BAD.

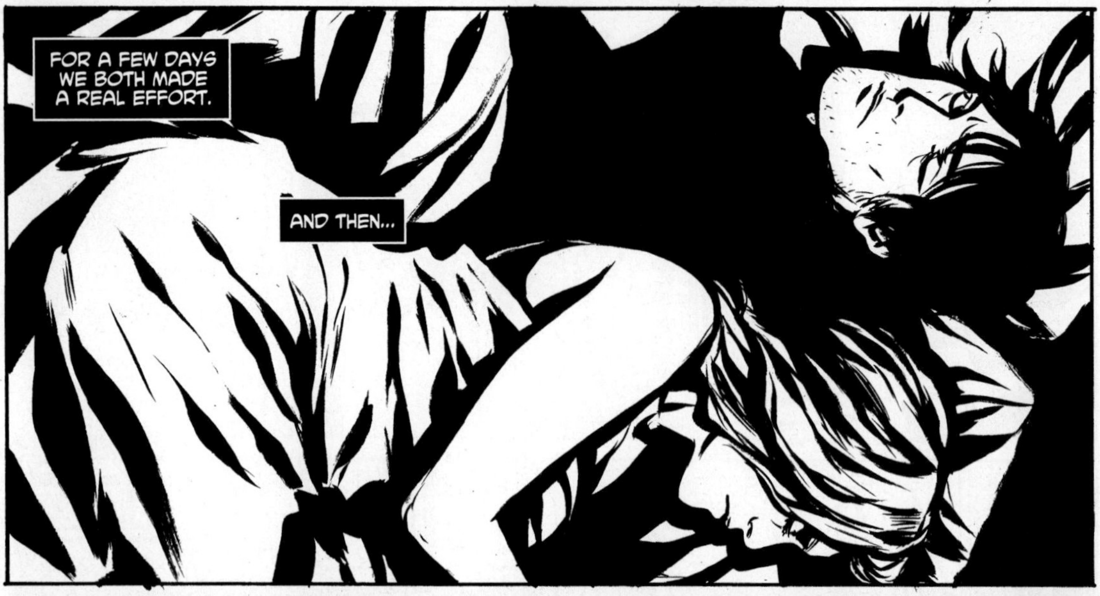
FOR A FEW DAYS WE BOTH MADE A REAL EFFORT.
AND THEN...

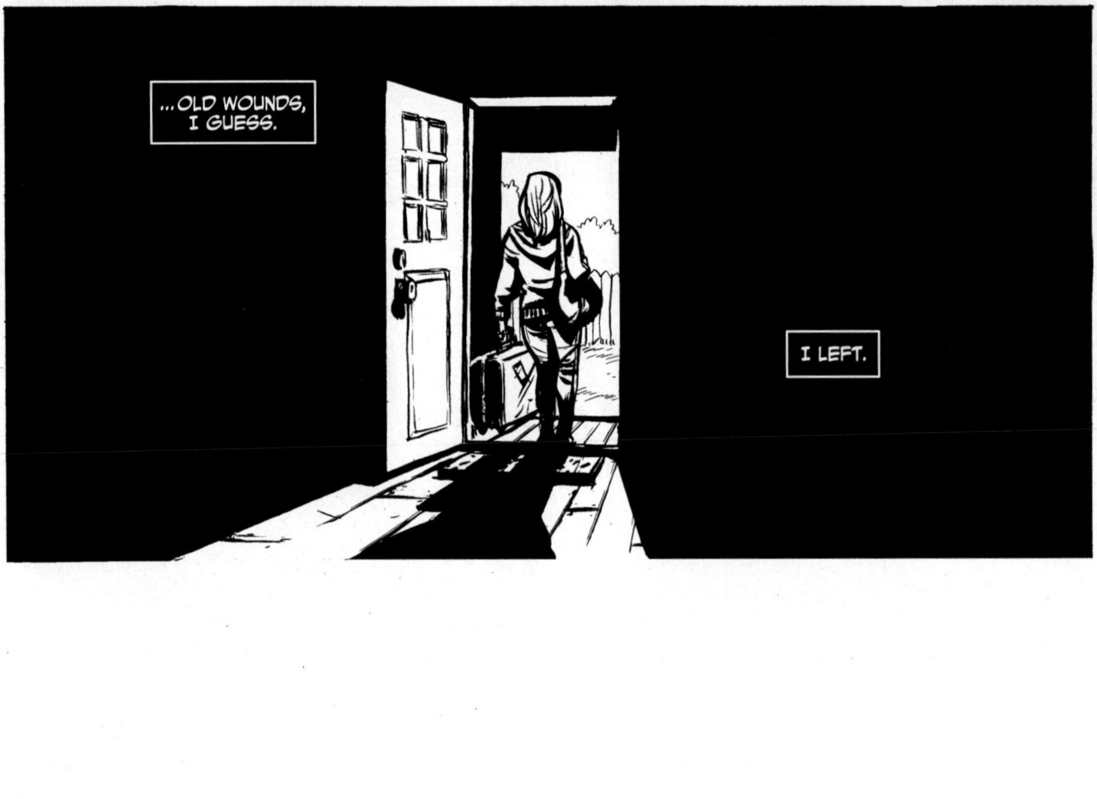
...OLD WOUNDS, I GUESS.
I LEFT.

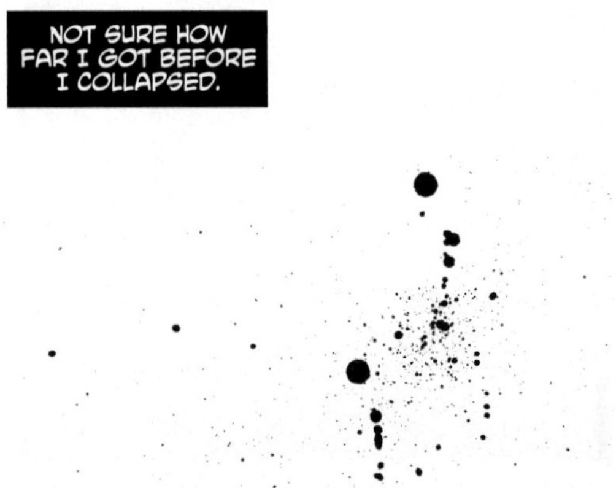
NOT SURE HOW FAR I GOT BEFORE I COLLAPSED.

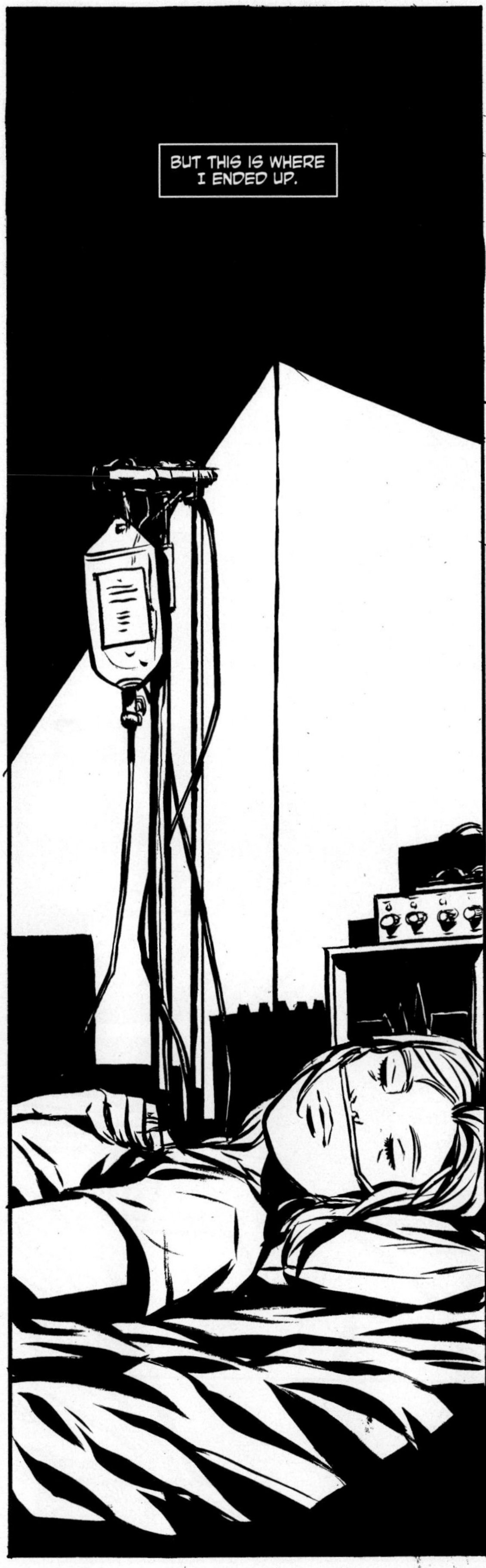
BUT THIS IS WHERE I ENDED UP.

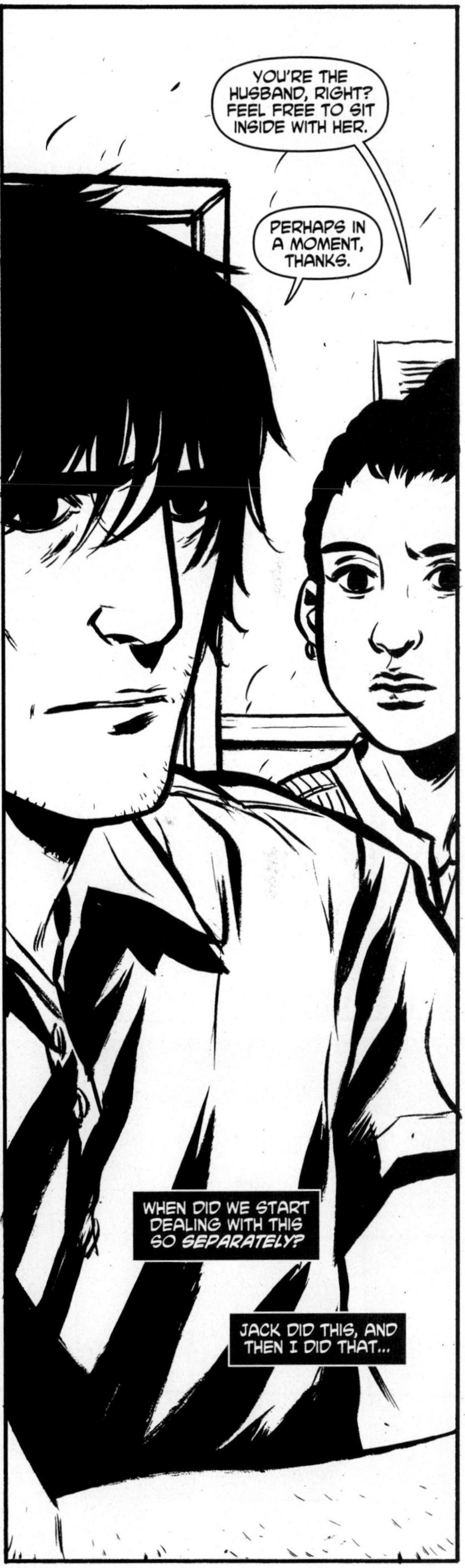
YOU'RE THE HUSBAND, RIGHT? FEEL FREE TO SIT INSIDE WITH HER.
PERHAPS IN A MOMENT, THANKS.
WHEN DID WE START DEALING WITH THIS SO *SEPARATELY?*
JACK DID THIS, AND THEN I DID THAT...

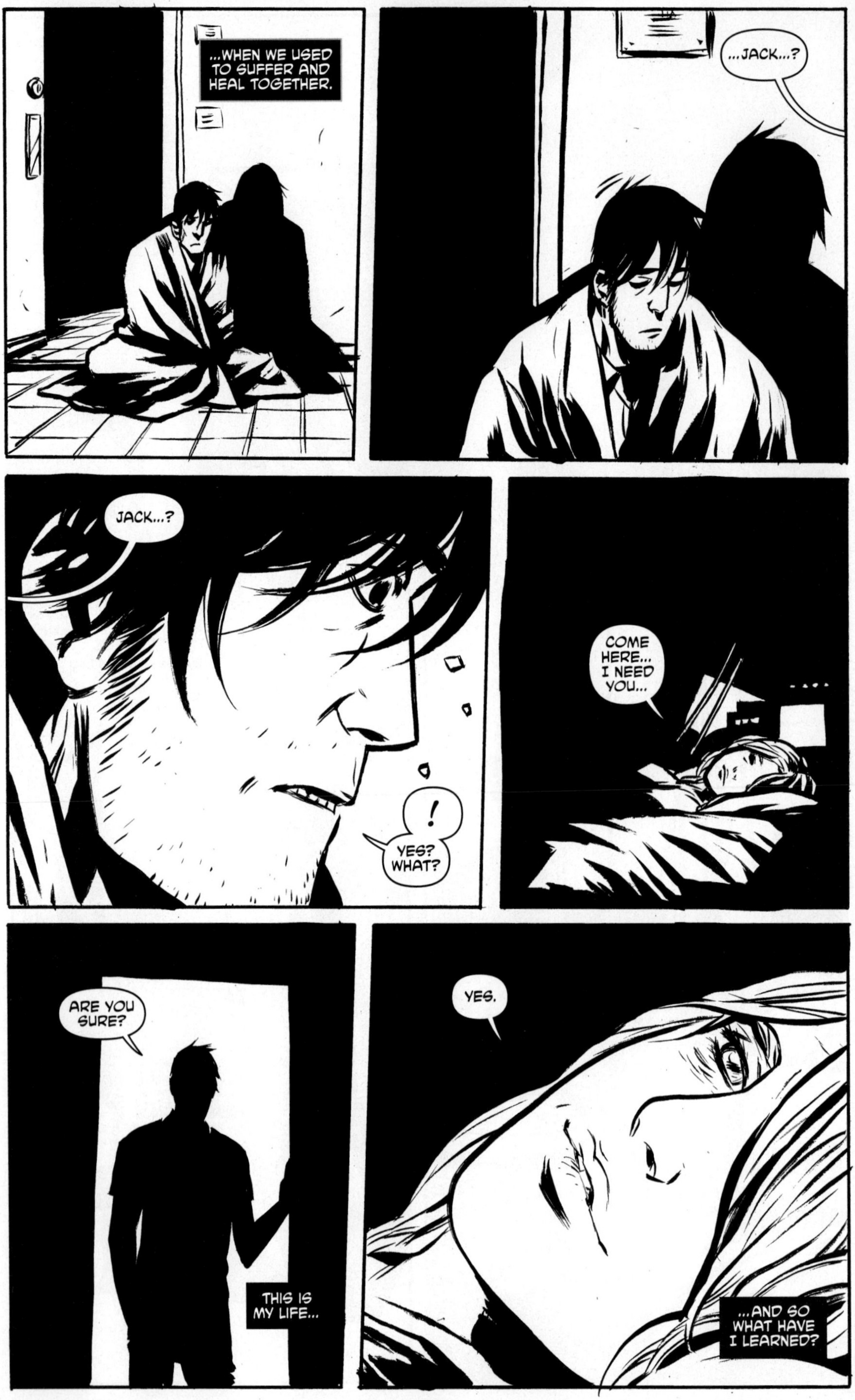
...WHEN WE USED TO SUFFER AND HEAL TOGETHER.
...JACK...?
JACK...?
!
YES? WHAT?
COME HERE... I NEED YOU...
ARE YOU SURE?
THIS IS MY LIFE...
YES.
...AND SO WHAT HAVE I LEARNED?

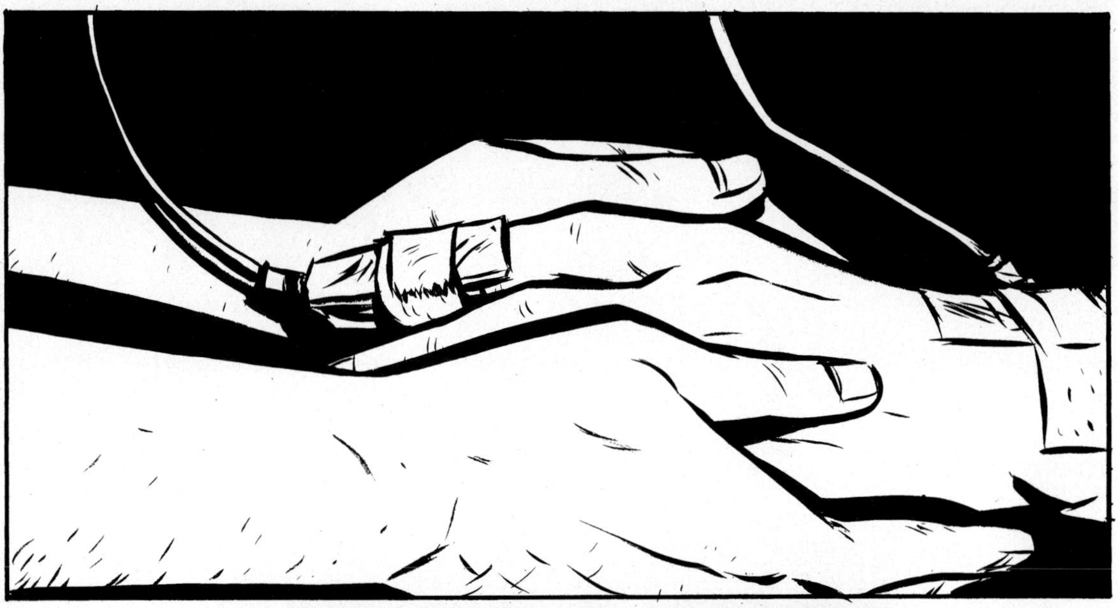

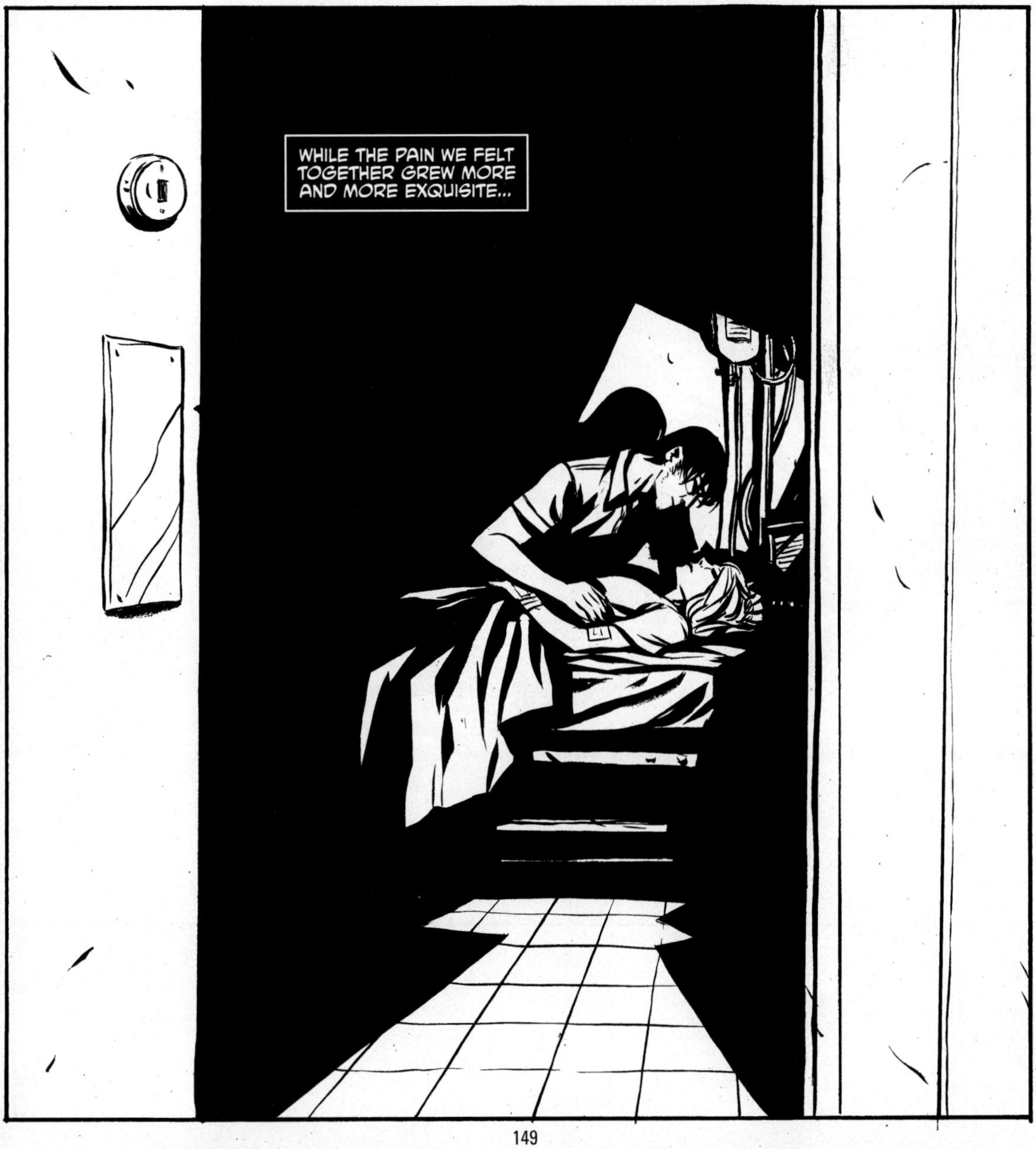
WHILE THE PAIN WE FELT TOGETHER GREW MORE AND MORE EXQUISITE...

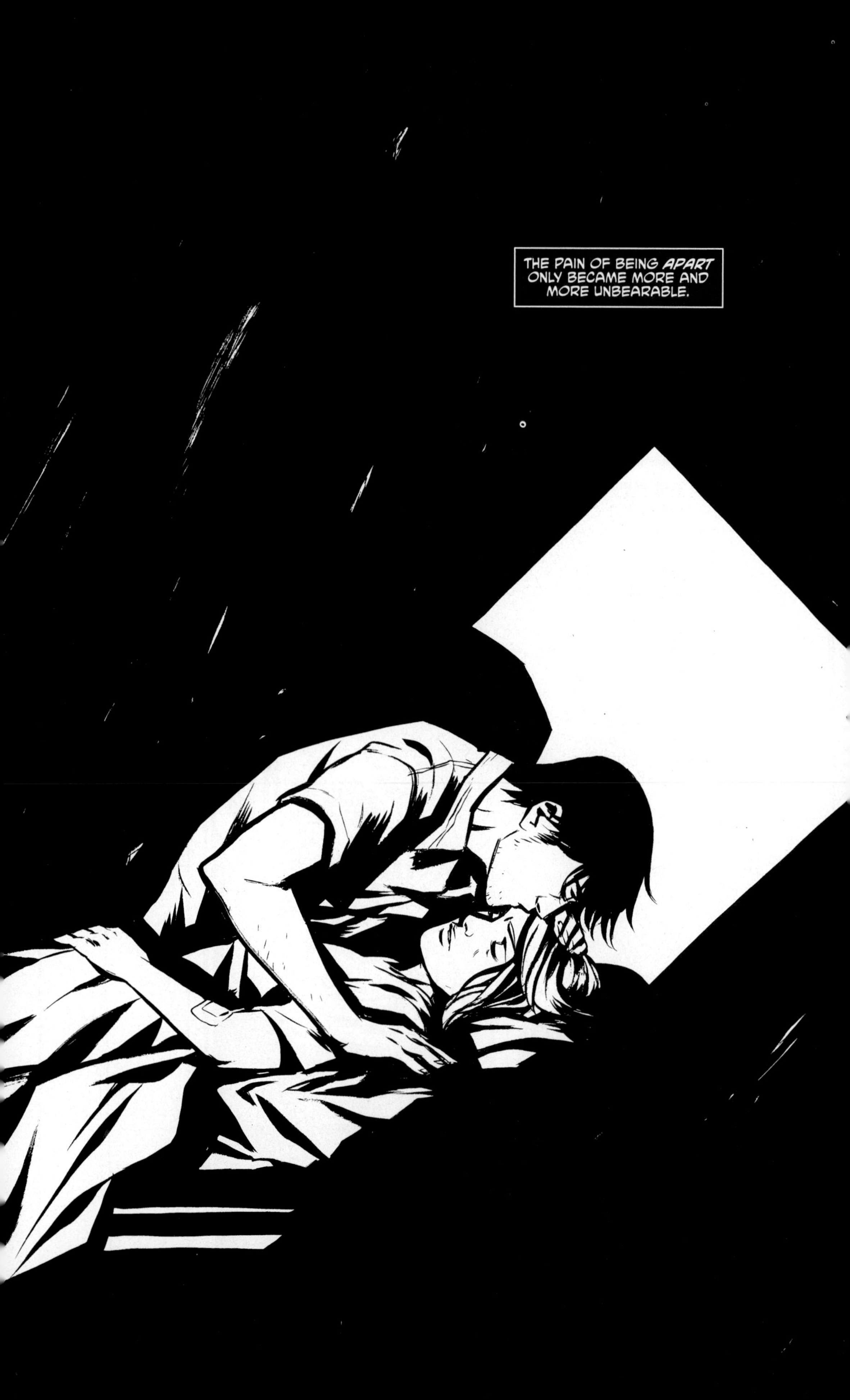
THE PAIN OF BEING APART ONLY BECAME MORE AND MORE UNBEARABLE.

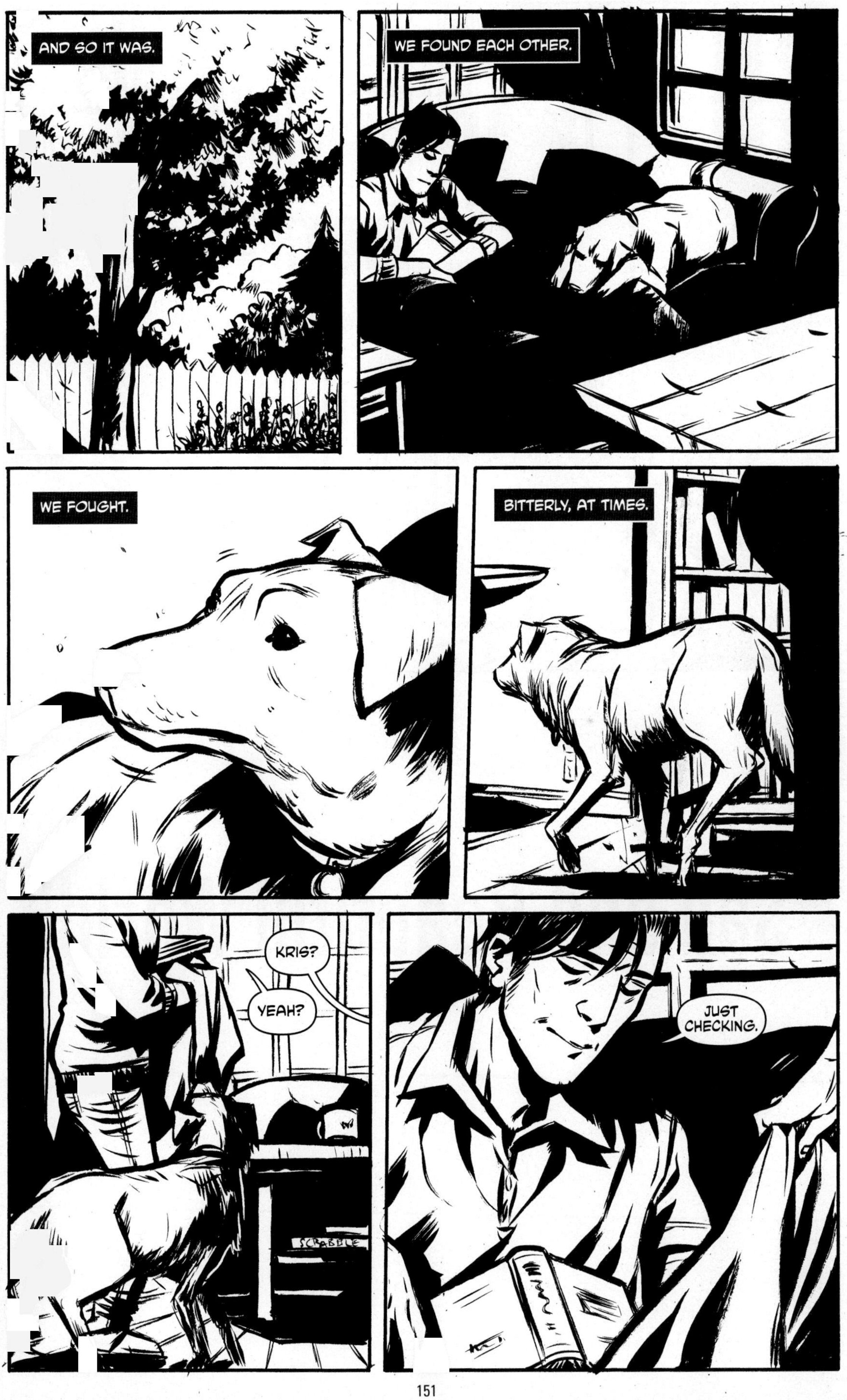
AND SO IT WAS.
WE FOUND EACH OTHER.
WE FOUGHT.
BITTERLY, AT TIMES.
KRIS?
YEAH?
SCRABBLE
JUST CHECKING.

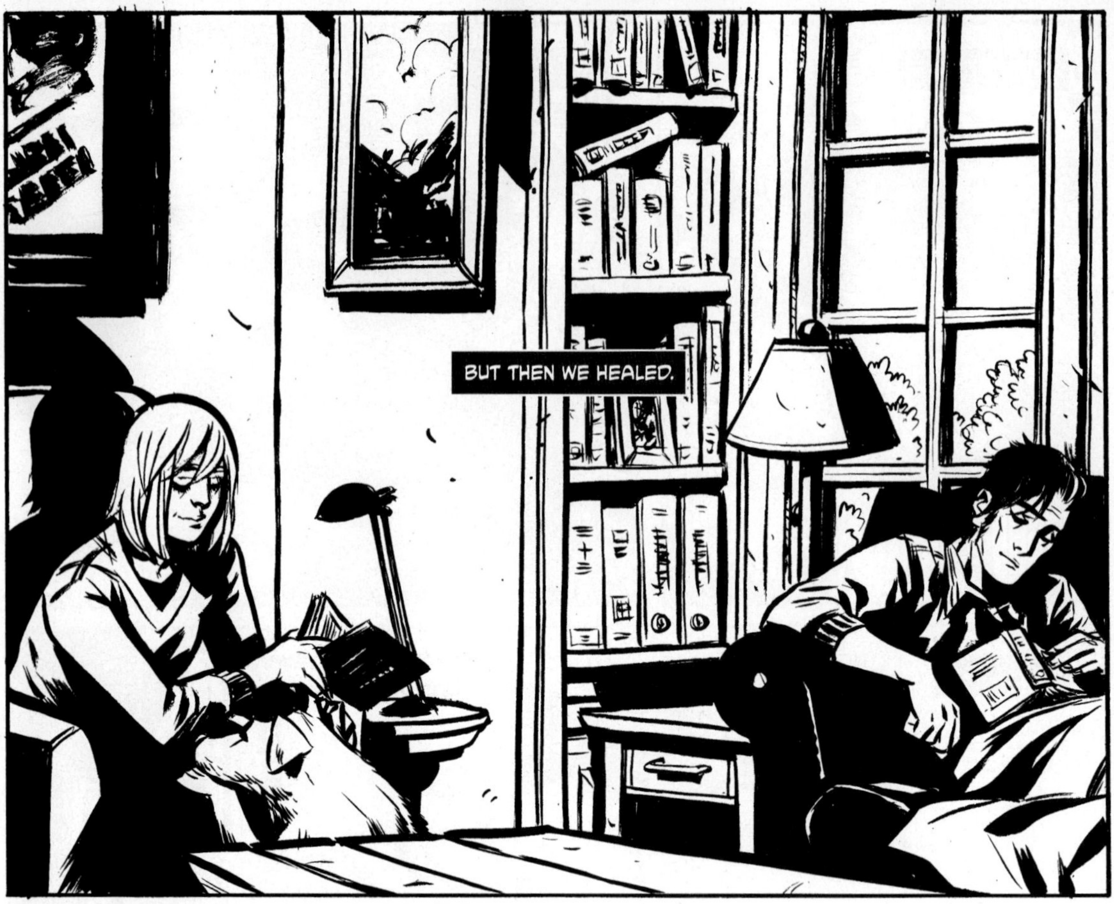
BUT THEN WE HEALED.

"Sad and Beautiful World"

1

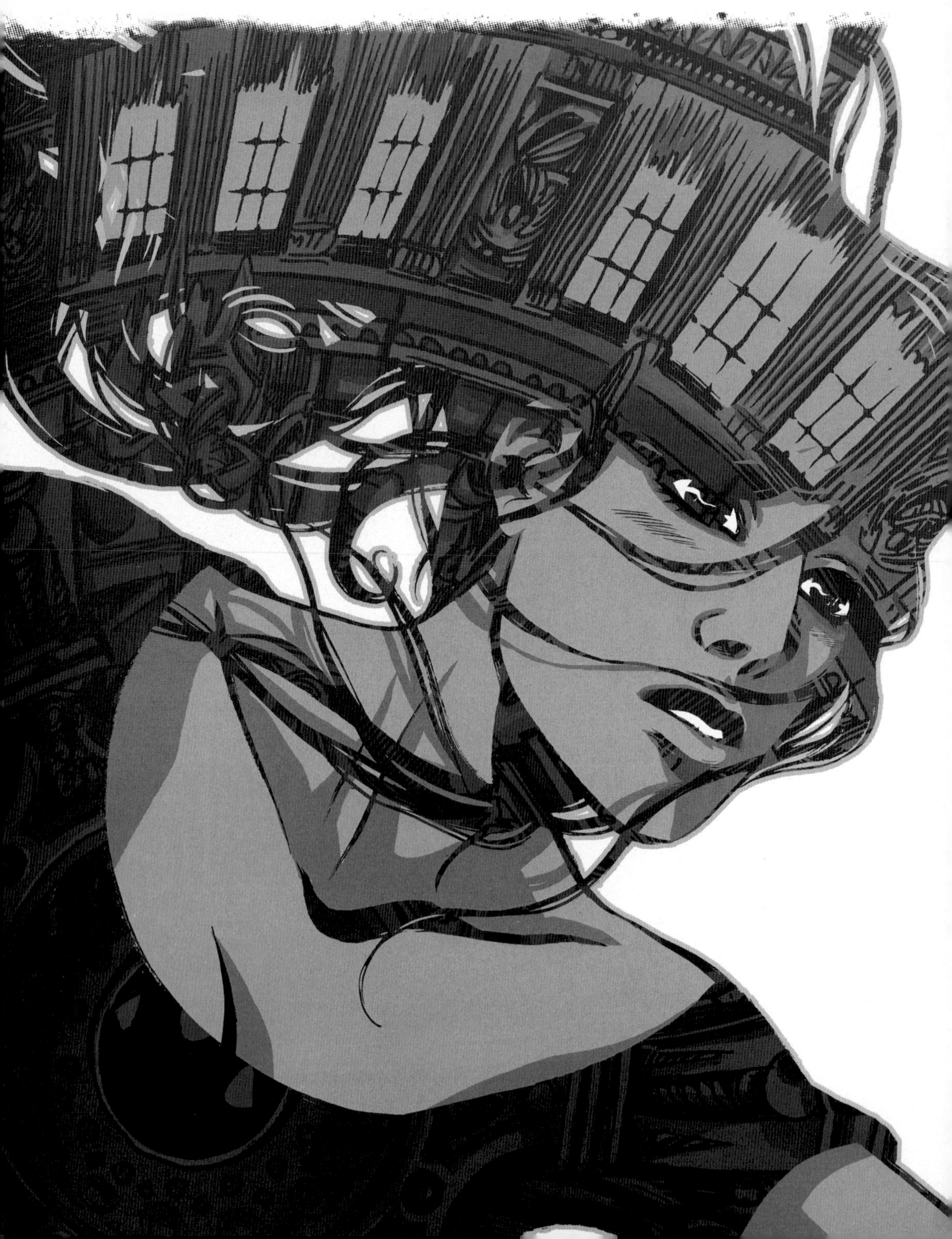

2

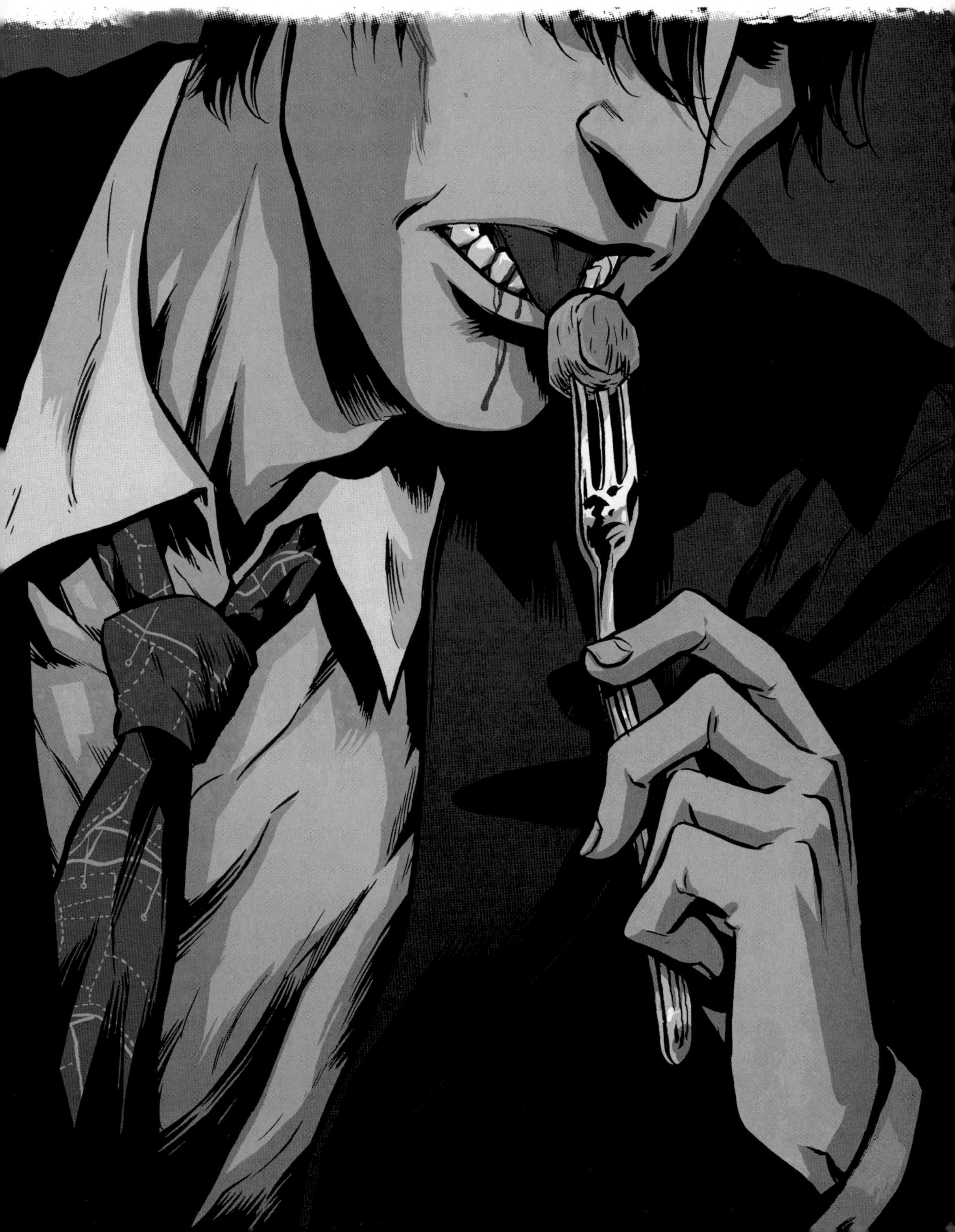

3

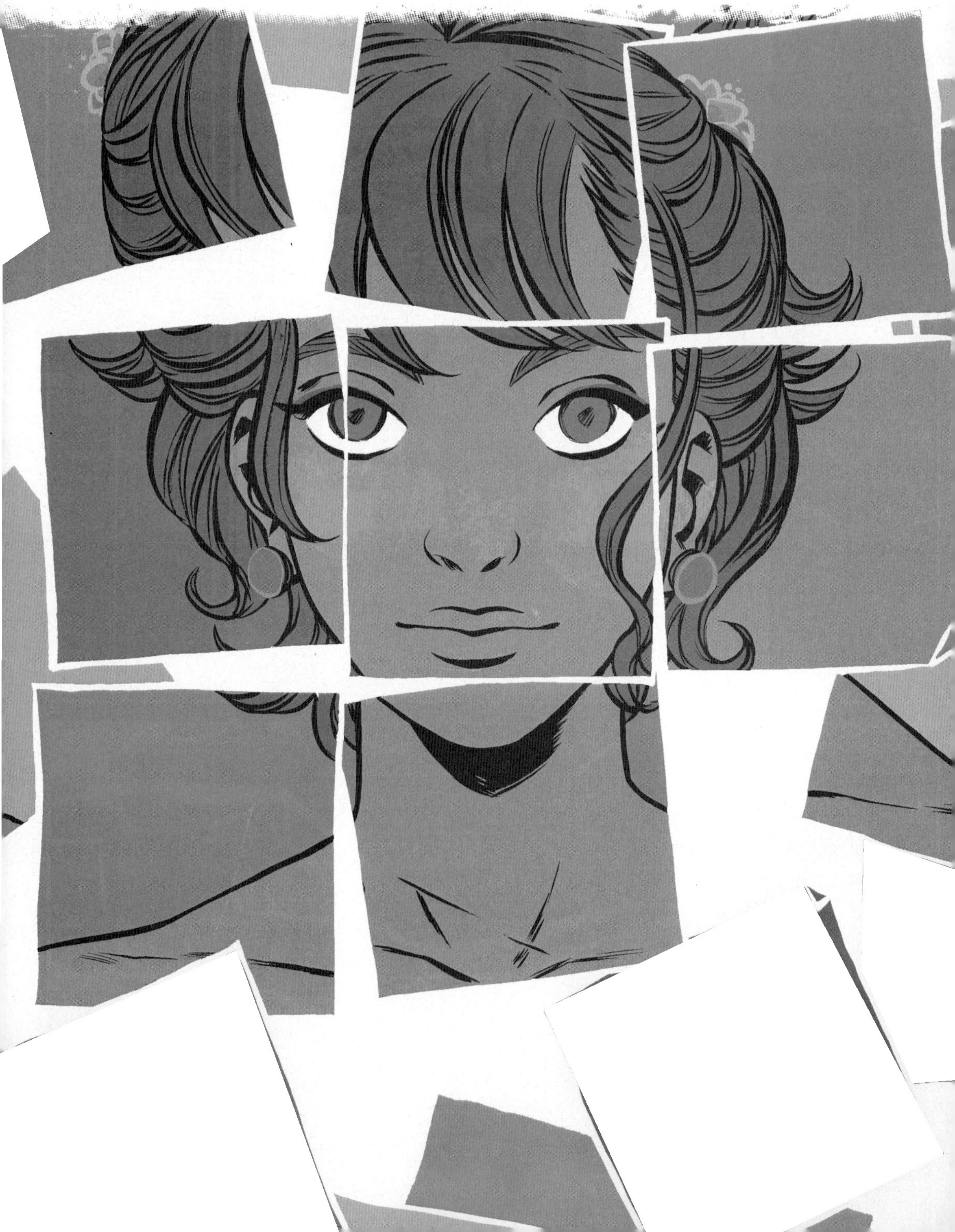

4

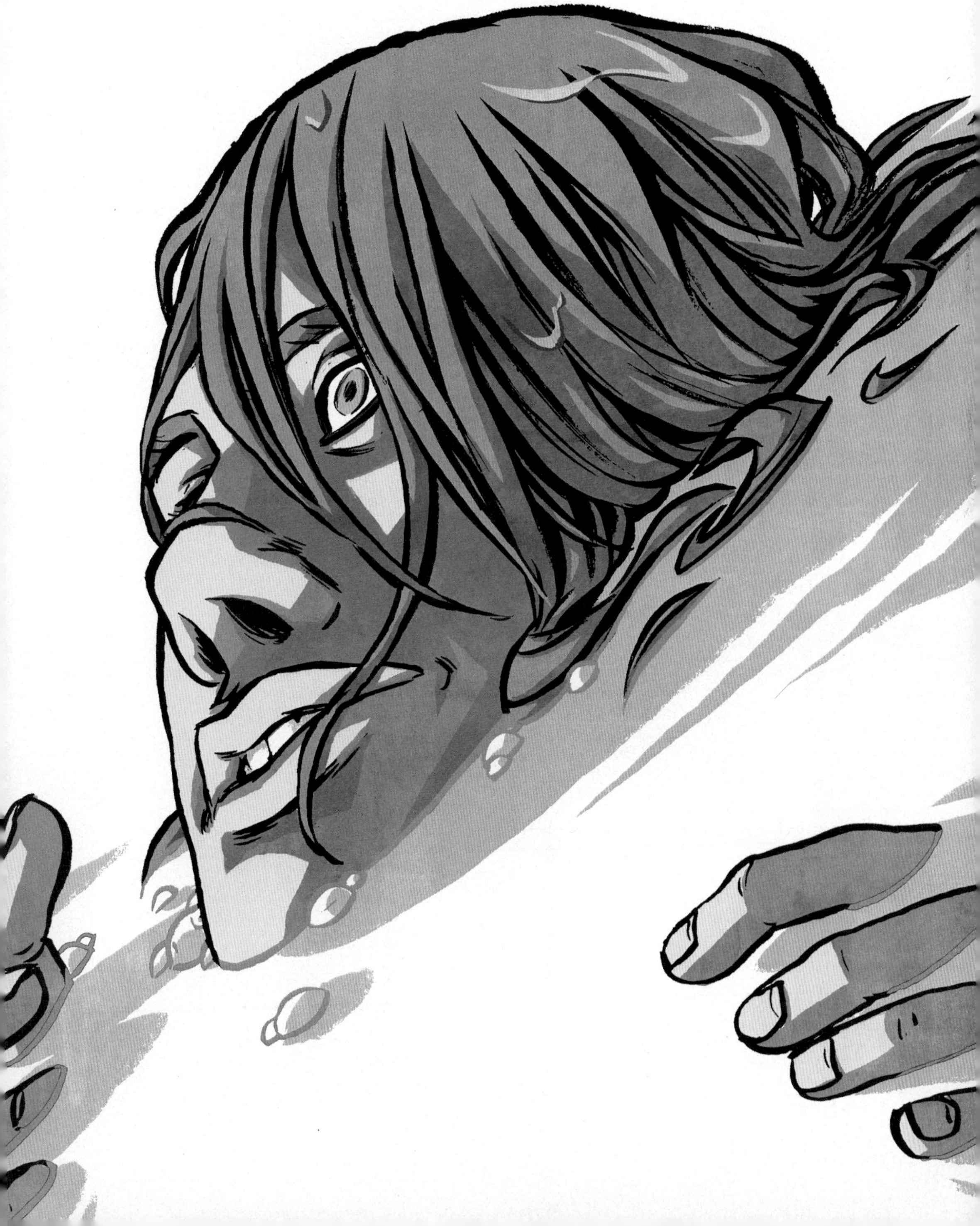

5

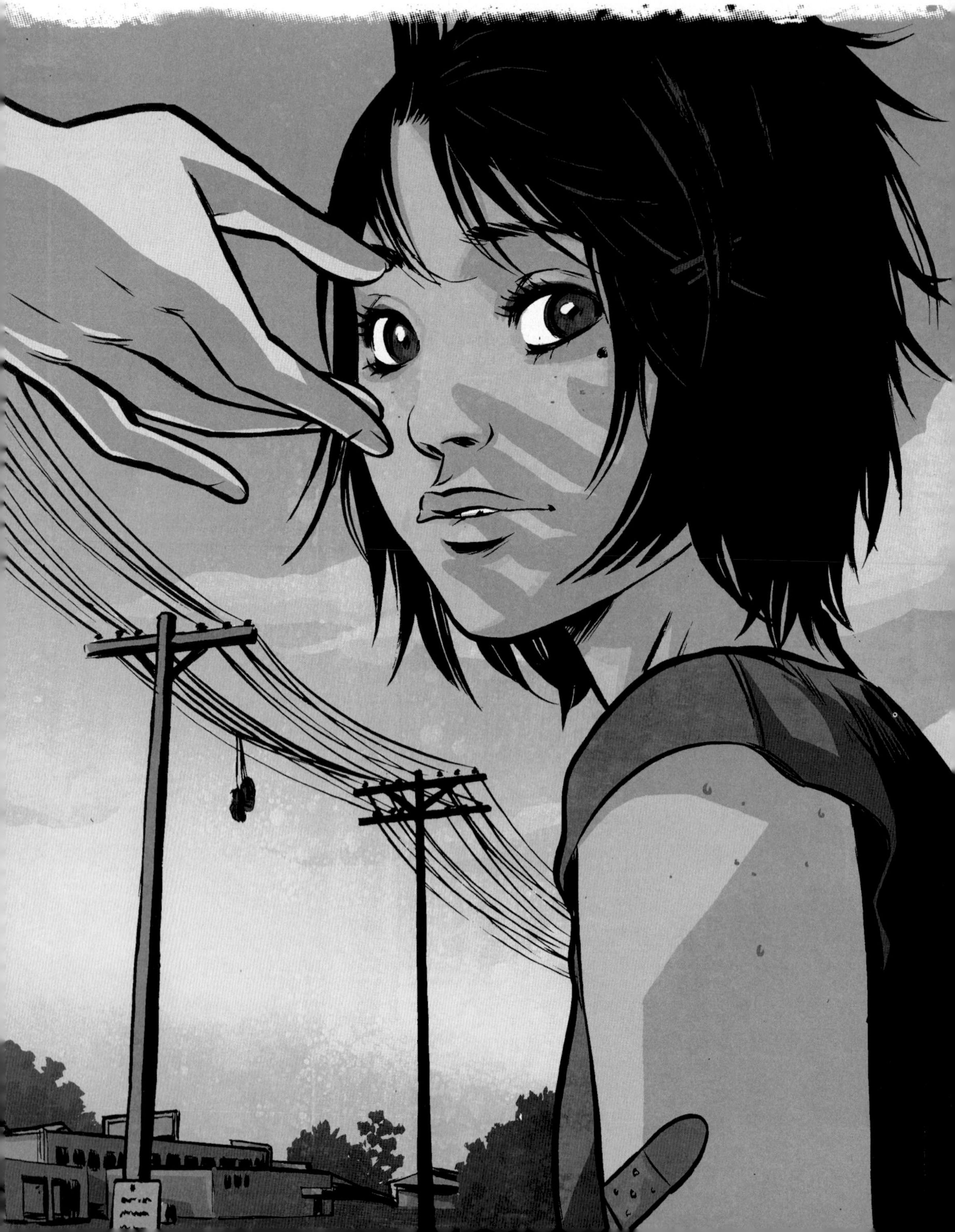

6

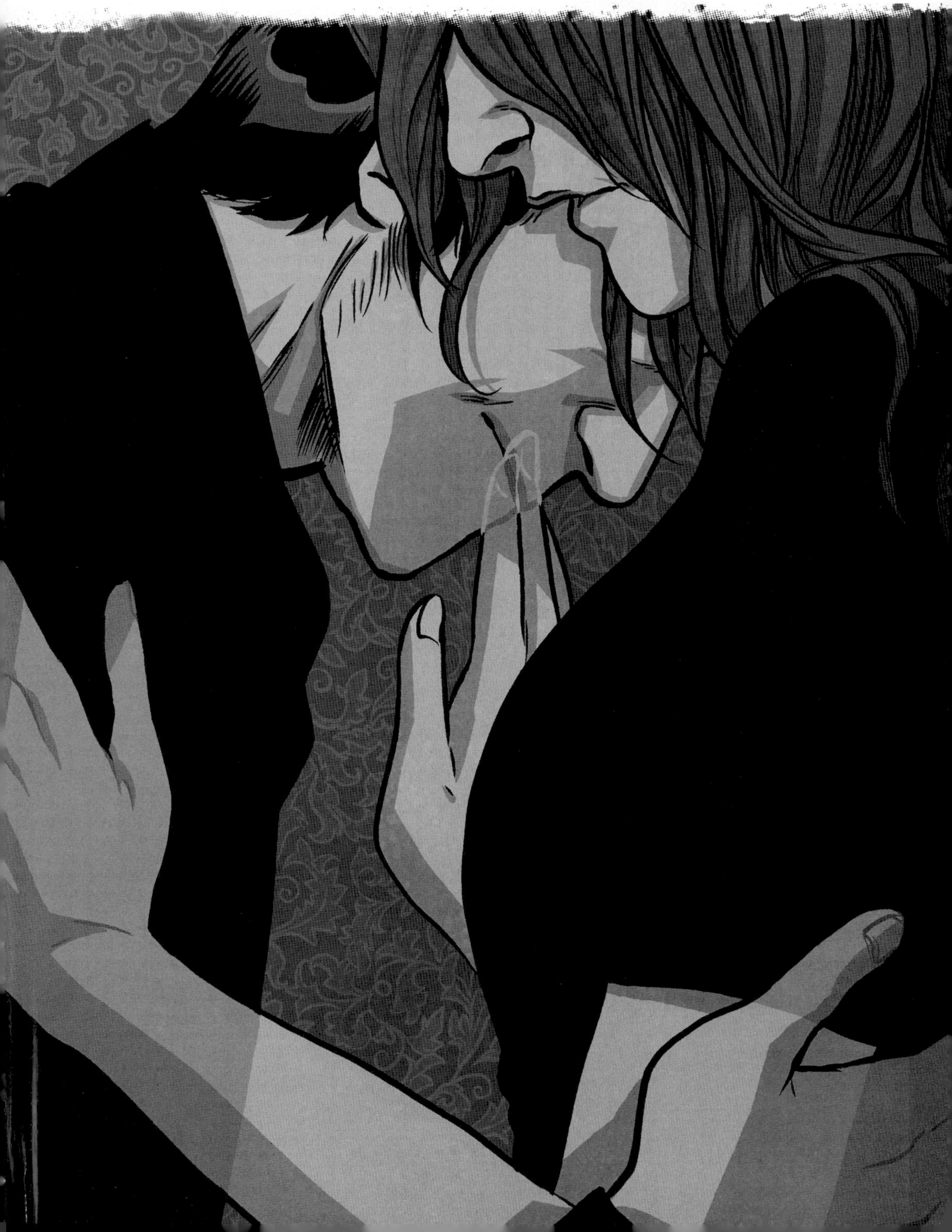

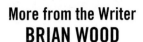